The MICHELIN Guide

Chicago

RESTAURANTS
2013

Michelin Travel Parner

Société par actions simplifiées au capital de 11 629 590 EUR
27 Cours de L'Île Seguin - 92100 Boulogne Billancourt (France)
R.C.S. Nanterre 433 677 721

© **Michelin et cie, Propriétaires-éditeurs**
Dépot légal Octobre 2012
Made in Canada
Published in 2012

The MICHELIN Guide
One Parkway South
Greenville, SC 29615 USA
www.michelinguide.com
michelin.guides@us.michelin.com

Dear Reader

*W*e are thrilled to present the third edition of our MICHELIN Guide to Chicago.

Our dynamic team has spent this year updating our selection to wholly reflect the rich diversity of Chicago's restaurants and hotels. As part of our meticulous and highly confidential evaluation process, our inspectors have anonymously and methodically eaten through all of the city's neighborhoods and suburbs to compile the finest in each category for your enjoyment. While these inspectors are expertly trained food industry professionals, we remain consumer driven: our goal is to provide comprehensive choices to accommodate your comfort, tastes, and budget. Our inspectors dine, drink, and lodge as 'regular' customers in order to experience and evaluate the same level of service and cuisine you would as a guest.

We have expanded our criteria to reflect some of the more current and unique elements of the city's dining scene. Don't miss the scrumptious "Small Plates" category, highlighting those establishments with a distinct style of service, setting, and menu; and the comprehensive "Under $25" listing which also includes a diverse and impressive choice at a very good value.

Additionally, you may follow our Michelin Inspectors on Twitter @MichelinGuideCH as they chow their way around town. Our anonymous inspectors tweet daily about their unique and entertaining food experiences.

Our company's two founders, Édouard and André Michelin, published the first MICHELIN Guide in 1900, to provide motorists with practical information about where they could service and repair their cars, find quality accommodations, and a good meal. Later in 1926, the star-rating system for outstanding restaurants was introduced, and over the decades we have developed many new improvements to our guides. The local team here in Chicago enthusiastically carries on these traditions.

We sincerely hope that the MICHELIN Guide will remain your preferred reference to the city's restaurants and hotels.

Contents

© MICHELIN

Contents

Contents

© City of Chicago / GRC

5

The MICHELIN Guide

"This volume was created at the turn of the century and will last at least as long".

This foreword to the very first edition of the MICHELIN Guide, written in 1900, has become famous over the years and the Guide has lived up to the prediction. It is read across the world and the key to its popularity is the consistency in its commitment to its readers, which is based on the following promises.

→ Anonymous Inspections

Our inspectors make anonymous visits to hotels and restaurants to gauge the quality offered to the ordinary customer. They pay their own bill and make no indication of their presence. These visits are supplemented by comprehensive monitoring of information—our readers' comments are one valuable source, and are always taken into consideration.

→ Independence

Our choice of establishments is a completely independent one, made for the benefit of our readers alone. Decisions are discussed by the inspectors and the editor, with the most important decided at the global level. Inclusion in the guide is always free of charge.

→ The Selection

The Guide offers a selection of the best hotels and restaurants in each category of comfort and price. Inclusion in the guides is a commendable award in itself, and defines the establishment among the "best of the best."

How the MICHELIN Guide Works

→ Annual Updates

All practical information, the classifications, and awards, are revised and updated every year to ensure the most reliable information possible.

→ Consistency & Classifications

The criteria for the classifications are the same in all countries covered by the Michelin Guides. Our system is used worldwide and is easy to apply when choosing a restaurant or hotel.

→ The Classifications

We classify our establishments using XXXXX-X and 🏨🏨🏨-🏠 to indicate the level of comfort. The ❀❀❀-❀ specifically designates an award for cuisine, unique from the classification. For hotels and restaurants, a symbol in red suggests a particularly charming spot with unique décor or ambiance.

→ Our Aim

As part of Michelin's ongoing commitment to improving travel and mobility, we do everything possible to make vacations and eating out a pleasure.

The MICHELIN Guide

How to Use This Guide

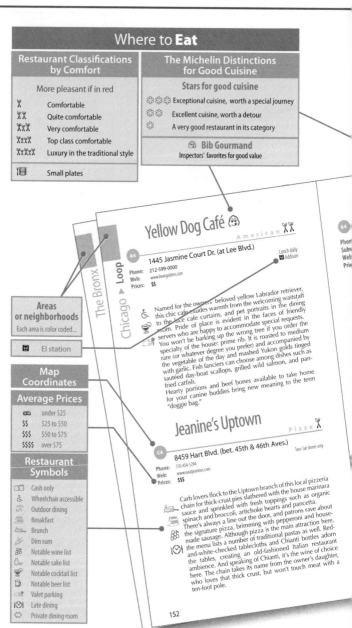

Where to **Eat**

Restaurant Classifications by Comfort

More pleasant if in red

X	Comfortable
XX	Quite comfortable
XXX	Very comfortable
XXXX	Top class comfortable
XXXXX	Luxury in the traditional style
▤	Small plates

The Michelin Distinctions for Good Cuisine

Stars for good cuisine

🏵🏵🏵 Exceptional cuisine, worth a special journey

🏵🏵 Excellent cuisine, worth a detour

🏵 A very good restaurant in its category

🏵 **Bib Gourmand**
Inspectors' favorites for good value

Areas or neighborhoods

Each area is color coded...

▥	El station

Map Coordinates

Average Prices

🍸	under $25
$$	$25 to $50
$$$	$50 to $75
$$$$	over $75

Restaurant Symbols

🕙	Cash only
🦽	Wheelchair accessible
🌲	Outdoor dining
🍳	Breakfast
🥞	Brunch
🥢	Dim sum
🍷	Notable wine list
🍶	Notable sake list
🍸	Notable cocktail list
🍺	Notable beer list
🅿	Valet parking
🕯	Late dining
🍽	Private dining room

Yellow Dog Café 🏵

A4 | American XX

The Bronx ▶ Loop / Chicago

A4 1445 Jasmine Court Dr. (at Lee Blvd.)

Lunch daily
▥ Addison

Phone: 212-599-0000
Web: www.ilovegolders.com
Prices: $$

Named for the owners' beloved yellow Labrador retriever, this chic cafe exudes warmth from the welcoming waitstaff to the lace cafe curtains, and pet portraits in the dining room. Pride of place is evident in the faces of friendly servers who are happy to accommodate special requests. You won't be barking up the wrong tree if you order the specialty of the house: prime rib. It is roasted to medium rare (or whatever degree you prefer) and accompanied by the vegetable of the day and mashed Yukon golds tinged with garlic. Fish fanciers can choose among dishes such as sautéed day-boat scallops, grilled wild salmon, and pan-fried catfish.

Hearty portions and beef bones available to take home for your canine buddies bring new meaning to the term "doggie bag."

Jeanine's Uptown

Pizza X

C4 8459 Hart Blvd. (bet. 45th & 46th Aves.)

Tues-Sat dinner only

Phone: 310-454-5294
Web: www.eatatjeanines.com
Prices: $$$

Carb lovers flock to the Uptown branch of this local pizzeria chain for thick-crust pies slathered with the house marinara sauce and sprinkled with fresh toppings such as organic spinach and broccoli, artichoke hearts and pancetta. There's always a line out the door, and patrons rave about the signature pizza, brimming with pepperoni and house-made sausage. Although pizza is the main attraction here, the menu lists a number of traditional pastas as well. Red-and-white-checked tablecloths and Chianti bottles adorn the tables, creating an old-fashioned Italian restaurant ambience. And speaking of Chianti, it's the wine of choice here. The chain takes its name from the owner's daughter, who loves that thick crust, but won't touch meat with a ten-foot pole.

152

A4
Phone
Subw
Web
Price

8

Where to **Stay**

Average Prices	Hotel Symbols	Hotel Classifications by Comfort
Prices do not include applicable taxes	**149 rooms** Number of rooms & suites	More pleasant if in red
$ under $200	♿ Wheelchair accessible	🏠 Comfortable
$$ $200 to $300	🏋 Exercise room	🏠 Quite comfortable
$$$ $300 to $400	💆 Spa	🏠 Very comfortable
$$$$ over $400	🏊 Swimming pool	🏠 Top class comfortable
	🏢 Conference room	🏠 Luxury in the traditional style
Map Coordinates	🐾 Pet friendly	
	📶 Wireless	

...a's Palace ✿ ✿

Italian ✕✕✕✕

...euther Pl. (at 30th Street)

Dinner daily

...-5309
...- 8 Av
...onyasfabulouspalace.com

Home cooked Italian never tasted so good than at this unpretentious little place. The simple décor claims no big-name designers, and while the Murano glass light fixtures are chic and the velveteen-covered chairs are comfortable, this isn't a restaurant where millions of dollars were spent on the interior.

Instead, food is the focus here. The restaurant's name may not be Italian, but it nonetheless serves some of the best pasta in the city, made fresh in-house. Dishes follow the seasons, thus ravioli may be stuffed with fresh ricotta and herbs in summer, and pumpkin in fall. Most everything is liberally dusted with Parmigiano Reggiano, a favorite ingredient of the chef.

For dessert, you'll have to deliberate between the likes of creamy tiramisu, ricotta cheesecake, and homemade gelato. One thing's for sure: you'll never miss your nonna's cooking when you eat at Sonya's.

153

Manhattan ► Chelsea

David Burlington/Getty Images

The Fan Inn

🏠

D1

135 Shanghai Street, Oakland

Phone: 650-345-1440 or 888-222-2424
Web: www.superfaninnoakland.com
Prices: $$

45 Rooms
5 Suites

🏋

💆

John A. Rizzo/Getty Images

...oused in an Art Deco-era building, the venerable Fan Inn ...ently underwent a complete facelift. The hotel now fits ...with the new generation of sleekly understated hotels ...ring a Zen-inspired aesthetic, despite its 1930s origins.

...othing neutral palette runs throughout the property, ...uated with exotic woods, bamboo, and fine fabrics. ...e lobby, the sultry lounge makes a relaxing place for ...mixed cocktail or a glass of wine.

...pens and down pillows cater to your comfort, while ...n TVs, DVD players with iPod docking stations, ...ess Internet access satisfy the need for modern ...les and credenzas morph into flip-out desks. ...ater, fax or scanner? It's just a phone call away. ...st, the hotel will even provide office supplies.

...alf of the accommodations here are suites, ...xury factor ratchets up with marble baths, ...ng areas, and fully equipped kitchens. ...nn doesn't have a restaurant, the nearby ...rly everything you could want in terms of ...dumplings to haute cuisine.

315

San Francisco ► Civic Center

How to Use This Guide

9

Where to Eat

Chicago

Andersonville, Edgewater & Uptown
Lincoln Square · Ravenswood

This rare and diverse collection of spirited neighborhoods in Chicago's north side is like a real-world Epcot theme park, with visitors easily flitting from one immigrant ethnic tradition to the next, and all the while sampling international cuisines, but without a passport. Lauded as one of the most bewitching neighborhoods in the Windy City, Andersonville also struts a plethora of quaint "Places to Stay" including popular bed-and-breakfasts and charming hotels. A food mecca of sorts, the **Andersonville Farmer's Market** (held every Wednesday) houses a cluster of bakeries, fresh farm produce, and Oriental fruit orchards.

Swedish Spreads

From the art on the lamppost banners to the Swedish American Museum Center, you can see the influence of Andersonville's historical roots upon arrival on Clark Street. Happily, much of that can be explored with your taste buds, starting the day at **Restaurant Svea**. This well-known hangout is also home of the hearty Viking breakfast that may unveil Swedish-style pancakes, sausages, roasted potatoes, and toasted *limpa* bread (to name a few of the offerings).

Meanwhile, **Wikström's Gourmet Foods** is one of the last standing Swedish emporiums of packaged and prepared favorites, still stocked with everything needed for a traditional smörgåsbord, from homey Swedish meatballs and herring, to lingonberry preserves.

Locals yearning for authentic baked goods eagerly take a number and wait in line at the **Swedish Bakery**. Many of its traditional baked treats are available in individual sizes, as well as larger portions perfect for those looking to entertain. For more instant gratification, scout a seat at the counter by the window and enjoy that miniature yet exquisite coconut-custard coffeecake right away, perhaps with a complimentary cup of coffee.

Andersonville also caters to its worldly community with the well-tread **Middle East Bakery & Grocery**. Make a massive meze feast from spreads, breads, olives, and an impressive range of hummus among other goodies available in the deli. Or, choose to stock up on dried fruits, spices, rice, rosewater, nuts, and teas from the grocery section. Either way, you will have ample options for a magnificent Middle Eastern menu.

All Italia

On the pizza front, **Great Lake** has received many accolades for its pizza, despite the infamously long lines and a lack of interest in expansion that, according to some hungry pizza lovers, is downright un-

American. Nonetheless, these delicious, Chicago-style pies are made with the country's premium ingredients—its menu is a virtual Who's Who of local, organic vegetable farmers and heirloom breeders. Whether you choose to dine in or take out, their fabulous pies usually feature organic tomato sauce, farmer's cheese, and a flurry of herbs paired with deliciously fresh green garlic, spring onions, mortadella, or chorizo. After this indulgence, stop by **The Coffee Studio** for a cup of joe prepared by what critics have named one of the country's best boutique coffee shops. Superlatives aside, take home a pretty little green box of chocolate-dipped *glacée* fruits to devour all by yourself.

An Asian Affair

Further uptown, Argyle Street is renowned for being a pocket of intermixed East Asian culture—even the Argyle Red Line El stop is thematically decorative. A terrific concentration of Chinese, Thai, and Vietnamese delis, as well as bakeries, herbalists, noodle shops, and restaurants line these streets; and there is endless tasting to be done along these blocks. Speaking of which, **Sun Wah BBQ** is a forever-cherished spot for Cantonese cuisine. Walk in and be greeted by their glistening selection of bronzed meats. These are offered on their own or over rice for a complete meal. The real draw in Edgewater is its art deco architecture, especially evident along Bryn Mawr Avenue and Lake Michigan's beaches. This neighborhood also boasts a vibrant community that convenes at **The Metropolis**

Café, an offshoot of Chicago's lauded Metropolis Coffee Company. Watch a crowd of students, professionals, and locals gulp down oodles of their creative coffee quenchers.

Hot Dog Haven

This is Chicago, so there's always a good hot dog nearby, and one of the best red-hots uptown is as thrilling as it is easy to spot. Just look for the iconic pitchfork piercing a sausage over the name **Wolfy's**, and know that you have arrived. Try the classic dog, but know that by the time the limitless listing of toppings are piled on, the meat will be invisibly buried beneath piccalilli, pickles, peppers, and other impossibly colored yet divine condiments.

LINCOLN SQUARE AND RAVENSWOOD

Evidence of the German immigrants who helped develop Lincoln Square still lingers in this quaint expanse. Highlights include a century-old apothecary as well as new, yet Old World-inspired butchers and specialty items that abound at **Gene's Sausage Shop**. For a fine menu of chops, steaks, free-range poultry, smoked sausages, and bacon in its many glorious forms, plan to sample the wares of **Lincoln Quality Meat Market**. The **Lincoln Square Farmer's Market** has long been loved and frequented (on Tuesdays); they now showcase a Thursday evening market, replete with live music alongside a medley of fruits, vegetables, and flowers, which remains a draw for locals with day jobs.

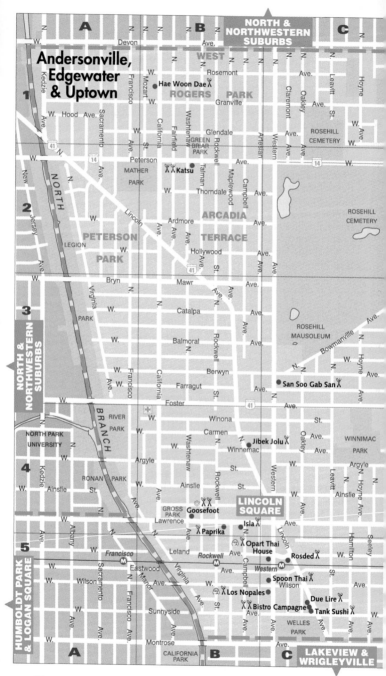

Andersonville, Edgewater & Uptown

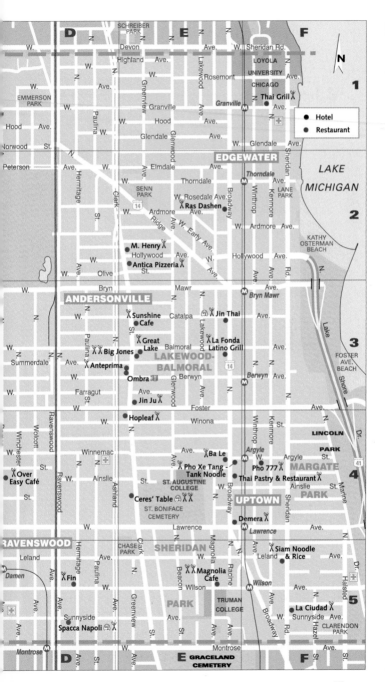

N

EDGEWATER

LAKE
MICHIGAN

- ● Hotel
- ● Restaurant

LOYOLA
UNIVERSITY
CHICAGO

✕ Thai Grill

EMMERSON
PARK

KATHY
OSTERMAN
BEACH

SENN
PARK

✕ Ras Dashen

M. Henry ✕

● Antica Pizzeria ✕

ANDERSONVILLE

✕ Sunshine
● Cafe

✕ Jin Thai

✕ Great
Lake

✕ La Fonda
Latino Grill

✕ ✕ Big Jones

**LAKEWOOD-
BALMORAL**

FOSTER
AVE.
BEACH

✕ Anteprima

● Ombra ▤

● Jin Ju ✕

● Hopleaf ✕

LINCOLN

PARK

✕ Over
● Easy Café

✕ Ba Le

MARGATE

✕ Pho Xe Tang -
Tank Noodle

Pho 777 ✕

● Thai Pastry & Restaurant ✕

PARK

● Ceres' Table ✕

ST. AUGUSTINE
COLLEGE

UPTOWN

ST. BONIFACE
CEMETERY

● Demera ✕

RAVENSWOOD

CHASE
PARK

SHERIDAN

✕ Siam Noodle
& Rice

✕ Fin

✕ ✕ Magnolia
Cafe

PARK

TRUMAN
COLLEGE

● La Ciudad ✕

● Spacca Napoli ✕

**GRACELAND
CEMETERY**

17

Anteprima

  Italian

 E3

5316 N. Clark St. (bet. Berwyn & Summerdale Aves.)

Phone: 773-506-9990   Dinner nightly
Web: N/A
Prices: $$

Berwyn

Along an attractive stretch of Clark, warm and welcoming Anteprima is a great little stop no matter the occasion. From the painted landscapes and bustling atmosphere to the regionally inspired menu, this place exudes a rustic vibe and feels steeped in all things Italian.

Don't wave away the bread basket—tender focaccia, rosemary *grissini*, and sliced country bread are irresistible. The menu begins with snacks like grilled polenta with slow-cooked greens and tomato, then moves on to pastas, sized as appetizers or entrées. Sample an array of traditional dishes like pan-roasted, marinated rabbit with cabbage, pancetta, and pickled green tomatoes, but pay attention to the full list of daily specials. Top it all off with some homemade limoncello.

Antica Pizzeria

  Italian

 E2

5663 N. Clark St. (bet. Hollywood & Olive Aves.)

Phone: 773-944-1492   Dinner Wed – Mon
Web: www.anticapizzeriachicago.com
Prices:

Antica Pizzeria's chef hails from Catania and serves up a roster of pizza and pasta that brings a decidedly Sicilian attitude to the regional Italian menu. The pizza here–chewy, crusty, and tender–is a bit thinner than their Neapolitan-style cousins and is proffered with myriad toppings that include the *fattoressa* (inspired by the chef's own mother) that piles on cooked ham, hard-boiled eggs, green peas, and mushrooms. Pastas are numerous and entrées offer the likes of grilled swordfish with *salmoriglio* sauce and eggplant *caponata*.

The comfortable and friendly room brings on a rustic mien showcasing bright yellow walls hung with black-and-white photography, wood furnishings, and a visible workstation installed with a wood-fired brick oven.

Andersonville, Edgewater & Uptown

Ba Le

E4

5014 N. Broadway (at Argyle St.)

Lunch & dinner daily

Phone: 773-561-4424
Web: www.balesandwich.com
Prices: 💰💰

🚇 Argyle

Moving just a few doors down did exactly what the owners hoped it would. This storefront is still the north side's hot spot for authentic French-Vietnamese sandwiches; but now within a more sleek sphere, starring an L-shaped counter overlooking Broadway (also a first-rate perch for people-watching).

The menu is heavy on *banh mi* variations, that tasty ensemble made with crusty French bread and swelled with fixings like grilled pork, cilantro, and house-pickled daikon. The affordable price tags plus large portions make for a sweet pair with leftovers for later. Natives in the know gulp down the quirky Vietnamese FOCO pennywort drink; while salads, pastries, desserts, sodas, and teas round out the menu and sate the more prudent palate.

Big Jones

E3

5347 N. Clark St. (bet. Balmoral & Summerdale Aves.)

Lunch & dinner daily

Phone: 773-275-5725
Web: www.bigjoneschicago.com
Prices: $$

🚇 Berwyn

Bistro tables, genteel brocade wallpaper, and iron chandeliers set the scene, but you know you're getting a real Southern experience when your meal starts with a pitcher of sweet tea and basket of honey butter-slathered cornbread. From start to finish, Big Jones showcases the best of the South from classic dishes like gumbo *ya-ya* in a dark, smoky roux; shrimp and grits with tasso gravy; and a can't-miss version of red velvet cake.

Aficionados of Lowcountry cooking keep coming back for Big Jones' frequent period dinners including the Boarding House Lunch ca. 1933 prix-fixe starring fried chicken, hoppin' John, and voodoo greens. Meanwhile, Bourbon lovers can't help but work their way down the vast whiskey and artisanal spirits list.

19

Bistro Campagne

French

4518 N. Lincoln Ave. (bet. Sunnyside & Wilson Aves.)

Phone: 773-271-6100
Web: www.bistrocampagne.com
Prices: $$

Lunch Sun
Dinner nightly
 Western (Brown)

This quaint little bungalow feels like a romantic bistro secreted away in the French countryside. A small, inviting bar offers an aperitif, as scenes of Parisian life line the walls and leaded glass windows play with your views of the outside world. The vibe is warm, romantic, and fun for small groups.

The country French menu features the tried-and-true classics made with local and organic ingredients. Meals begin with warm crusty baguettes wrapped in paper—a perfect accompaniment for soaking up the buttery *escargot au beurre d'ail*. Or, try the duck confit with wild mushroom duxelles and hazelnuts in puff pastry with Madeira reduction, followed by half of the beautifully roasted *poulet roti forestière*. End with profiteroles or possibly an Armangac.

Ceres' Table

Mediterranean

4882 N. Clark St. (bet. Ainslie St. & Lawrence Ave.)

Phone: 773-878-4882
Web: www.cerestable.com
Prices: $$

Dinner Mon – Sat

 Lawrence

Unpretentious, perfectly casual, and always good, Ceres' Table does honor to the chef's Sicilian heritage as well as the Roman goddess of the harvest for which it is named. Inside, the mood is always lively and the full bar is popular among solo diners. A floral mosaic near the entry gives way to painted concrete floors and a dining room bathed in dark and azure shades of blue; sheer curtains divide a few of the bare wood tables.

The mostly Mediterranean menu may focus on Italy but shows American flair. Expect freshly chopped lamb tartare with cornichons and capers, garnishes of mint and horseradish; or pan-roasted duck breast and sausage with vinegar-braised black kale. Wednesdays offer a $40 prix-fixe for three courses and a glass of wine.

Demera

Ethiopian

 E4

4801 N. Broadway (at Lawrence St.)

Phone: 773-334-8787 — Lunch & dinner daily
Web: www.demeraethiopianrestaurant.com
Prices: $$ — Lawrence

A short skip off the red line at Lawrence, this bright corner location is as welcoming for a quick bite or drink and good people watching as it is for an authentic Ethiopian feast. On the weekends Demera also welcomes musicians for live performances, promising that this spot goes beyond other ethnic eateries.

As is tradition, Demera serves *injera*, the spongy, pancake-like bread used as a utensil on a communal plate. Its tangy flavors pair wonderfully with the *ye beg alicha* dish of tender lamb in a rich and creamy aromatic green sauce; as well as the *ye-kwanta firfir*, featuring beef tips stewed in a spicy *berbere* sauce. Don't skip the Ethiopian tea, which is an oregano tea infused with anise, clover, and cinnamon. Sweeten with honey and savor.

Due Lire

Italian

C5

4520 N. Lincoln Ave. (bet. Sunnyside & Wilson Aves.)

Phone: 773-275-7878 — Dinner Tue – Sun
Web: www.due-lire.com
Prices: $$ — Western (Brown)

Contemporary Italian cuisine comes to this Lincoln Square address courtesy of Naples native Massimo Di Vuolo and Chef Kevin Abshire. Di Vuolo's warm welcome is a gracious entrée to this trattoria bearing a perfectly neighborhoody ambience with its casual décor of parchment-colored walls and polished dark wood furnishings.

The kitchen presents a tastefully edited canon of preparations beginning with *antipasti* such as local Italian sausage with rapini; *arancino* Milano dotted with asparagus and fontina; or drunken mussels in Belgian-style ale with pretzel-roll crostini. The selection of *primi* may offer a spot-on risotto whirled with charred ramps and nuggets of langoustine; while main dishes may include grilled ahi tuna with Sicilian caponata.

Fin

Asian

D5

1742 W. Wilson Ave. (at Hermitage Ave.)

Phone: 773-961-7452
Web: www.finsushibar.com
Prices:

Lunch & dinner Tue – Sun

 Montrose (Brown)

While this may not be an authentic Japanese restaurant, it is in fact a flavorful, fresh, and budget-friendly hybrid of sushi-meets-Thai cuisine. Inside this pleasant Ravenswood enclave, find a white-dominated room complemented by chocolate brown accents, plenty of windows, a cheerful staff, and bright disposition.

Enjoyably prepared nigiri and sashimi of fine quality contribute to an extensive menu bolstered by a plethora of maki. Standard rolls like spicy tuna coated with tempura crunch seem humble against the likes of a crunchy plantain, cream cheese, and avocado maki as featured among the listing of special rolls. Entrées bring a Thai accent in the likes of shrimp pad Thai; duck with red curry sauce and organic soba; or tom yum fried rice.

Great Lake

Pizza

E3

1477 W. Balmoral Ave. (bet. Clark St. & Glenwood Ave.)

Phone: 773-334-9270
Web: N/A
Prices: $$

Dinner Wed – Sat

 Berwyn

How have Lydia Esparza and Nick Lessins gotten people to say such nice things about Great Lake for years? Consider pizza their bribe of choice. For inside this tiny, communal spot simply dressed with wood floors, exposed brick walls, a dozen seats, and a pizza-burning oven, they are cooking no more than two or three pies at a time. But envision one as perfectly charred with a thin crust that is at once crisp, chewy, and crunchy, laden with fresh tomato sauce and creamy Farmer's cheese, another with homemade spicy chorizo, crème fraîche, onions, and herbs. Fresh salads from local purveyors help bide the time once you've scored a table.

Mind that service is minimal and these lines are long. Really long. Still, the BYO policy does help ease the wait outside.

Goosefoot ✿

B4

2656 W. Lawrence Ave. (bet. Talman & Washtenaw Aves.)

Phone:	773-942-7547
Web:	www.goosefoot.net
Prices:	$$$

Dinner Tue – Sat

🚊 Rockwell

♿

Anthony Tahlier

This quiet, commercial strip is the home and first solo endeavor of Chef Chris Nugent, whose talent and passion just might be capturing the city's culinary zeitgeist. Goosefoot's square, aqua-blue room is comfortable, welcoming, and adorned with little more than a few mini Rodin sculptures and drawings for impact. The ambience isn't loud but celebratory; everyone here is having a good time.

Plan to bring your own bottle, though they are equipped with all the decanters, coolers, and stemware that a dedicated oenophile might require. Eight course menus (no à la carte) might begin with dishes that combine improbable flavors with complexity and pleasure, as in the plump, butter-poached scallop on a bed of mushrooms, with lobster sauce, licorice root essence, and fragrant Madras curry. Delicate ingredients like supremely fresh and perfectly seared *loup de mer* might be paired with leek confit, lemon sauce, tapioca pearls, and a bold, bright tear of fennel purée and pollen. Beef tenderloin can seem irreproachable, perhaps poached in consommé, set atop sautéed goosefoot greens and mushroom ragout, encircled in Bordelaise-shallot jus.

For dessert, chocolate mousse is a wafer-shattering event.

Andersonville, Edgewater & Uptown

23

Hae Woon Dae

B1

6240 N. California Ave. (bet. Granville & Rosemont Aves.)

Phone: 773-764-8018 — Lunch Sat – Sun

Web: www.letseat.at/haewoondaebbq — Dinner nightly

Prices:

 Located in a low-slung strip mall and labeled by a plain black awning, Hae Woon Dae looks simple and unimpressive. While appearances may be lacking, the tasty Korean specialties served inside more than satisfy.

Mandoo, pan-fried or boiled dumplings; three varieties of savory Korean-style pancakes; and *yookhwae* (spiced beef tartare) start off the list of hearty specialties that include soul warming stews and casseroles. Of special note is the barbecue selection. Each table features a recessed pit into which a cauldron of glowing wood charcoal is lowered for tabletop grilling. Serving scissor-cut strips of sizzling marinated *kalbi* brushed with fermented chili paste and wrapped in cool crisp daikon and romaine, Hae Woon Dae offers pizzazz indeed.

Hopleaf

E4

5148 N. Clark St. (bet. Foster Ave. & Winona St.)

Phone: 773-334-9851 — Lunch & dinner daily

Web: www.hopleaf.com

Prices: $$ — Berwyn

 Hopleaf's long-awaited expansion into the space next door is complete, and beer geeks have double the reason (and room) to patronize the charmingly gritty tavern—spiffed up with a glassed-in kitchen and marble counter. A wood-burning oven takes the chill off in cold weather, while a back patio remains as lush as ever during those sun-filled days.

American gastropub food pairs sublimely with draft and bottled craft beers, ranging from Chicago's own Goose Island to obscure Euro brews including an ample Belgian assortment. Forget onion rings with your drink: instead try Barbār beer-battered Gunthorp Farms rabbit confit with a side of Thumbelina carrots; grilled Broken Arrow Ranch quail with fennel and black grapes; or a classic pot of steamed mussels.

Isla

B4

2501 W. Lawrence Ave. (bet. Campbell & Maplewood Aves.)

Phone: 773-271-2988
Web: www.islapilipina.com
Prices:

Lunch & dinner Tue – Sun

Western (Brown)

A favored spot for Filipino cuisine in Lincoln Square, Isla now sports a freshened look to accompany its friendly vibe and heaping plates. The former steam-table setting offers pale mint green walls hung with artwork for sale, sleek seating, and cheerful signs scrolled in Tagalog that welcome and thank diners for their patronage.

The menu is well endowed in distinct pork specialties: crispy *pata*, deep-fried pork knuckle; *paksiw na lechon*, tangy pork stew with peppercorns and soy sauce; and *inihaw na baboy*, marinated and grilled pork strips served with tart vinegar dipping sauce. Saving room for dessert may prove challenging, but the *halo-halo* could tempt—an otherworldly colorful layering of ice cream, crushed ice, candied fruit, beans, and flan.

Jibek Jolu

Asian

B4

5047 N. Lincoln Ave. (bet. Carmen & Winnemac Aves.)

Phone: 773-878-8494
Web: www.jibekjolu.us
Prices:

Lunch & dinner daily

Jibek Jolu (translates as Silk Road) is a tasty spot serving the cuisine of Kyrgyzstan. The culinary makeup of this landlocked Central Asian republic melds the influences of Turkish, Russian, Persian, and Chinese cuisines to produce a unique representation of the region.

To start, the menu utilizes halal products to offer meat-stuffed pastries, as in the *cheburek* (fried lamb turnover), along with soups that include *borsh*, and an incredibly crunchy Korean carrot salad with julienned carrots, onion, garlic, parsley, and dried chilies. *Lagman*, hand-pulled wheat noodles tossed with a stew of tender seared beef, sweet peppers, and daikon, is featured among the entrées that may also reveal *pelmeni* and charcoal-grilled cubes of marinated chicken.

Andersonville, Edgewater & Uptown

Jin Ju

Korean

5203 N. Clark St. (at Foster Ave.)

Phone: 773-334-6377
Web: www.jinjurestaurant.com
Prices: **$$**

Dinner Tue – Sun

A sexy spot on a stretch of bustling Clark Street, Jin Ju spins out luscious Korean classics with aplomb. Inside, dim lighting, dark wood furnishings, and lush red walls create a sophisticated coziness, while servers are gracious and attentive.

The menu showcases a range of specialties to start, like plump *mandoo*, batter-fried spicy chicken wings, or *paj un*, a savory Korean-style pancake filled with the likes of kimchi, served sliced in wedges with a tangy soy and rice vinegar dipping sauce. The *dak tori tang* could warm the coldest day in the Windy City—its fiery red pepper broth is brought to the table bubbling and brimming with braised chicken, potato, carrots, and leafy herbs served with sticky rice, along with a tasty assortment of *banchan*.

Jin Thai

Thai

5458 N. Broadway (at Catalpa Ave.)

Phone: 773-681-0555
Web: www.jinthaicuisine.com
Prices: 💰

Lunch & dinner daily

🚇 Bryn Mawr

♿ It's an auspicious beginning for a restaurant to have its space blessed by Buddhist monks—and though it sounds like urban legend, neighbors attest that this really happened at Jin Thai. Benevolent Buddha figures continue to keep watch over the dining room, their serene vibe amplified by the hospitality of husband-and-wife team Chai and Jintana Roongseang.

This might be the place to convince your pad Thai-loving friends to try a new menu offering. The standards are available, but lively creations like Vietnamese crêpes plump with tofu, coconut flakes, shrimp, and cucumber make a case for sampling other items on the menu. *Nam tok* doesn't fall prey to sogginess here; grilled steak gets a kick from fresh mint, cilantro, lime, chilies, and onion.

Katsu

 Japanese

2651 W. Peterson Ave. (bet. Talman & Washtenaw Aves.)

Phone: 773-784-3383   Dinner Wed – Sun
Web: N/A
Prices: $$

Lovingly run by Chef Katsu Imamura and his wife, this charming Japanese spot offers sushi fans countless reasons to head over to Katsu's counter. Mrs. Imamura is a gracious presence in the dining room and, despite its age, the setting is attractively maintained. Its minimal décor bears personality, as in a sepia-toned print of Johnny Cash in the bathroom and robotic action figures stationed at the sushi bar.

Raw fish is the focus, prepared as sushi, sashimi, or *chirashi*. The deluxe platter brings pleasing mouthfuls of embellished nigiri–yellowtail with slivers of green onion, super-white tuna topped by caviar, and *amaebi* with tobiko–along with sashimi and *tamagoyaki*. The tasty cooked fare includes veal liver sautéed with garlic chives.

La Ciudad

Mexican

4515 N. Sheridan Rd. (bet. Sunnyside & Windsor Aves.)

Phone: 773-728-2887   Lunch & dinner daily
Web: www.laciudadgrill.com
Prices: Wilson

La Ciudad is a family-owned favorite that seems to smile upon this rather gritty strip-mall neighborhood. Inside is a contemporary space with deep red walls hung with black-and-white prints of bustling Mexico City. Cherry red walls lined with contemporary white chairs and upbeat Latin music brighten the mood.

Be sure to start by reviewing the white board for specials like guava empanadas or *pozole Sinaloan*, brimming with chunks of avocado, chicken, and hominy. Burrito fans will relish the grilled version here, stuffed, plump, and perfectly wrapped. The menu is teeming with different *sopes*, while beef ribs, and pork chops supplement classic enchiladas and tacos.

It is BYOB, but they offer all the fruit-flavored mixers to complete a margarita.

Andersonville, Edgewater & Uptown

La Fonda Latino Grill

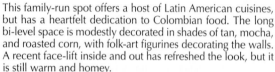

Latin American

E3

5350 N. Broadway (bet. Balmoral & Berwyn Aves.)

Phone: 773-271-3935
Web: www.lafondalatinogrill.com
Prices: $$

Lunch Tue – Fri
Dinner Tue – Sun
 Berwyn

This family-run spot offers a host of Latin American cuisines, but has a heartfelt dedication to Colombian food. The long bi-level space is modestly decorated in shades of tan, mocha, and roasted corn, with folk-art figurines decorating the walls. A recent face-lift inside and out has refreshed the look, but it is still warm and homey.

While the lunch buffet is popular, the regular menu is offered at any time. The two-dollar empanadas are not only a bargain, but are deliciously stuffed with beef and raisins or spinach and mushroom. Potent potables like the *mangorita* or sangria pair festively with grilled steaks or *cazuela de mariscos* full of seafood in a creamy tomato broth. Beans, rice and tostones are staples of any Colombian feast here.

Los Nopales

Mexican

C5

4544 N. Western Ave. (bet. Sunnyside & Wilson Aves.)

Phone: 773-334-3149
Web: www.losnopalesrestaurant.com
Prices:

Lunch & dinner Tue – Sun
 Western (Brown)

Beyond the deceptively small green awning, find a true fiesta that is as pleasing to the eyes as it is to the stomach. The tidy space is not large but feels big and bright with decorative cacti, holiday lights, and avocado walls trimming the two dining areas. Despite the little thatch-roofed cabana bar, they are BYOB.

The house-made chips and creamy puréed salsas (one with avocados and tomatillos, the other *chile de arbol*) are worth a visit on their own, as are the delicious *picaditas*. *Nopales*–crisp green cactus paddles–appear throughout the menu, perhaps sliced and grilled in a salad to accompany that delicious char-grilled skirt steak special with *frijoles borrachos* (drunken beans) and tortillas nestled in an embroidered kerchief.

Magnolia Cafe

E5

1224 W. Wilson Ave. (at Magnolia Ave.)

Phone: 773-728-8785
Web: www.magnoliacafeuptown.com
Prices: $$

Lunch Tue – Sat
Dinner Tue – Sun

Wilson

French sophistication meets casual American allure at this refined local bistro. A garden of tasseled lampshades hang from exposed wood beams, framed prints of the namesake flower blossom from rustic brick walls, and soft jazz soothes frayed edges after a rough day—note half-price bottles of wine on Tuesday nights can also help in that department.

Fresh fish specials like a shrimp and tuna tartare timbale held together by a soy-based vinaigrette and laced with golden tobiko change daily; but regulars heave a sigh of relief knowing that signature crab cakes are a staple. Not feeling the fish? Tuck into a hanger steak with frites, or a grilled double-cut pork chop fit for Fred Flintstone before taking a forkful of flourless chocolate-banana cake.

M. Henry

E2

5707 N. Clark St. (bet. Edgewater & Hollywood Aves.)

Phone: 773-561-1600
Web: www.mhenry.net
Prices: ⊖⊖

Lunch Tue – Sun

Bryn Mawr

Before settling into the sunny dining room teeming with happy hippies and trendy hipsters, take a good hard look at the shelves of pastries and cakes. These flaky, sugary confections are possibly the crown jewels of this farmhouse-esque sanctum, so plan on leaving room at the end for at least one of the sweets.

After deciding on dessert—maybe the likes of Belgian chocolate cookies, apple cake, or brioche cinnamon rolls—it's probably wise to move on to savory fare like "Fannie's killer fried egg sandwich" with Gorgonzola and bacon; apple-maple chicken sausage; or even a roster of other globally inspired sandwiches. If you're going sweet all the way, pancake and French toast variations abound, and bottomless cups of coffee wash it all down.

Ombra

Italian

E3

5310 N. Clark St. (bet. Berwyn & Summerdale Aves.)

Phone:	773-506-8600	Lunch Sat – Sun
Web:	www.barombra.com	Dinner nightly
Prices:		Berwyn

A spinoff of nearby cousin Acre, Ombra shares a main entry with the flagship but not the seasonal menu, instead focusing on Italian small plates. Raised booths upholstered with old leather jackets, orbital lights papier-mâchéd with weathered strips of newsprint, and wooden plank dividers telegraph a casual-cool mood.

Peruse the *salumi*, cheese, wine, and other daily specials listed on the chalkboard, or pick from the dozens of *cicchetti* displayed behind glass at the dining counter. Panko-crusted trotter terrine set over an acidic arugula salad is at once rich and crunchy; whereas cold composed salads with grilled chicken, olives, and raisins are antipasti on steroids. Negronis, Bellinis, and pours of house-made grappa or limoncello keep the bar hopping.

Opart Thai House

Thai

C5

4658 N. Western Ave. (bet. Eastwood & Leland Aves.)

Phone:	773-989-8517	Lunch & dinner daily
Web:	www.opartthai.com	
Prices:		Western (Brown)

While it may be mixed in and among the other local Thai eateries, this well-kept spot sets itself apart with its highly spiced and hearty food. The trio of rooms combines a mix of natural wood and dark stone tile floors, with intricate teak carvings accenting the exposed brick.

The large menu features an expansive selection of noodles, stir-fries, and soups. Be forewarned: they aren't playing games with the little spicy indicators, so if it says it's hot, it really is. Slices of char-broiled beef (*neau sa-ded*) are tasty and tender, with a sweet-sour sauce that brings a creeping heat. Curries are a popular highlight, as in the spicy, yellow *haeng musaman* with coconut milk, chicken, and potatoes. It's BYOB, but a liquor store is on the corner.

Over Easy Café

 American

D4

4943 N. Damen Ave. (bet. Ainslie & Argyle Sts.)

Phone: 773-506-2605 Lunch Tue – Sun
Web: www.overeasycafechicago.com
Prices: Damen (Brown)

This place takes the life's work of the hen seriously—from the menu to the décor. Exposed brick and red tin ceilings hug the cozy room, where tables are snug, the vibe is friendly and communal, and a painting of Humpty Dumpty stands sentinel over the dining counter.

Breakfast sandwiches like the "carbonara" with Parmesan and provolone, are a highlight; and many of the dishes have Latino flair, like sassy eggs with chorizo, guacamole, cheddar, and ancho ketchup. Sweeter starts are offered with the likes of an upside-down apple pancake with cinnamon-butter and whipped cream, or pumpkin pie French toast. Lunches may reveal a red chili chicken torta.

Complimentary coffee is waiting in the tiny foyer if there is a wait, and this alone is worth the wait.

Paprika

 Indian

B4

2547 W. Lawrence Ave. (bet. Maplewood Ave. & Rockwell St.)

Phone: 773-338-4906 Dinner Tue – Sun
Web: www.paprikachicago.com
Prices: **$$** Rockwell

Chef Shah Kabir and his family know hospitality. Prepare to be swept up in their warmth and care (with maybe a splash of kitsch) the minute you enter this richly colored space, adorned with artifacts, and even the chef himself at the door, welcoming guests to sit and sip a cool, refreshing *lassi*.

From aromatic, homemade curries to tasty twists on *dahls* (*turka dahl ki shabzi* is a revelation), everything is fresh and fragrant. Bengali fish curry is a notable attraction—its flavors mild yet lively with mustard seeds, firm and fresh green beans, and silky-sweet onions. A very nice selection of vegetarian dishes might include the veggie samosa, its soft, light shell stuffed with spices, potatoes, peas, and cauliflower, served with a trio of tangy chutneys.

Pho 777

Vietnamese 🍴

F4

1063-65 W. Argyle St. (bet. Kenmore & Winthrop Aves.)

Phone: 773-561-9909   Lunch & dinner Wed – Mon
Web: N/A
Prices: 😑   🚇 Argyle

This strip of Argyle Street is destination No. 1 when it comes to Vietnamese food. The décor may not distinguish Pho 777 from the pack, but good quality makes it an easy choice.

Of course, the namesake dish is a must. The broth of the *tai bo vien pho* (beef noodle soup with round steak and meatballs) is scented with cardamom, ginger, and clove. It might be a bit mild but tables are topped with an assortment of chili pastes and oils to spice things up. Start off with some spring rolls, filled with rice noodles, shrimp, mint, carrots, bean sprouts, and basil, served with a punchy peanut sauce. Charbroiled pork rice plates, catfish simmered in a clay pot, and an assortment of flavored bubble teas (think: papaya, taro, plum, and mango) complete the menu.

Pho Xe Tang - Tank Noodle

Vietnamese 🍴

E4

4953 N. Broadway (at Argyle St.)

Phone: 773-878-2253   Lunch & dinner Thu – Tue
Web: www.tank-noodle.com
Prices: 😑   🚇 Argyle

Also known as "Tank Noodles," Pho Xe Tang is one of the highlights of Little Saigon. Tables are dotted with caddies containing chopsticks, plastic and steel flatware, *sriracha*, soy sauce, and pickled jalapeños. Unlike other nearby eateries, Pho Xe Tang has a louder vibe, with lots of pulsating bass in its music.

No visit to a Vietnamese restaurant would be complete without slurping up *pho*, traditionally served with a plate of lime wedges and fresh greens (bean sprouts, fresh mint, basil, and sliced jalapeños). The *pho tai nam ve don* is as good a choice as any; its tender skirt steak spiced with star anise and cinnamon. Starters like the papaya salad and steamed rice flour roll provide additional (and authentic) tastes.

Ras Dashen

E2

5846 N. Broadway (bet. Ardmore & Thorndale Aves.)

Phone: 773-506-9601
Web: www.rasdashenchicago.com
Prices: $$

Lunch & dinner daily

 Thorndale

Welcoming and all-embracing, Ras Dashen is a good pick for both the neophyte to Ethiopian cuisine as well as the loyal enthusiast who wants authentic eats. The friendly staff is committed to both the food and your enjoyment, always happy to explain the drink offerings or the *mossab* (communal serving plate), all to the backdrop of pleasant Ethiopian folk music.

As is traditional, dishes are served with *injera*, the fermented pancake-like bread used to ladle food like *yebeg wat*, a dish of tender lamb cubes stewed in a spicy *berbere* sauce. For dessert, expect the likes of warm and creamy bread pudding made with *injera*, spices, and flax seeds.

A fully stocked bar in the back mixes a list of signature "Ras Dashen" cocktails and beers from Africa and beyond.

Rosded

C5

2308 W. Leland Ave. (bet. Lincoln & Western Aves.)

Phone: 773-334-9055
Web: N/A
Prices:

Lunch & dinner Tue – Sun

 Western (Brown)

This BYOB Thai fave has seen quite a bit of traffic in its day, as evidenced by the lived-in feel of the tiny, eleven-table dining space. But we get it. Belly-pleasing dishes keep the place packed for lunch and dinner, while maintaining a hearty take-out business to boot.

Soups, noodles, rice dishes, curries, and salads are offered in vast varieties on the menu; as are yummy mains like flaky catfish fritters, battered and deep-fried, smothered with a glaze of sweet chili sauce and fragrant Thai basil; or Rama chicken with curry-peanut sauce. Try the *pad prik khing*—curried green beans with a choice of meat; or smoky, tender pork satay, marinated in flavorful yellow curry, grilled, and served with a dipping sauce and zesty cucumber salad.

Andersonville, Edgewater & Uptown

San Soo Gab San

Korean

C3

5247 N. Western Ave. (bet. Berwyn & Farragut Aves.)

Phone: 773-334-1589
Web: N/A
Prices: 😊😊

Lunch & dinner daily

Beloved by families by day and large groups on the late night, this neighborhood standby appeals to locals and visitors thanks to the grill-top tables offering do-it-yourself feasts and lived-in décor.

A meal commences with the typically mammoth parade of *banchan* including several types of kimchi, sesame oil-flavored vegetables, cold noodle salads, and even a steaming bowl of savory soup. The sheer number served forgives a few misses in quality. The massive menu shows all the classics like *dol sot bi bim bap* and *bulgogi*. Try the giant *mandoo* accompanied by a pungent, spicy dipping sauce, as well as char-broiled chicken in a smoky-sweet glaze. San Soo Gab San is open almost all night, perfect for a boozey Korean barbecue feast with friends.

Siam Noodle & Rice

Thai

F5

4654 N. Sheridan Rd. (at Leland Ave.)

Phone: 773-769-6694
Web: www.siamnoodleandrice.com
Prices: 😊😊

Lunch & dinner Tue – Sun

🚇 Wilson

This cozy mainstay opened its doors over twenty years ago and has been going strong ever since. Family-run and charming to boot, this Thai favorite churns out scrumptious specialties with a unique home-style twist; collard greens get sprinkled into a number of dishes, like *pad see ew*, and sliced ham hocks are stewed Thai-style over rice in the *kao kha moo*.

To start, settle into a glass-topped table and try the papaya salad, neatly piled high with julienned green papaya, basil, and chilies topped with pungent dried shrimp, all perfectly drenched in a bright lime dressing. Meat lovers should explore the list of chef's specials, like basil meatballs—sliced and stir-fried with strips of green chili and bamboo shoots, tossed in a salty-sweet sauce.

Spacca Napoli

Pizza ✗

D5

1769 W. Sunnyside Ave. (bet. Hermitage & Ravenswood Aves.)

Phone: 773-878-2420
Web: www.spaccanapolipizzeria.com
Prices:

Lunch Wed – Sun
Dinner nightly
Montrose (Brown)

A warm greeting awaits, just bypass the door at the corner and enter on Sunnyside, under the *Vera Pizza Napoletana* sign—you are in the right place for authentic Neapolitan pizza. Named for the historic street that bisects Naples, Spacca Napoli is the Chicago home to the thin-crusted and truly authentic Neopolitan pie. This should be no surprise, as it is equipped with an extraordinary Bisazza glass-tiled pizza oven and Naples-trained Chef/owner Jon Goldsmith.

The menu is built around a dozen or so perfectly blistered pizzas; they arrive uncut to your table to stay hot and simply topped with myriad mozzarella options or as more lavish specials decked with egg, truffles, and *guanciale*. Couple this with chilled antipasti and wine in juice glasses.

Spoon Thai

Thai ✗

C5

4608 N. Western Ave. (bet. Eastwood & Wilson Aves.)

Phone: 773-769-1173
Web: www.spoonthai.com
Prices:

Lunch & dinner daily

Set along a strip of Western Avenue that is rich in Asian offerings, Spoon Thai is certainly worthy of consideration. The room is simple but clean and warmed by the affable service.

Look past the spring rolls and satay for a more enriching experience. Homemade Thai sausages and the *yum pla muk* salad of squid tossed with spicy lime dressing and fragrant herbs are two fine preludes. The array of vibrant cooking goes on to feature the likes of *ka nom jeen nam ya*, ground catfish in curry sauce over wide noodles; and intriguing house specialties such as banana blossom salad, a meaty combination of chicken and shrimp with slivers of tender banana blossom in a warm coconut milk sauce bright with lime and red chili and showered with crispy shallots.

35

Sunshine Cafe

E3

J a p a n e s e

5449 N. Clark St. (bet. Catalpa & Rascher Aves.)

Phone: 773-334-6214   Dinner Tue – Sun
Web: N/A
Prices: 🚇 Bryn Mawr

While many dining establishments succeed at being hospitable, it's an absolute pleasure when one encounters an ambience that is truly welcoming and laid-back, case in point Sunshine Cafe. The setting is modest but does bear one note of embellishment: a bright yellow sign that reads "You are my sunshine."

This sprightly spot showcases home-style Japanese cooking that is hearty and heartwarming. Starters include *shu mai*, potato croquettes, and *inari zushi* (fried tofu skin pouches filled with seasoned sushi rice). Entrées, accompanied by miso soup and green tea, focus on broiled fish, tempura and donburi. The *katsu don* is a bowl of top quality rice decked with slices of tender, panko-crusted pork tenderloin, sautéed onions, egg, and light brown sauce.

Tank Sushi

C5

J a p a n e s e

4514 N. Lincoln Ave. (at Sunnyside Ave.)

Phone: 773-769-2600   Lunch & dinner daily
Web: www.tanksushi.com
Prices: $$ 🚇 Western (Brown)

Step aside, sushi purists. This diverse gang of chefs whips up a frenzy of artful and innovative creations, throwing fried bananas into a maki alongside lobster and spiced honey mayo; and drizzling butter-soy sauce, red *tobiko*, and chives over tender chunks of steamed king crab. Traditional maki, classic sashimi, and various nigiri also line the multi-page menu, as do hot and cold small plates like the decadent crisp chopstick roll stuffed with mushrooms and cream cheese.

Happy hour specials offer selections at half price, though there's usually a crowd to contend with. Grab a spot in the sleek, modern space and refresh with a flight of fragrant sake—there's an ample selection to choose from. End the feast with tasty mango *mochi*.

Thai Grill

Thai ✂

F1

1040 W. Granville Ave. (bet. Kenmore & Winthrop Aves.)

Phone:	773-274-7510	Lunch & dinner Tue – Sun
Web:	www.thaigrillchicago.com	
Prices:	⎈⎈	🚊 Granville

♿ In the ground floor of the Sovereign building, Thai Grill & Noodle Bar sports a more contemporary (and less clichéd) take on the typical Thai eatery. Amid the grey walls, striped zebrawood tables, and dark banquettes, find locals, families, and students from nearby Loyola enjoying tasty renditions of Thai standards and sipping tapioca "bubble" teas.

Diners who are new to Thai cuisine, or just shy about the heat of their food, should not fear as these dishes are friendly to western palates. Expect the likes of papaya salad with dried shrimp and citrus dressing, catfish with red curry and Kaffir lime leaves, and Thai coconut custard. A vegetarian menu might include *massaman curry jay* (tofu, vegetables, coconut milk, and peanuts) or grilled tofu satay.

Thai Pastry & Restaurant

Thai ✂

E4

4925 N. Broadway (bet. Ainslie & Argyle Sts.)

Phone:	773-784-5399	Lunch & dinner daily
Web:	www.thaipastry.com	
Prices:	$$	Argyle

Thriving since 2000 in the stretch of North Broadway known as Little Saigon, this unassuming restaurant and bakery showcases authentic Thai cooking from Chef/owner Aumphai Kusub. Traditional artifacts on the walls and ceramic serving vessels brought to each table echo the delicate and colorful handiwork of the individual cakes and pastries on display.

Savory dishes favor classic preparations and flavors that balance spice, creaminess, and acidity. These might feature chicken *massaman* curry; lightly fried crab Rangoon; or *nam tok* with tender sliced beef, chilies, and mint. But it's the pastry and ice cream parade loaded with treats like *klong klang*, taro custard, and curry puffs that's truly eye-catching. Take some home to assuage a late-night craving.

37

Bucktown & Wicker Park

Ukranian Village · West Town

Finesse and Flair

Like many of the Windy City's neighborhoods, Bucktown and Wicker Park has seen its fair share of transition. Ranging from Polish immigrants to wealthy businessmen (who have built stately mansions on Hoyne and Pierce avenues), it has been home to people from all walks of life. But, don't let the hushed residential streets and bewitching brownstones fool you—this neighborhood still knows how to mix it up. While you're more likely to run into bankers than Basquiats these days, Bucktown and Wicker Park remains an international hotbed of creative energy and trendsetting style.

Shopping Sanctum

Shake out the remains of your piggy bank before arriving. After all, this neighborhood has some of the most stylish shopping in the Midwest. It is worlds away from the international chains of the Magnificent Mile. Instead, think über-cool indie shops. Don't have time to travel the world for funky home accessories, or love the flea market look but don't want to get out of bed on the weekends? Fake the well-traveled look and visit Fenway Gallery, where you can pick up an exotic home accessory or two. To experience a taste of Wicker Park's vast and vivid music scene, be sure you make

the time to stop by Reckless Records and get schooled on the latest underground band. You can even get creative and design your own t-shirt at the appropriately named T-Shirt Deli—and rest assured, as this is only the beginning of a wonderful journey.

Gathering of the Arts

The neighborhood shows off its artistic roots by hosting two of the city's largest festivals. Wicker Park Fest is an annual two-day music festival held each July that features no less than 28 bands. The Around the Coyote festival held each fall shines a spotlight on local artists practicing creative and visual arts. Wicker Park is also home to a number of art galleries, including the unique 4Art Inc., where artists create their works during the opening night show.

Even starving artists can find something to eat in foodie-friendly Bucktown and Wicker Park. Hot dog fanatics simply must take a tour of the famed **Vienna Beef Factory**—visitors are bound to be blown away by the production lines of products made here. After a view of the manufacturing line, indulge your appetite by dining in the large employee cafeteria. Parched after all this meat eating? Quench your thirst by heading straight for **Black Dog**

Gelato, where you can savor outstanding whisky gelato bars dipped in milk chocolate and candied bacon; or taste unusual flavors like goat cheese-cashew-caramel.

Fascinating Foods

Bucktown and Wicker Park locals also love and savor the flavors and tastes of the **Butcher & Larder**. Husband & wife, Rob & Allie Levitt are the meat and potato behind this Noble Square butcher shop. Since leaving Mado in 2010, the couple has focused on the dwindling profession of artisan butchery and supporting local farmers in the process. Whole animal butchery isn't seen much these days, but the Levitts even offer classes on how to break down whole animals and produce wonderful sausages, terrines, and cured bacon, also available in their shop. Go whole hog and bone up on your cooking skills at **Cooking Fools**, and you won't ever be teased about your tiramisu again.

If you're planning to entertain friends with an elaborate meal at home, be sure to swing by the **Wicker Park & Bucktown Farmer's Market** for a full range of fresh produce, glorious cheeses, and other specialty items. And while basking in cheese paradise, don't forget to grab a pie at **Piece**—hugely frequented by natives due to its rep as Chicagoland's most favored pizza place. However, Piece has garnered a following that comes by not only for their crunchy pizzas, but also for their hand-crafted beers and delicious spectrum of appetizers, sandwiches, and desserts. Sweet tooths worth their salt certainly know all about **Red Hen Bread**. Atkins would turn over in his grave if he ever got a taste of the bread and pastries from this terrific bake shop. Lauded as an exceptional carrier of high quality artisan breads and pastries," Red Hen sates scores with the likes of croissants, muffins, scones, cookies, tarts, quiches, and Red Hen Signature treats. Think your mama makes good pie? Grab a fork and taste a lip-smacking piece from **Hoosier Mama Pie Company**. Run by Paula Haney, the former pastry chef at Trio, it's a little slice of paradise. And of course, no bakeshop is complete without cake, and **Alliance Bakery**'s window display of cakes is quite stupendous.

Crowning Cocktails

Speaking of stupendous, lull on the late night at **Violet Hour**, the speakeasy that serves some of the most heavenly cocktails in town. Slurp up these concoctions while chowing on toasty treats like spiced nuts, deviled eggs with smoked paprika and goat cheese, and smoky chili cheese mini-dogs topped with mustard and onion. **Marie's Rip-Tide Lounge** is a bit of retro fun. With such soulful beats emanating from a jukebox and an incredibly energetic vibe, this hopping lounge draws a regular roster of late night revelers. Marie, now in her 70s, lives upstairs and decorates this frozen-in-time space for all of the holidays. The perennially-packed **Moonshine Brewing Company** showcases a solid and serious beer collection, with packs brewed on-site; while **Silver Cloud** is foolproof for

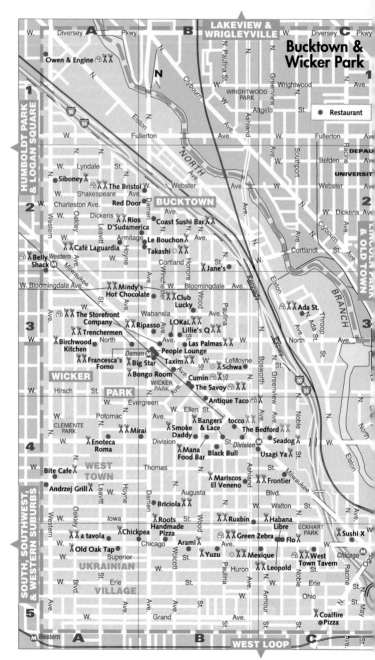

LAKEVIEW &
WRIGLEYVILLE

W. Diversey A Pkwy.   B   W. Diversey C Pkwy.

Owen & Engine

N

WRIGHTWOOD
PARK

W. Ave.   Wrightwood   Ave.

Greenview

● Restaurant

Clybourn

Elston

Fullerton   Ave.   N. NORTH   Fullerton   Ave.

HUMBOLDT PARK & LOGAN SQUARE

Ashland   Southport   Racine   DEPAU
UNIVERSIT

W. Lyndale   St.   Belden   Ave
Siboney   The Bristol W.   Webster   Ave.
W. Shakespeare   Ave.
Red Door
W. Charleston Ave.   BUCKTOWN   W. Dickens Ave
W. Oakley   Dickens   St.
Rios   Coast Sushi Bar
D'Sudamerica   Cortlandt   St.
Armitage   Le Bouchon   Ave.
Café Laguardia   Takashi
Cortland   St.
Jane's
Belly   Western   Honore
Shack   Cortland

Milwaukee

WICKER

W. Bloomingdale Ave.   Bloomingdale   Ave.   Kennedy
Mindy's   Club   Ada St.
Hot Chocolate   Lucky
The Storefront   Wabansia   LOKaL   Ave.
Company   Ripasso   Lillie's Q
Trenchermen   North   Las Palmas   North   Ave.
Birchwood   People Lounge
Kitchen   Damen   Big Star   Taxim   LeMoyne
Francesca's   Bongo Room   Cumin   Schwa
Forno   The Savoy
W. Hirsch   St.   Antique Taco
PARK   WICKER
PARK
W.   Evergreen
W. Potomac   Ellen St.
CLEMENTE   Mirai   Bangers   tocco
PARK   Smoke   & Lace   The Bedford
Daddy   St. Division   Seadog
Enoteca   Division   Mana   Black Bull   Usagi Ya
Roma   WEST   Food Bar
Bite Cafe   TOWN   Thomas
Andrzej Grill   Mariscos   Frontier
El Veneno   Milwaukee
Augusta   Walton   St.
Briciola   Blvd.
Roots   St.   Ruxbin   Habana
a tavola   Chickpea   Handmade   Libre
Pizza   Green Zebra   ECKHART
Old Oak Tap   Chicago   Arami   Flo   PARK   Sushi X
UKRAINIAN   Yuzu   Mexique   West
Superior   Leopold   Town Tavern
W.   Erie   St.
VILLAGE   Huron
W. Blvd.
Ohio
Ave.   Grand   Coalfire
Pizza

Western   WEST LOOP

40

sidewalk boozing, chicken pot pie, or a grilled cheese sandwich. This comfort food haven makes one feel completely at home by virtue of its casual vibe and interior that is flooded with warmth. Whether you're here for "small bites," "big bowls," or a crowning cocktail, Silver Cloud is sure to be a crowd-pleaser and reeks of Bucktown.

Late Night Fun

Definitely defining the 'tude of the 'hood is the **Cellar Rat Wine Shop**. If you thought exceptional wines at excellent value was never a possibility, think again, as this place will prove you wrong. Displaying a splendid array, this neighborhood delight never fails to satisfy, no matter the day or time. Carry on your Saturday night fever at **Salud**

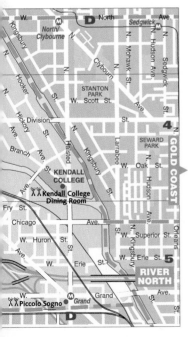

Tequila Lounge. Alongside an exquisitely delightful range of tequilas, Salud also salutes foodies with south-of-the-border spreads from gooey guacamole, crispy nachos, and quesadillas, to classic tortas, tacos, and other deliciousness. Straight from the horse's mouth, eat well but drink better at **Angels and Mariachis**. This bar may be rustic-looking, but it reverberates nightly with a raucous set. Watch them groove to the beats of rock and country, whilst sipping and savoring a menu of eats 'n treats. From martinis, margaritas, tequila, and cerveza, to a range of Mexican faithfuls, this cantina struts it all.

Wholesome Ways

Local Folks Food is a family-run enterprise whose chief charge is to develop delicious, natural, and gourmet condiments (mustard and hot sauce anyone?) perfect for slathering upon burgers. Find these tangy, tantalizing treats at the lauded **Green Grocer** and know that they will elevate your burger to ethereal. And finally, much to every foodie's delight, Bucktown and Wicker Park also features **Olivia's**, a fantastic and fabulously unique marketplace. This particular paragon is replete with the finest quality products, including hard-to-find specialty items displayed beside a plethora of organic, locally made items, as well as everyday brands. Choose your favorite foods, a precious collection of artisan cheeses, then your best beverage (from an incredible selection of wine and beer), and end the affair with a dramatic ensemble of flowers before heading home to execute an elegant and enticing dinner party.

Ada St.

Contemporary ✕✕

1664 N. Ada St. (bet. Concord Pl. & Wabansia Ave.)

Phone: 773-697-7069 · Dinner Wed – Sun
Web: www.adastreetchicago.com
Prices: $$

North/Clybourn

Give your eyes a minute to adjust to the lobby's twinkling candelabras, before strolling down a dim corridor to arrive at this hip and happy dining room. Guests congregate around picnic and ping-pong tables on the Astroturf patio, or lounge inside on banquettes covered in repurposed wool Army blankets.

The vinyl collection is as impressive as the cocktail list. Enjoy a deep cut from Marvin Gaye while soothing your soul with an applejack julep. The small plates menu builds from simple *salumi* and cheese, to salmon tartare tossed with bacon lardons, trout roe, and smoky, crispy salmon skin; or rare grass-fed beef tenderloin with a horseradish vinaigrette. It's first come, first served for the bar and patio; otherwise, opt for a table reservation.

Andrzej Grill

Polish ✕

1022 N. Western Ave. (bet. Augusta Blvd. & Cortez St.)

Phone: 773-489-3566 · Lunch & dinner Mon – Sat
Web: www.andrzejgrillrestaurant.com
Prices:

No trip to Chicago would be complete without a super filling, inexpensive, and authentic Polish feast. If you're not invited into someone's home for such a satisfying meal, the homey Andrzej Grill is as good a choice. The diminutive, no-frills stop is as popular for take-out as dining in.

Service is efficient and straightforward, which can be said of the food, too. For less than $10, diners can fill up on the Polish platter, which includes a crisp potato pancake; stuffed cabbage roll (tender leaves of cabbage surrounding a steamed filling of herb-scented rice); a smoky, well-seasoned, grilled kielbasa; and that star of the Polish culinary world: plump *pierogi*. And on top of all this comes a side of tasty sauerkraut, made with cabbage and carrot.

Antique Taco

B4

Mexican 🍴

1360 N. Milwaukee Ave. (at Wood St.)

Phone: 773-687-8697

Web: www.antiquetaco.com

Prices: 💰

Lunch & dinner Tue – Sun

🚇 Damen (Blue)

Antique doesn't mean staid or out of touch when it comes to the food at Antique Taco. In fact, the flavor combinations here are nothing short of modern. Order at the walk-up counter and take a numbered wooden spool to one of the boxy varnished plank tables. The composed Mexican dishes may take a few minutes to cook and plate, but that's how you know they're coming out fresh.

Bold dishes like a tender masa biscuit ladled with luxurious lobster gravy; chorizo chili topped with beer-battered cheese curds and scallion *crema*; or habanero-tinged popcorn arrive on old-school china plates. Desserts like Abuelita's pop tart with Mexican chocolate and marshmallow are too good to pass up, but get them with your meal so you won't have to wait in line a second time.

Arami

B5

Japanese 🍴

1829 W. Chicago Ave. (bet. Wolcott Ave & Wood St.)

Phone: 312-243-1535

Web: www.aramichicago.com

Prices: $$

Dinner Tue – Sun

🚇 Division

Serenity and taste extend well beyond the dangling bamboo, moss, and riverstones in the front window at Arami, where unembellished fresh fish and light but artful Japanese cuisine have the chance to shine. Ask to sit in the back for a view of the sushi bar and absorb the wide sake selection or a Japanese spirit-infused cocktail while the chefs work with a deft touch.

Pristine freshness is evident in all of their raw offerings that may include the "secret hamachi" where opaque yellowtail is paired with the earthy flavors of mushrooms and truffle oil. Cooked items have revealed *togarashi*-seared tuna coupled with a crunchy seaweed salad; while warming braised short ribs served with pickled Asian pear and Fresno chiles keep things interesting.

Bucktown & Wicker Park

a tavola

A5

Italian ✗✗

2148 W. Chicago Ave. (bet. Hoyne Ave. & Leavitt St.)

Phone: 773-276-7567
Web: www.atavolachicago.com
Prices: $$

Dinner Mon – Sat

Don't bother looking for a sign: a tavola takes up residence in a stately brick house on an otherwise storefront-lined block in the Ukrainian Village—an ivy-covered façade is a dead giveaway in the summer. Stepping inside is like arriving at Chef/owner Dan Bocik's home for a dinner party, where a convivial and gracious atmosphere reigns from the three-seat wine bar and gorgeous original wood floors, to the serene back patio.

A concise menu offers straightforward Italian food, though who needs frills when pillows of gnocchi with crispy sage and brown butter; or on-point beef tenderloin with roasted rosemary potato coins are so effective on their own? Dessert follows the same simple blueprint with a tangy lemon curd-filled shortbread tart.

Bangers & Lace

B4

Gastropub ✗

1670 W. Division St. (at Paulina St.)

Phone: 773-252-6499
Web: www.bangersandlacechicago.com
Prices: $$

Lunch & dinner daily

 Damen (Blue)

Brat and brew lovers take note: this hopping gastropub is taking things far beyond your average ballgame fare. "Bangers" get serious sprucing up here. Smoked venison sausage is served in a toasted challah roll and topped with rhubarb jam, candied bacon bits, black currants, and house-made beer mustard; a French garlic sausage is wrapped in soft brioche cornbread with orange marmalade, foie gras mousse, and maple butter; and a veal brat is paired with melted Gouda and sauerkraut.

Exposed brick walls lined with beer taps, blackboards with daily specials, and lace curtains all give warmth to the hipster-packed space. The thirty-plus beer list includes locally crafted brews as well as a slew of international and regional offerings.

The Bedford

B4

American XX

1612 W. Division St. (at Ashland Ave.)

Phone: 773-235-8800

Web: www.bedfordchicago.com

Prices: $$

Dinner Mon – Sat

Damen (Blue)

This old bank continues to service its community, but now as a restaurant honoring the foods of America's Midwest. Look for the doorman to find the portal that "deposits" you down the slate stairwell and into the glamorous Bedford. The bar and dining room turns back the clock with vaults, safe deposits, and Americana pictures. If scenes from family road trips come to mind, you're on track. Either way, it is idyllic for a romantic tryst.

Peruse the nibbles as you nestle: Grandma Ann's deviled eggs with hot sauce are a perfect intro for a roasted beet salad with candied fennel and pumpernickel. Pan-seared strip steak paired a potato purée and knob onions; or a chocolate-strawberry pie filled with fresh berries will hook any cool Chicagoan.

Belly Shack

A2

Fusion X

1912 N. Western Ave. (at Milwaukee Ave.)

Phone: 773-252-1414

Web: www.bellyshack.com

Prices: ⊖⊖

Lunch & dinner Tue – Sun

Western (Blue)

Everything feels like a fantastic burst of flavor at Chef/owner Bill Kim's Asian-Latin snack shop. Hip crowds fill this minimalist-urban spot burrowed beneath the El, line up to order at the counter, grab a number, and get their own silverware and soft drinks (BYOB) as their funky fusion dishes are prepared.

Vegetarian and vegan options abound, as in the *Boricua bulgogi*, made with marinated tofu (or chicken), crispy plantains, brown rice, and hoisin sauce. Hot and sour soup with hominy, chicken, and cilantro is proof that this innovative kitchen knows exactly what it's doing with Latin-meets-Asian flavors.

Belly Shack's delicious soft serve swirls together such playful flavors as Vietnamese cinnamon and caramel with outrageous success.

Big Star

Bucktown & Wicker Park

B3

Mexican

1531 N. Damen Ave. (bet. Milwaukee & Wicker Park Aves.)

Phone: 773-235-4039

Web: www.bigstarchicago.com

Prices:

Lunch & dinner daily

Damen (Blue)

The team behind Blackbird, Avec, and Publican have built one heck of a rollicking hot spot here for Wicker Park scenesters. Loud music, a grungy but hip vibe, and abundant drink specials keep the lofty garage-like space filled to the rafters. Arrive seriously early to claim a spot at the bar, or just go with the standing room flow and raise a glass with 200 of your closest friends and neighbors.

Order up an outstandingly refreshing michelada or prepare to succumb to the addictive La Paloma. Highlights of the tasty menu include a satisfying *queso fundido*, smoky tacos *al pastor*, a killer Sonoran hot dog plus some solid guacamole. With three dollar shots and pitchers of Schlitz you'll want to keep the food coming to survive the booze consumption.

Birchwood Kitchen

A3

American

2211 W. North Ave. (bet. Bell Ave. & Leavitt St.)

Phone: 773-276-2100

Web: www.birchwoodkitchen.com

Prices:

Lunch Tue – Sun

Dinner Tue – Fri

Damen (Blue)

Birchwood Kitchen's periwinkle façade sparkles like a gem from a stretch of brick storefronts lining North Avenue. Daily specials written on a cookie sheet and old church pews lining the exposed brick walls hint of quirky country charm and mirror the ethos of the utterly fresh and ever-changing menu, which might include a quiche with country pork sausage and slivered apple, or house-cured gravlax. The café takes pride in supporting local edibles like Burton's maple syrup and the Metropolis Coffee Company.

Prepared foods in a glass case make the idea of a picnic completely sensible and inspiring, and homemade sweets beg to be wrapped up for dessert. It's hard to pin down a choice from the jars of soft cookies, banana nut bread, and gooey brownies.

Bite Cafe

American ✗

A4

1039 N. Western Ave. (bet. Cortez & Thomas Sts.)

Phone:	773-395-2483	Lunch & dinner daily
Web:	www.bitecafechicago.com	
Prices:	$$	

Though Bite's black-framed windows barely stand out on its block of industrial brick storefronts, gals with a roller derby edge serve up unforgettably bold dishes inside. Grab a seat at the small back counter or take up residence at distressed oak tables armed with powder blue metal chairs, and settle in for an eccentric but filling ride.

Eat all day, if you can: breakfast *poutine* gilds the lily with poached eggs atop house-cut fries, cheese curds, and smoked bacon gravy. Lunch? How about a fried chicken leg sandwich with pickled cabbage slaw and Tabasco aïoli? Dinner could be bison Salisbury steak or a Porterhouse pork chop paired with watermelon and tomato salad. And don't stop before dessert; there's pie, pound cake, or ice cream to be had.

Black Bull

Spanish

B4

1721 W. Division St. (bet. Hermitage Ave. & Paulina St.)

Phone:	773-227-8600	Dinner Tue – Sun
Web:	www.blackbullchicago.com	
Prices:		Division

Like a matador brandishing his cape, the red neon silhouette of a bull draws hungry diners to this tiny, no-reservations tapas bar on Division Street. Inside, stacks of earthenware plates on glossy black communal tables and Andalusian ceramic wall tiles give the sultry interior the feel of an authentic but modern Spanish pintxos bar. Glasses of red and rosé sangria abound, though the Iberian Peninsula gets fair play on the wine list as well.

Snack on marinated olives while perusing the menu, where traditional tapas get a bit of finesse. *Pulpo a la Gallega* is braised, grilled, and dusted with paprika for a double punch of smokiness. The classic combination of *jamon Serrano*, Manchego cheese, and fresh tomato on sliced baguette is a sexy, salty mess.

Bucktown & Wicker Park

Bongo Room

American

B3

1470 N. Milwaukee Ave. (bet. Evergreen Ave. & Honore St.)

Phone: 773-489-0690
Web: www.thebongoroom.com
Prices:

Lunch daily

Damen (Blue)

This cheery spot with a jaunty name has offered Wicker Park residents a hearty start to the day since 1993. Fuel up on eggs any style, banana and bacon flapjacks with warm praline sauce and fresh banana, or the super-stuffed breakfast burrito—though be forewarned that any one of these may send you back home for a nap. Come midday, treats like the chicken and pear club or spinach, golden beet, and duck confit salad will sate you until sundown, but keep in mind they don't serve dinner.

The sunny room, offset by an upbeat staff, is fitted with yellow-painted furnishings and a dining counter that doubles as an excellent roost for those who are best left alone until after that all-important first cuppa'.

Also try their South Loop and Andersonville locations.

Briciola

Italian

B4

937 N. Damen Ave. (bet. Augusta Blvd. & Iowa St.)

Phone: 773-772-0889
Web: www.briciolachicago.com
Prices: $$

Dinner nightly

Division

After decades of cooking and traveling, Chef/owner Mario Maggi was ready to open a small place—just a crumb, or "la briciola," of a restaurant. This tiny trattoria nestled between Ukrainian Village's brick buildings is indeed a speck of warmth and charm, festooned with party lights on the patio and mustard-toned walls inside.

Traditional Italian cuisine gets personalized tweaks from the chef. *Carpacci* may include paper-thin octopus, beets, or beef; *macaroncini alla Briciola* folds diced Tuscan sausage into a spicy garlic-sage sauce; and a hefty bone-in pork chop, pounded thin, breaded, and pan-fried until golden, is a house classic dressed with arugula and shaved Parmesan.

A bottle from the wine shop down the block makes the meal even more convivial.

The Bristol

B2

American 🍴🍴

2152 N. Damen Ave. (bet. Shakespeare & Webster Aves.)

Phone: 773-862-5555
Web: www.thebristolchicago.com
Prices: $$

Lunch Sun
Dinner nightly

At The Bristol, Chef/owner Chris Pandel aims to reward boldly carnivorous cravings head-on, sending out strongly satisfying plates–often highlighting less appreciated cuts–in a comfortable and convivial setting.

There is always plenty to munch on while cocktailing here, perhaps accompanying your numerous sips of an autumn gimlet with crispy chicken skin dipped in ranch dressing, beet crostini crowned with *lardo* and pistachios, or chickpea pancakes topped with piperade and parsley to please even the most timid tastes. Larger plates include specials such as smoked salmon with bacon-dill dumplings and *piment d'Esplette*. Timid and adventurous palates meet for dessert to share a monumental finale like caramel pot *de crème* with café dolce and confit lemon.

Café Laguardia

A2

Cuban 🍴🍴

2111 W. Armitage Ave. (bet. Hoyne Ave. & Leavitt St.)

Phone: 773-862-5996
Web: www.cafelaguardia.com
Prices: ⊖⊖

Lunch & dinner daily

🚇 Western (Blue)

A portrait of one of history's most fervent Cuba-lovers, Ernest Hemingway, hangs on the wall in this second-generation Cuban haunt. Red-topped tables are paired with chairs upholstered in a riot of animal prints, lending the place a marked south-of-the-border expat feel.

The menu renders an armchair trip to Cuba, with an affordable sampling of filling sides and entrées. A particular bargain is the Taste of Cuba platter, which shows off the kitchen's specialties: *picadillo criollo*, a ground beef dish with raisins and olives, is hot and flavorful; the fried pork medallions are crunchy, caramelized, and tender; and the ham croquette sports an appealing (and golden) exterior. Black beans, white rice, and grease-free fried plantains complement the meaty menu.

Chickpea

Middle Eastern

B5

2018 W. Chicago Ave. (bet. Damen & Hoyne Aves.)

Phone: 773-384-9930 — Lunch & dinner daily
Web: www.chickpeaonthego.com
Prices: ⊜⊜

Chickpea's modern and traditional mash-up comes through loud and clear—a blast of Led Zep from the kitchen blends with a snake charmer tune from the Genie pinball machine in the corner. Adding to the medley is an iconic Coca-Cola sign in Arabic that hangs under ornate brass lamps and lanterns.

Chef Amni Suqi's menu matches the décor with its combo of Middle Eastern flavors and simple preparations. Tabbouleh and *kibbeh* enliven and refresh the palate, and flaky, honey-soaked baklava is made in-house. Daily dinner specials pull from Suqi's Palestinian culinary repertoire, and may include *koosa mihshee* or *malfoof waraq dawalli*. Vegetarians will eat well and happily at Chickpea, as approximately half the menu is not only veggie-centric but vegan.

Club Lucky

Italian XX

B3

1824 W. Wabansia Ave. (at Honore St.)

Phone: 773-227-2300 — Lunch Mon – Fri
Web: www.clubluckychicago.com — Dinner nightly
Prices: $$ — 🚇 Damen (Blue)

An Italian-American supper club for the ages, Club Lucky has played the part since 1990 and its glass block windows, red vinyl booths, and linoleum tiled-floor look no worse for the wear. Grab a signature "killer martini" and come to rest upon a round red cushioned stool in the front cocktail lounge. Alternatively, settle in for a big traditional spread at any of the black Formica tables.

All the classics are represented proudly from minestrone with perfectly al dente pasta shells among cannellini beans, greens, and potatoes; and golden brown chicken Parmesan with homemade marinara; to baked meaty littleneck clams. Should you need a little red sauce for the road, Club Lucky sells its packaged version along with salad dressing and freshly baked bread.

Coalfire Pizza

C5

Pizza

1321 W. Grand Ave. (bet. Ada & Elizabeth Sts.)

Phone: 312-226-2625
Web: www.coalfirechicago.com
Prices:

Lunch & dinner Tue – Sun

Chicago (Blue)

Few restaurants are as aptly named as Coalfire. The pizzas from this local favorite are cooked in an oven fueled by a coal fire. That 800-degree fire sets the stage for the kitchen and the menu.

The menu does include a few other Italian favorites like salads and calzones, but really there's no reason to consider them, because you (and everyone else in town) are here for the pizza, and that in itself says a great deal. These are not Chicago-style pies; rather, an American spin on 14-inch Neapolitan-style pies. Pick from one of nine combos or create your own. Options include fresh or regular mozzarella cheese, thin sliced hot salami, and pesto. A decent beer and wine list round out the offerings, but bring patience, since they don't take reservations.

Coast Sushi Bar

B2

Japanese

2045 N. Damen Ave. (bet. Dickens & McLean Aves.)

Phone: 773-235-5775
Web: www.coastsushibar.com
Prices: $$

Lunch Sat – Sun
Dinner nightly

Dimly lit but not sedate in the least, Coast Sushi Bar is high volume—both in the amount of fish it sends out to its animated guests and the mix of chatter and thumping music that nearly overpowers the food. Japanese chefs donned in matching T-shirts and baseball caps crank out rolls at a dizzying pace behind the slender Formica counter, crowned by a glass case loaded with pristine seafood.

Spring for real wasabi root alongside sushi like hamachi and madai, neatly sliced and draped elegantly over rice; or signature maki like the White Dragon with shrimp tempura. While you have to BYOB, a litany of appetizers like jalapeño-spiked miso soup, or tropical ceviche sporting fresh seafood in a cilantro-lime marinade make for divine accompaniments.

Cumin

B3

1414 N. Milwaukee Ave. (bet. Evergreen & Wolcott Aves.)

Phone:	773-342-1414	Lunch Tue – Sun
Web:	www.cumin-chicago.com	Dinner nightly
Prices:		Damen (Blue)

Polished wood, steel, and leather accents, and white linen tables draped with butcher paper make it clear this isn't your run-of-the-mill, divey Indian joint. Whether for the well-priced lunch buffet or for the à la carte dinner menu, diners come out en masse for Cumin's flavorful food and creative, original cocktails.

Contemporary versions of Nepali and Indian dishes split the menu. *Mirchi masala naan*, stuffed with green chilies and spices and baked to order, comes out flaky and moist from the kitchen. Tender white and dark meat bathed in a golden-hued almond and cashew curry makes for an exemplary chicken *sahi korma*; thick mango lassi served over ice does the trick of balancing the palate after pummeling it with the pleasures of heat and spice.

Enoteca Roma

A4

2146 W. Division St. (bet. Hoyne Ave. & Leavitt St.)

Phone:	773-772-7700	Dinner nightly
Web:	www.enotecaroma.com	
Prices:	**$$**	Division

Roman goddess Letizia Sorano presides over the candlelit cavern housing Enoteca Roma, a rustically welcoming spot with a big heart and an appetite for sharing. Adventurous and studious oenophiles can test themselves with multiple wine flights, and casual noshers can pick through antipasti, *salumi,* and nearly a dozen kinds of bruschetta.

Come early for the square Roman-style pizza, because when the dough runs out, it's gone for the night. Late arrivals can still get a bowl of Letizia's lasagna, arriving screaming hot in a round crock and bubbling over with venison Bolognese, béchamel, gooey mozzarella, and salty Parmesan. If the irresistible brownie of the day isn't enough, sleep on it and grab more treats next door at Letizia's Natural Bakery.

Flo

C5

Southwestern

1434 W. Chicago Ave. (bet. Bishop St. & Greenview Ave.)

Phone: 312-243-0477
Web: www.flochicago.com
Prices:

Lunch Tue – Sun
Dinner Tue – Sat
Chicago (Blue)

The name says "cozy down home diner" and the décor might straddle the line between modern and quaint, but Flo's café and bar is straight outta New Mexico, letting diners saddle up for a taste of the Wild West in Noble Square. The bar's small but quick to stir up a mimosa or Bloody Maria to start brunch on the right note.

An always-cranking kitchen serves breakfast through mid-afternoon featuring seriously flavorful dishes like the signature breakfast burrito with roasted poblanos and pickled jalapeños that will tide you over till dinner. Heaps of zucchini and corn lighten up turkey chili; while *carnitas* tacos come with all the bells and whistles. No matter what's on the plate, a drizzle of the kitchen's homemade red and green chile sauces are a must.

Francesca's Forno

B3

Italian

1576 N. Milwaukee Ave. (at Damen Ave.)

Phone: 773-770-0184
Web: www.miafrancesca.com
Prices: $$

Lunch Sat – Sun
Dinner nightly
Damen (Blue)

Francesca's Forno underwent a slight yet propitious face-lift, so say good-bye to those huge portions of pastas and *primi* in favor of lighter, ingredient-driven Italian thrills. Old-timers shouldn't sweat as the reduced portions have brought about reduced prices—now groups can indulge in many more Lilliputian dishes instead of attacking one Gulliver.

Enveloped in walls of windows, wooden floors, glass light fixtures, and a pressed-tin ceiling, fans hanker for their sumptuous *cicchetti*. Expect the likes of *granturco arrostito*, sweet corn with truffle oil and Grana Padano; Padrón peppers in spicy *pomodoro*; and *orecchiette con salsiccia* tossing crumbled sausage, tender rapini, and Calabrian chilies that may have a soft mien, but explode with flavor.

Frontier

American ✗✗

C4

1072 N. Milwaukee Ave. (bet. Division & Noble Sts.)

Phone: 773-772-4322
Web: www.thefrontierchicago.com
Prices: $$

Lunch Tue – Sun
Dinner nightly
Chicago (Blue)

Corral a crew of carnivores and mosey on in to this sexy saloon-style eatery for a good ole fashion meat-feast. Dining in numbers comes in handy at Frontier, where banquet options like "Whole Animal Service" get you and a dozen cohorts an entire house-smoked pig, goat, lamb, or wild boar, plus a starter and lip-smacking sides. (Equally handy is remembering to order this five days in advance.)

Bend an elbow at the handsome bar with one of several craft beers or specialty drinks, which pair perfectly with snacks such as dilled habanero pickles, deviled eggs, or pristine fresh oysters. Grub on tasty apps like duck confit tacos (corn tortillas plump with onion, yucca, salsa verde, and *queso fresco*); lollipop chicken wings; or lamb spareribs.

Green Zebra 😊

Vegetarian ✗✗

C5

1460 W. Chicago Ave. (at Greenview Ave.)

Phone: 312-243-7100
Web: www.greenzebrachicago.com
Prices: $$

Lunch Sun
Dinner nightly
Chicago (Blue)

Chef/owner Shawn McClain stays true to his roots at this perennial Noble Square pearl, which has kept its minimalist, organic, and sustainable sensibility well-intact over the years. Green Zebra telegraphs its intentions through recycled wood frames of living lichen and moss reliefs adorning the walls, and a number of organic and biodynamic wines among their international listings. If that doesn't' scream "green," the rooftop garden supplies the kitchen with its bounty whenever possible.

Graze freely with friends on the all-vegetarian menu which might include standouts like crispy sweet potato dumplings sopping up walnut-sage *pistou* and crab-apple ketchup; or mustard and caraway spaetzle punctuated by hon shimeji mushrooms and smoked cipollini onions.

Habana Libre

C u b a n

C5

1440 W. Chicago Ave. (bet. Bishop & Noble Sts.)

Phone: 312-243-3303   Lunch & dinner daily
Web: www.habanalibrerestaurant.com
Prices: $$ Chicago (Blue)

The spirit of Cuba is more than alive and well—it's a celebration amid the festive faux banana tree, swaying paper lanterns, and Latin tunes at Habana Libre. Let time ease by as the kitchen pulls together a pleasant parade of plantains in versatile forms: mashed and fried into cups that hold tender, beefy strings of *ropa vieja*; or cut wide and smashed, thin as a slice of bread, then fried into *tostones*, layered with mayo, braised chicken, and grilled onions for a fantastically messy *jibarito* sandwich.

Instead of settling for the pedestrian bottled red sauce on hand, ask for the fresh jalapeño-laced salsa verde, and dollop it all over dishes like succulent *lechon asado*, which dodges the "dry pork" bullet that befalls so many versions of the entrée.

Jane's

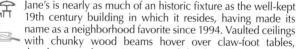

A m e r i c a n

B2

1655 W. Cortland St. (bet. Marshfield Ave. & Paulina St.)

Phone: 773-862-5263   Lunch Fri – Sun
Web: www.janesrestaurant.com   Dinner Tue – Sun
Prices:

Jane's is nearly as much of an historic fixture as the well-kept 19th century building in which it resides, having made its name as a neighborhood favorite since 1994. Vaulted ceilings with chunky wood beams hover over claw-foot tables, thereby complementing exposed brick walls hung with artwork while emphasizing a rustic and homey vibe.

Global accents and vegetarian specialties on the menu showcase the kitchen's wide-ranging definition of comfort food. If the freshly ground half-pound sirloin burger topped with pancetta, grilled pineapple, mozzarella, and chipotle aïoli isn't enough, mashed potatoes and salad on the side should leave you fulfilled. Lighter fare like an Asian chicken salad, or bowl of Jane's corn chowder are ideal taste bud teasers.

Kendall College Dining Room

International   ✗✗

D4

900 North Branch St. (at Halsted St.)

Phone: 312-752-2328
Web: http://culinary.kendall.edu
Prices: $$

Lunch Mon – Fri
Dinner Tue – Sat
🚇 Grand (Blue)

Imagine that dining out could be a sneak peek at a future Michelin-starred chef. That's a real possibility in this dining room and kitchen, which doubles as a test space for culinary arts students. Forgive the jitters as servers-in-training deliver your meal, which you can watch being prepared through floor-to-ceiling windows onto the kitchen.

The lunch prix-fixe menu includes three courses for under $20, with dishes such as a green gazpacho and a buttermilk panna cotta that rivals what may be served in nearby fine restaurants. Additionally, enjoy many other fine dining indulgences, such as an amuse-bouche, intermezzos, and very good bread.

It is not just the chefs who come from the school: many of the herbs and vegetables are grown in campus gardens.

Las Palmas

Mexican   ✗✗

B3

1835 W. North Ave. (at Honore St.)

Phone: 773-289-4991
Web: www.laspalmaschicago.com
Prices: $$

Lunch Wed – Sun
Dinner nightly
🚇 Damen (Blue)

What looks like a small but bright and cozy hangout is a deceptively creative Mexican spot. Inside, find a warm and lively space with vibrant artwork that can seem psychedelic after too much mezcal, and a glowing yet intimate glassed-in atrium. The garden is a warm-weather oasis for inventive margaritas and mojitos muddled to order with mint and fresh fruit.

Likewise, the menu tweaks Mexican standards with 21st century details. A crisp, light chili relleno bursts with Manchego, goat, and Chihuahua cheeses plus a hint of *epazote*. Pineapple- and tequila-marinated skirt steak is perfectly tender atop rum-soaked roasted plantains and mango salsa. Who would pair sangria gelée and cocoa nib brittle with simple bread pudding? Las Palmas, that's who.

Le Bouchon

 B2

French

1958 N. Damen Ave. (at Armitage Ave.)

Phone: 773-862-6600
Web: www.lebouchonofchicago.com
Prices: $$

Lunch & dinner Mon — Sat

 Damen (Blue)

In lieu of intercontinental travel, head straight for Le Bouchon. One step inside this endearing restaurant and you'll think you've died and gone to bistro heaven. Pressed-tin ceilings, red walls, tile floors, framed pictures of Paris, and cramped tables only enhance its authenticity.

Still, Le Bouchon embodies more than the classic bistro look. Wholesome and fuss-free preparations of French comfort food headline the menu, as Chef/owner Jean-Claude Poilevey flits about from table to table. This kitchen knows how to soothe the soul with its cooking, as in salad Lyonnaise with a perfectly poached egg and crisp bacon lardons; steaming bowls of bouillabaise brimming with clams, mussels, and shrimp; or the smooth, lovely chocolate marquis.

Leopold

C5

Belgian

1450 W. Chicago Ave. (bet. Bishop & Noble Sts.)

Phone: 312-348-1028
Web: www.leopoldchicago.com
Prices: $$

Dinner Tue — Sun

Chicago (Blue)

Having cradled a potpourri of cultures and cuisines, it is only fitting that Chicago's own Leopold adds to the influx of beer-friendly Belgian options in West Town. Let the wafting aromas lure you inside—the serene front lounge is a nice place to linger and will divert thoughts of moules and frites.

Inside, fans fill chic nailhead chairs set atop dark wood floors. The dining room hugs a glass-lined bar and rightly so, they have all the booze and brews to match. This is upscale bar food which flaunts French and German influences, yet standouts like a tart filled with garlicky escargots and melted Grayson; *potatis korv*, pork and veal sausages with currant mustard; and crispy waffles licked with maple gelato and Bourbon butter are nothing if not divine.

Lillie's Q

Barbecue

B3

1856 W. North Ave. (at Wolcott Ave.)

Phone: 773-772-5500
Web: www.lilliesq.com
Prices: $$

Lunch & dinner daily

 Damen (Blue)

A note to traditionalists: the goods here are referred to as urban barbecue, so expect a few tasty tweaks on some cherished favorites. Meats are massaged with "Carolina Dirt"—the house dry rub—and then may be given a glaze; or finished with one of five flavorful sauces, all of which can be found neatly lined on the tables. Feast on tangy apple-glazed baby back ribs, tender tri-tip, smoky baked beans, hush puppies, and fried pickles.

The popular spot rocks a rustic chic style, with exposed ducts and brick walls; metal chairs beneath wooden tables; and filament bulbs in iron fixtures. Service pieces follow the theme—steamy sides roll out in cast iron dishes, meats on paper-lined metal trays, and cold bevs in old-fashioned Mason jars.

LOKaL

American

B3

1904 W. North Ave. (bet. Winchester & Wolcott Aves.)

Phone: 773-904-8113
Web: www.lokalchicago.com
Prices: $$

Lunch Sat – Sun
Dinner Tue – Sat

 Damen (Blue)

This European-flecked American café gets the urban vibe going with its stylish interior dressed in square tables, white molded chairs, and large canvases of modern art. The lounge area hosts guest DJs who pump up the volume when the lights go down, augmenting the retro feel.

At LOKaL, lunch and dinner offer wholly different experiences, but each is worthy on its own. Lunches are a simpler affair (see: a flurry of sandwiches and salads); while the dinner menu is more complex (showcasing the likes of bison steak with pepper cress mashed potatoes, lobster *pierogi*, and braised rabbit salad). LOKaL is lauded for its fresh, first-rate ingredients that may present themselves, for example, in an artisan greens salad with rhubarb vinaigrette.

Mana Food Bar

Vegetarian

B4

1742 W. Division St. (bet. Paulina & Wood Sts.)

Phone: 773-342-1742
Web: www.manafoodbar.com
Prices: ⊜⊜

Lunch Sat
Dinner nightly
🚇 Division

Mana is tiny, trim, and trendy—if you dine here frequently, so is your waistline. Loosely translated, its name means "life force in nature" and this concept sets the tone for its cross-cultural vegetarian cuisine.

The menu is tinged with exotic spices and house-made chili sauces, ensuring that the meatless versions of Korean *bulgogi* with seared tofu are just as flavorful as their carnivorous counterparts. Spicy sesame noodles with peanuts, pea pods, and carrots; as well as their signature black-bean and mushroom sliders have veggie-lovers swooning. Portion sizes can be adjusted to fit any appetite in an array of hot and cold offerings.

The industrial-chic space is offset by a full bar serving sake-based cocktails and freshly squeezed juices.

Mariscos El Veneno

Seafood

B4

1024 N. Ashland Ave. (at Cortez St.)

Phone: 773-252-7200
Web: N/A
Prices: $$

Lunch & dinner daily

🚇 Division

Searingly hot sauces steal the show at Mariscos El Veneno, focused on the seafood-centric cuisine of the Mexican state Nayarit. Look past the fish tank in the rear to appreciate the bustling activity and tantalizing aromas escaping from the kitchen. Service is friendly and fast, though speaking Spanish can be useful here.

The kitchen turns out serious heat and wonderful complexity in each gartantuan dish. *Pulpo especial*, a house signature, smothers tender octopus with creamy and spicy stewed onions. Bright red *camarones* arrive sizzling in a diabolical hot sauce, and piquant sour tomatillo salsa dresses *tacos de pescado*, made with their own soft corn tortillas. Cool down with a piña colada mousse pie, layered over a thick chocolate cake base.

Mexique ✿

Mexican 🍴

C5

1529 W. Chicago Ave. (bet. Armour St. & Ashland Ave.)

Phone: 312-850-0288
Web: www.mexiquechicago.com
Prices: $$

Lunch & dinner Tue – Sun

📺 Chicago (Blue)

Rafael Iriarte

There's nothing dramatic about the standard brick storefront that houses Mexique; this restaurant reserves its fireworks for inside. The décor features splashes of orange, boldly colorful art installations, and glittering light fixtures that pop against creamy white walls and wooden banquettes. A bar stretching more than half the length of the narrow space, punctuated by orange-backed barstools, draws diners back toward simple but elegant white linen-covered tables.

French and Mexican ingredients plus techniques marry with satisfying and electrifying fashion, as in the salmon mousse *tamal* steamed in banana leaves, ladled with crimson salsa Veracruzana that gets a tart punch from strips of lemon confit. Here, tender braised veal short ribs arrive atop roasted parsnip purée, and gain tremendous depth from a slaw of sliced fennel, Serrano chilies, and oranges. Dessert guacamole is an inspired mash-up of avocado pastry cream, strawberry compote, and sweet tortilla chips.

A glass-framed semi-open kitchen lets diners watch Chef Carlos Gaytan at work. Take a breather from the parade of creative dishes to idle here or read the graffiti-style adulations that visiting chefs left along the wall.

Mindy's Hot Chocolate

Contemporary

B3

1747 N. Damen Ave. (bet. St. Paul Ave. & Willow St.)

Phone: 773-489-1747
Web: www.hotchocolatechicago.com
Prices: $$

Lunch Wed – Sun
Dinner Tue – Sun
 Damen (Blue)

After a brief closure for remodeling and some tweaking, owner Mindy Segal has flung open the floor-to-ceiling glass doors once more—re-opening as Mindy's Hot Chocolate Craft Food & Drink. Now that's a mouthful, but the lofty, industrial-chic space allures with rich brown hues on leather banquettes, a long wooden bar, and painted concrete floors. As the handle indicates, sweets are only part of the temptations on offer. A full lineup of savory fare like house-ground lamb sausage with creamy cheese on flatbread, shares menu space with Segal's renowned desserts. Six varieties of hot chocolate are served with homemade marshmallows; and the cookie cart is an instant favorite, stocked with a dozen choices like gingersnap and snickerdoodle for a buck each.

Mirai

Japanese

B4

2020 W. Division St. (bet. Damen & Hoyne Aves.)

Phone: 773-862-8500
Web: N/A
Prices: $$

Dinner nightly

 Damen (Blue)

Mirai is a bit like Disney World. You know it's not real, but who cares? The Japanese food is westernized and by no means traditional, but unless you're dining out with Mr. Miyagi, rest assured that nobody will cry foul.

Bold and appetizing flavors beg to take center stage. It's really all about the sushi at this spot—just look around and you'll find most devotees feasting on sashimi, *unagi*, and maki. If raw fish doesn't float your boat, take a shot at one of the house specialties like *kani nigiri*, a baked king crab concoction. There is also a surfeit of hot dishes, think chicken *togarashi* with spicy, sweet, and tangy flavors. Affable and alert service and a relaxed atmosphere, especially on the front patio, make this a hit with area residents.

Old Oak Tap

 American 🍴

2109 W. Chicago Ave. (bet. Leavitt St. & Hoyne Ave.)

Phone: 773-772-0406   Lunch Tue – Sun
Web: www.theoldoaktap.com   Dinner nightly
Prices: **$$**

Though it may seem like a bar, this classy and cool tavern has the tasty starters and creative sandwiches to give the impressive docket of international and domestic craft beer second billing. Pick a table near the fireplace, under the dramatic oak mirror, or just settle into the bar scene, but by all means arrive hungry for the likes of crunchy, spicy, and sweet *sriracha* wings with wasabi aïoli—so beautifully powerful that they may order an accompanying draft themselves. Other options include homemade soft pretzels, duck confit quesadillas, and the *porchetta* sandwich.

Weekends can be a mob scene behind the huge oak door, with conversations and music loud enough to make the chandeliers swing. The large patio is all the rage during warmer months.

Owen & Engine

Gastropub 🍴🍴

2700 N. Western Ave. (at Schubert Ave.)

Phone: 773-235-2930   Lunch Sat – Sun
Web: www.owenengine.com   Dinner nightly
Prices: **$$**

This Victorian pub's glossy black façade hints at what awaits—think Pippa and Kate look-alikes chatting with bearded guys in skinny jeans. The constants are polished woods, a long inviting bar, studded black leather, and beer. Lots and lots of beer...Belgians, Brits, Germans, and a few Americans get along swimmingly over good food without pretense.

Mole pork rinds, pork rillettes, and oysters are spot-on snacks. Roasted bone marrow is deliciously hefty, while fish and chips get highbrow with malt vinegar aïoli and pea purée. Fun and simple, the Tuesday burger special includes beer and shot for an additional buck.

Parking is a bit dodgy but once inside, the Clash and a Pimm's Cup will have you springing for that "five-dollar six-pack for the kitchen."

People Lounge

Spanish

 B3

1560 N. Milwaukee Ave. (at Damen Ave.)

Phone: 773-227-9339
Web: www.peoplechicago.com
Prices: $$

Dinner nightly

 Damen (Blue)

For pub-hoppers who take their food as seriously as they take their brews, the tapas-inspired menu at People Lounge sets a new standard for bar nibbles. Smartly situated in a century-old Victorian home near the epicenter of Wicker Park, seating at communal tables or along the 30-foot oak bar is often at a premium during peak hours, when the sangria flows freely around this brown-shaded den.

Once a square of bar turf has been claimed from the ubiquitous gaggles of ladies blowing off steam through drink specials, work your way through inspired dishes like seared scallops garnished with Serrano ribbons; seared, chilled ahi tuna with wasabi mashed potato-filled crispy wontons; and braised skirt steak set upon a menagerie of cornichons, capers, and Manchego.

Piccolo Sogno

 D5

Italian

464 N. Halsted St. (at Milwaukee Ave.)

Phone: 312-421-0077
Web: www.piccolosognorestaurant.com
Prices: $$

Lunch Mon – Fri
Dinner nightly

 Grand (Blue)

In an area better known for its nightclubs than restaurants, Piccolo Sogno ("little dream" in Italian) stands out as a quaint trattoria, awash in a restful shade of blue with sparkling chandeliers. Come on a warm evening to enjoy the lovely outdoor terrace—beneath a canopy of trees and twinkle-lights, this is a favorite date-night spot.

Their straightforward Italian menu draws a corporate crowd at lunch with pastas or thin-crust Neapolitan pizzas. Evenings lure well-dressed couples perusing the carefully chosen Italian wine list and delving into *sformato di zucca* (local squash flan with Parmesan cream), four-cheese ravioli, or hearty Berkshire pork shank with Tuscan kale and house-cured pancetta.

River North welcomed Piccolo Sogno Due this past summer.

Red Door

International

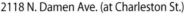

B2

2118 N. Damen Ave. (at Charleston St.)

Phone: 773-697-7221
Web: www.reddoorchicago.com
Prices: **$$**

Lunch Sat – Sun
Dinner nightly

Don't look for a sign—an imposing red door near a red fire hydrant is the only indication that imaginative (read: eclectic) gastropub eats can be found inside. Servers behind the gracefully curving wooden bar shake and stir funky concoctions, also pouring a respectable list of American and European microbrews. Long red aprons on the staffers and red cotton napkins on the chunky wooden tables play off the name.

In the summer, the back patio is the place for sharing small plates like fried oyster *ssäm* with crunchy kimchi and tasso ham; snacks like bacon-wrapped artichokes with chicken liver; or boozy snow cones at long candlelit communal tables. It's like a global neighborhood barbecue and you don't have to bother cleaning up at the end of the evening.

Rios D'Sudamerica

Peruvian ✕✕

B2

2010 W. Armitage Ave. (bet. Damen & Hoyne Sts.)

Phone: 773-276-0170
Web: www.riosdesudamerica.com
Prices: **$$**

Lunch & dinner daily

 Damen (Blue)

It's simply called "Rios" by its regulars, all of whom seem to adore drinking and dining in this two-story space flanked by cream walls and murals of icons like Macchu Picchu and the Christ the Redeemer statue towering over Rio de Janeiro. Posh lounge seating for pre-dinner caipirinhas gives way to white tablecloths throughout this cavernous dining room.

Peruvian food takes center stage, but the menu spans South and Central American traditions. A standout *tamal Peruano* stuffed with tender slices of pork loin and hard-boiled egg, pairs seamlessly with sautéed *lomo saltado al pisco* and *camarones enrollado en cangrejo* that pay tribute to the miles of Pacific coastline. A $13 Sunday *criollo* buffet lets Peruvian cuisine fans sample to their hearts' content.

Ripasso

Italian 🍴🍴

B3

1619 N. Damen St. (bet. North & Wabansia Aves.)

Phone: 773-342-8799   Dinner Tue – Sun
Web: www.ripassochicago.com
Prices: $$ 🚇 Damen (Blue)

Pale sage stucco walls and silvery pressed-tin ceilings bring light and life to this brand-new Bucktown charmer, dedicated to spotlighting regional Italian cuisine as the progenitor of farm-to-table dining. Its all-Italian wine list follows suit, underscoring the country's obscure winemaking expanses alongside old favorites.

The menu spins with the month, but may include standouts like warm spinach *sformato* with flaky mushroom strudel; or homemade pappardelle in a creamy sauce chock-full of pork, veal, beef, and lamb, that's made even richer by a touch of truffle oil. Weekly farmhouse dinners focusing on the varied culinary traditions of "the boot," family-style specials, and prix-fixe options make dining with a crowd a smart and satisfying choice.

Roots Handmade Pizza

Pizza 🍴

B5

1924 W. Chicago Ave. (bet. Winchester & Wolcott Aves.)

Phone: 773-645-4949   Lunch & dinner daily
Web: www.rootspizza.com
Prices: $$ 🚇 Division

In a town synonymous with deep-dish, it takes a certain amount of chutzpah to bring a new pizza style to Chicago. Roots does just that and succeeds winningly with Quad Cities-style pizza from the Iowa-Illinois border: a round, hand-tossed pie scissor-cut into rectangular strips with a key ingredient–malt in the crust–that adds a bronzed edge and subtle sweetness.

Quality ingredients abound: finely ground sausage is liberally sprinkled across the signature Quad Cities pie, and fresh mozzarella, hand-pulled each day, arrives in breaded planks for a take on the ubiquitous appetizer. Little touches, like the exclusively Midwestern brews on tap and the plate of warm washcloths that come with the check, make the spot an endearing neighborhood player.

Ruxbin

B4

851 N. Ashland Ave. (at Pearson St.)

Phone: 312-624-8509

Web: www.ruxbinchicago.com

Prices: $$

Dinner Tue – Sun

Division

Eclectic and maybe a tad bizarre, this über-popular Noble Square gem is as successful as it is freewheeling (note the no-reservations and BYOB policy). The funky setting is comprised of all things refurbished, reclaimed, and repurposed to fashion a timeless interior (see the cookbook pages decoupaged on the ceiling). Yes, that is a bench made of seatbelts and what's that door leading to the bathroom? It's an old revolving darkroom door.

Discover a comparably assorted offering of American bistro fare made with talent and globetrotting flair. The limited, seasonal menu may include crispy eggplant with roasted beets, cucumber, frisée, and honey-cardamom yogurt; hanger steak with kimchi-potato hash and *guajillo* ketchup; or mussels in a sake-tomato broth.

The Savoy

B3

1408 N. Milwaukee Ave. (bet. Evergreen & Wolcott Aves.)

Phone: 773-698-6925

Web: www.savoychicago.com

Prices: $$

Lunch & dinner daily

Damen (Blue)

Wicker Park is headed to sea with The Savoy. Tall marble-topped round tables near the raw bar lead to raised booths in the dining room and a small curtained lounge in the rear. However, maritime-inspired accents like fish trap-style light fixtures and nautical rope carry the refined seafood shack theme throughout the space.

The raw bar is rife with juicy oysters, but don't miss out on an equally creative menu. Share a generous pile of partially shelled Alaskan snow crab claws and legs with a smoked tomato cocktail sauce; rich salmon rillettes with pickled fennel; or ahi lettuce wraps with julienned Napa cabbage, jalapeños, and a soy-ginger vinaigrette. With 40 kinds of absinthe properly diluted by elegant fountains, end the evening with a nightcap.

Schwa ✿

B3

1466 N. Ashland Ave. (at Le Moyne St.)

Phone: 773-252-1466 Dinner Tue – Sat
Web: www.schwarestaurant.com
Prices: $$$ 📺 Division

nickbellyszk

Bucktown & Wicker Park

First-timers who have survived the byzantine reservation process to score a seat at Schwa shouldn't be taken aback by the graffiti-tagged exterior. Forge ahead, through the storm-door patched with duct tape to enter this dining room, where ombre walls deepening from cream to blue are the only nod to design. Tightly packed bare tables and simple hardwood floors keep the focus on food.

This is a culinary playground, foregoing typical amenities in favor of a loose, high-volume vibe. Chef Michael Carlson and team are sincerely hospitable, despite the potential for intimidation from a kitchen of tattooed, facial-haired dudes rocking out while they cook and plate. Leave inhibitions and expectations at the duct-taped door, BYO bevy, and revel in the unconventional style.

Brief descriptions on the three- or nine-course menus downplay these complex and eclectic dishes. Expect the kitchen to riff on nostalgic tastes while inventing something totally new, as in passion fruit gelée studded with steelhead roe, papaya, lavender foam, and a salty shad roe beignet that honestly conjures Froot Loops. Foie gras rolled in cocoa nibs, pistachios, and curry powder is at once creamy, crunchy, and decadent.

67

Seadog

C4

1500 W. Division St. (at Greenview Ave.)

Phone: 773-235-8100
Web: www.seadogsushibar.com
Prices:

Dinner nightly

Division

Serving more than just sushi, this Noble Square restaurant is a fine choice to satisfy that craving for Japanese cuisine. An array of fine quality cuts are prepared by a trio whose smiling faces welcome arriving diners and their brown uniforms match the room's earthy aesthetic. From the counter's polished bronze-hued backdrop, the team sends forth the likes of tuna and jalapeño *temaki*; nine variations of spicy maki; a roster of signature rolls that unveil the little sea monster, constructed from white fish tempura, cream cheese, avocado, and *masago*; and non-piscine morsels such as an *oshinko* roll filled with pickled daikon.

Entrée's from the kitchen supplement the sushi bar selection and include standards like tempura, teriyaki, and *yakisoba*.

Siboney

A2

2165 N. Western Ave. (at Palmer Ave.)

Phone: 773-276-8776
Web: www.siboneychicago.com
Prices:

Lunch & dinner daily

 Western (Blue)

In many ways, Cuba's kitchens are an amalgam of the best Spanish, African, and Caribbean traditions. The neighborhood that houses Siboney (named for a city in Cuba) is likewise an amalgam and celebration of its culture. This is a lovely, bright, and tidy corner location graced with many windows for people-watching and a front lounge that hosts occasional music performances.

Siboney captures Cuba's vibrant cuisine by focusing on the country's staples (chicken, pork, lobster, and fish) and preparing them with authenticity, whether raw or stewed. The Cuban-style pork ribs are incredibly tender and sweet; the tantalizing bread pudding is spiked with lots of cognac; and the dark, rich coffee blended with milk and sugar will have you feeling truly *Cubano*.

Smoke Daddy

 Barbecue

B4

1804 W. Division St. (at Wood St.)

Phone: 773-772-6656

Web: www.thesmokedaddy.com

Prices:

Lunch & dinner daily

Division

Sometimes you just need to slow down: Southern drawls, slow-cooked barbecue, and blues usually do the trick. Such relaxing influences can be found at this neighborhood joint, with nightly live music and a mouthwatering menu of wood-smoked goods. A corrugated aluminum bar, low lighting, and 1950s-era photographs give "The Daddy" its laid-back, retro vibe.

Whether your tastes run to Memphis, Kansas City, or Carolina barbecue, the trifecta of tabletop sauces gives everyone a taste to crow about. Douse your pulled pork, brisket, or ribs, then buy a bottle of your fave for the home grillmaster. Ribs are smoky and tender, but the chicken a bit dry and not worth the calories. Save those for the pork-studded, smoky baked beans or the gooey macaroni and cheese.

The Storefront Company

Contemporary

B3

1941 W. North Ave. (bet. Damen Ave and Honore St.)

Phone: 773-661-2609

Web: www.thestorefrontcompany.com

Prices: $$

Lunch Sun
Dinner Tue – Sat

Damen (Blue)

If the stylized pastoral mural and fashionable off-the-runway farmhouse décor didn't immediately tip you off, the bread service should. Its freshly baked garlic-chive Parker House rolls in mini crocks, Parmesan *lavash*, and a butter pyramid dipped in pink Hawaiian salt is a clear sign this isn't any run-of-the-mill farm-to-table restaurant.

Chef Bryan Moscatello puts an avant-garde spin on contemporary seasonal cuisine, spooning beet-cured salmon and fennel pollen cream into fluted brioche cups; and topping cool, milky green cucumber panna cotta with mini flowering cukes and bouncy smoked trout roe. Artisanal libations like FEW Spirits from neighboring Evanston stock the bar, and are put to good use in cocktails—shaken, stirred, or on the rocks.

Sushi X

C5

Japanese

1136 W. Chicago Ave. (bet. May St. & Racine Ave.)

Phone: 312-491-9232
Web: www.rollingatsushix.com
Prices: $$

Lunch Mon – Fri
Dinner nightly

Chicago (Blue)

X doesn't mean anonymous in this instance; it's the Roman numeral ten, and now that this hip sushi joint has been around for a decade, the X seems almost prophetic. Additionally, there's nothing demure about this spot to begin with—inside the industrial chunk of a building, animé projected on dark walls, thumping background music, and low candle-lit lounge tables make Sushi X more of a club than an eatery.

Don't bother with plain nigiri here; instead go for signature "neo" and "mega" rolls. The Godzilla roll lives up to its name, filled with shrimp tempura, scallion, roe, avocado, and at least four other sauces and components. Non-sushi choices unveil hot and cold fusion dishes like Chinese-style red chicken in a red pepper-bean marinade with avocado.

Taxim

B3

Greek

1558 N. Milwaukee Ave. (bet. Damen & North Aves.)

Phone: 773-252-1558
Web: www.taximchicago.com
Prices: $$

Dinner nightly

Damen (Blue)

Though Taxim channels the spirit of Greece in its food, its Moroccan-esque décor takes inspiration from Turkey and other Mediterranean coastal neighbors. The large room glints with light from hanging Moorish lanterns and copper-topped tables. Share small plates on the sidewalk patio to take full advantage of Wicker Park people-watching.

Many of Taxim's dishes get a modern twist while remaining respectful to the islands' traditional cuisine. Wild Greek oregano and ouzo-preserved lemon offer a perfect balance to roasted Amish Miller Farms chicken; while *loukoumades* prove that no one can resist fried dough, especially when tossed in wildflower honey and topped with rosewater-infused pastry cream. The all-Greek wine list is an adventure for oenophiles.

Takashi ✿

Contemporary ✕✕

B2

1952 N. Damen Ave. (at Armitage Ave.)

Phone: 773-772-6170
Web: www.takashichicago.com
Prices: $$$

Lunch Sun
Dinner Tue – Sun
🚇 Damen (Blue)

Tylie Barbosa Photography

Discreetly set back from neighboring shops and restaurants, Takashi's red brick townhouse is emblematic of the subtle charms that unfold inside. This one-time artists' studio can't help but feel intimate, with tight-knit tables that fill up quickly with appreciatively murmuring diners. An austere silver and gray décor with discreetly deposited knickknacks warms up the cordial-cum-relaxed atmosphere as well as the fireworks of talent in the kitchen.

A red *daruma* talisman placed by the stairs for luck has clearly been working its magic. Japanese and French techniques mingle throughout the menu in a succession of well-executed dishes. An amuse of the house-made tofu nearly steals the show with tender creaminess offset by fragrantly gingered soy and two slices of bigeye tuna sashimi. A plump seared Maine scallop balances its sweetness with earthy trumpet royale mushrooms and a sharp yet mellow celery root-Parmesan foam; while creamy milk chocolate crème brûlée in a cleanly clipped eggshell marries pleasure and skill.

Chef Takashi, an expert in the art of Japanese noodle making, offers a Sunday noodle brunch with homemade ramen and soba, as well as a nightly non-noodle-focused omakase.

71

tocco

Italian ✕✕

B4

1266 N. Milwaukee Ave. (bet. Ashland Ave. & Paulina St.)

Phone:	773-687-8895
Web:	www.toccochicago.com
Prices:	$$

Dinner Tue – Sun

🚇 Division

Is this Rodeo Drive? Milan? No. It's Wicker Park, and that bronzed man in sunglasses and linen pants is your stylish host and owner, Bruno Abate. The fashion-focused window display and servers, who may as well be walking the runway while delivering your food, hint to the voguish theme. The room pulses with techno, pink faux-ostrich wall panels, garage doors that roll back to reveal the patio's colorful murals, and white plastic resin chairs filled with a gorgeous clientele, happy to have somewhere to wear this season's haute couture.

In addition to pastas and heartier entrées, the menu offers cracker-crisp artisanal pizzas, fresh from the wood-burning ovens, as in the *quattro stagioni* with olives, mushrooms, artichokes, and ham crowned with a fried egg.

Trenchermen

Contemporary ✕✕

B3

2039 W. North Ave. (bet. Hoyne & Milwaukee Aves.)

Phone:	773-661-1540
Web:	www.trenchermen.com
Prices:	$$

Dinner Mon – Sat

🚇 Damen (Blue)

"Trenchermen" is a slang term for hearty eaters and drinkers, and a place that includes "pickle tots" on its menu knows its namesake clientele pretty darn well. In the former Luxor Bathhouse building that most recently housed Spring, exposed black pipes, raw brick, and glossy tiles evoke these turn-of-the century baths—albeit one for the working man who also enjoys a sophisticated round of celery gin and tonics.

Chicken breast *bresaola* takes on focused flavors and textures after air-drying when paired with the aforementioned fried pickle-and-potato tots; beet-tinged yogurt steps in to balance the plate. Bacon-cured sweetbreads are equally over the top, and black olive- and sesame-crusted sea trout is incredibly satisfying and refined.

Usagi Ya

Japanese X

1178 N. Milwaukee Ave. (bet. Division St. & Haddon Ave.)

Phone:	773-292-5885	Lunch & dinner daily
Web:	www.usagiyasushi.com	
Prices:	**$$**	Division

Even at lunch, amoeba lights, vibey music, and nearly-naughty paintings give off a nightclub feel that complement the contemporary creative seafood at this funky sushi joint. Fish of paramount quality is handled delicately by the sushi chefs working at the open sake-lined bar overlooking the room.

Beyond the wide selection of rarely boring maki rolls and sushi options, Usagi Ya's menu shines with its unorthodox combinations. Top choices include sticky rice "snowballs" topped with fresh albacore tuna, white truffle soy sauce, and minced scallions; tempura-fried jalapeños stuffed with *unagi*, drizzled with sesame oil and cream cheese dressing; and Thai ocean noodles with plump shrimp, scallops, and squid wading in a spicy lemongrass broth.

West Town Tavern

American XX

1329 W. Chicago Ave. (at Throop St.)

Phone:	312-666-6175	Dinner Mon – Sat
Web:	www.westtowntavern.com	
Prices:	**$$**	Chicago (Blue)

Comfort fare may elicit simple memories of warm pies and full bellies, but hearty, home-style favorites transcend expectation at West Town Tavern. Sip wine amid loyal locals at the long oak bar; or settle into the warm dining space and peek into the semi-open kitchen.

Start with the wild mushroom chowder–a smoky sensation topped with crunchy blue cheese croutons–then dive into the juicy, braised pork tenderloin served over buttery cannelloni beans, wilted kale, roasted cherry tomatoes, and bits of bacon. Dessert cannot be skipped, as the buttery Bourbon-pecan pie with its sticky-sweet layer of brown sugar syrup is an impossibly rare treat. Drop in for one of the rotating weekly specials, whether it's Fried Chicken Mondays or Wagyu burger Tuesdays.

Yuzu

B5

1715 W. Chicago Ave. (bet. Hermitage & Paulina Sts.)

Phone: 312-666-4100	Lunch Mon – Sat
Web: www.yuzuchicago.com	Dinner nightly
Prices: ⊗⊗	Chicago (Blue)

Yuzu is new, but its sushi bar and *robata* grill come with a few features that are already broken-in: reclaimed weathered planks line the walls, and the crave-worthy counter is a slab of wood that's over a 100 years old. Décor elements like hand-painted manga murals, metal drafting stools, and Ball Jars (be sure to BYOB) provide rustic-retro contrast.

The menu's mix of cool sushi and hot *robata* items proves to be equally complementary. Each item off the grill is matched with simple sauces—perhaps beef short ribs glazed in *kalbi* sauce; or ahi brushed with white miso and Japanese mustard. Those in need of smaller bites should opt for creative and quirky maki which come in jumbo or small; and juicy watermelon slices for dessert are on the house.

Bib Gourmand 🏵
indicates our inspectors'
favorites for good value.

Chinatown & South Loop

Chinatown and the South Loop were two neighborhoods that for years didn't have much linking them, besides of course the north-south running Red Line El. Geographically, they may be close, but are worlds apart in terms of population, architecture, gentrification, and a gastronomic vibe.

Recent development has slowly but surely allowed for these two neighborhoods to meet in the middle. While, they are still very distinct, both expanses have managed to combine their old and new in ways that should appeal to any true gastronome residing in the Windy City.

Strolling Through South Loop

Revered as one of Chicago's oldest neighborhoods, the South Loop houses a number of buildings that were fortunately spared the Great Chicago Fire. In particular, Prairie Avenue is a concentration of magnificent homes that were built by some of the wealthiest in the city. Similarly, Glessner House and Clarke House are distinctive gems. Glimpses of all sorts of history can be toured through time-tested churches; Willie Dixon's Blues Heaven Foundation, whose main mission is to preserve the blues legacy; National Vietnam Veterans Art Museum; and other impressive landmarks. In previous incarnations, the South Loop (which begins south of Roosevelt Road) housed famed mob man Al Capone, Chess Records, and other buzzing industrial spaces. However, over the last 15 years, this neighborhood has undergone a serious transformation; and it now includes new condos and shopping, which have helped fuel a rash of fresh restaurants. Also home to Mayor Richard M. Daley, Columbia College, Museum Campus, and Soldier Field, it seems as if almost anything (or anyone) can be found in the South Loop.

Magnificent Munching

Nurse your sweet addiction at **Canady Le Chocolatier Ltd**. Their decadent selection includes dark, milk, or white chocolate filled with the likes of chocolate and cream, soft caramel, and sugar cream. Want a glimpse of the way real natives eat? Nearby **Manny's Coffee Shop and Deli** is ground zero for local politicians. Pastrami, corned beef, and crispy potato pancakes are solid here, and the speedy staff keeps the line moving. So follow suit, glimpse your pick, and grab it! Come to watch the wheeling and dealing, or just eat a giant pastrami on rye. Either way, you will feel satiated. Admired and applauded as one of Chicago's most authentic Italian markets, **Panozzo's** creative produce and talent brings a host of foodies, locals, and tourists alike. A welcoming landmark in the Windy City's vibrant South Loop, this glorified Italian deli's well-stocked shelves are arranged with carefully prepared foods. From cold and hot sandwiches and classic entrées, to crunchy salads and freshly-baked breads, they personify the art behind Italian home-style cooking.

PRINTERS ROW

These massive historical printing lofts were converted into a hotel, condos, and related retail spaces (such as browse-worthy used bookstores) before the rest of the area was gentrified. Now this multi-block strip is chockablock with restaurants, offices, stores, shops, as well as a Saturday farmer's market from June through October. Just north of the district is the looming Harold Washington Library Center, which serves as a city resource and showcases a beautiful glass-top garden on the ninth floor. On the south end is the landmark Dearborn Station, the oldest remaining train depot in all of Chicago. It is now a multi-use space for retail stores, both small and large corporate offices, and the like.

CHINATOWN

Chicago is home to the country's fourth largest Chinatown, with a population of about 15,000 ethnic Chinese. Chicago's Chi-town also boasts a good combination of original Chinese-American history and contemporary Chinese-American life. At Wentworth Avenue and Cermak Road, you'll find the Chinatown Gate, an old yet elaborate and ornate icon for this neighborhood. Outdoor mall **Chinatown Square** is *the* hub for much of the commercial activity. This two-story extravaganza cradles restaurants, retail spaces, boutiques, and banks. While strolling through this neighborhood, don't miss St. Therese Chinese Catholic Church, an edifice that points to the area's pre-Chinatown Italian roots. Much of the food served in restaurants here is classic Chinese-American fare, which is usually an amalgam of Sichuan, Cantonese, and Chinese-American favorites, mostly of the Midwest. Crab Rangoon anyone?

Stellar Sweets and Spicy Eats

Locals come here, not just to eat out, but to stock up on a gamut of good eats in order to dine in. **Hong Kong Noodle Company** is a factory and the place to go for wonton wrappers. **Mayflower Food** also has one of the largest selections of fresh noodles; and **Ten Ren Tea** is lauded for its extensive tea selection and unique tea-making gadgets. To top off a day of fun feasting and adventure, try a fresh-baked treat from **Golden Dragon Fortune Cookies**, or sweets from **Chiu Quon Bakery**. This Chinatown pearl shows a range of baked goods, dim sum, and desserts... gooey sesame balls perhaps? Those who need guidance can pick up a cookbook from the Chinese Cultural Bookstore and all the necessary gear at **Woks 'n' Things**. After these ethnic delights, saunter over to U.S. Cellular Field and home of the Chicago White Sox—the rare baseball park that serves veggie dogs alongside crispy house-made potato chips.

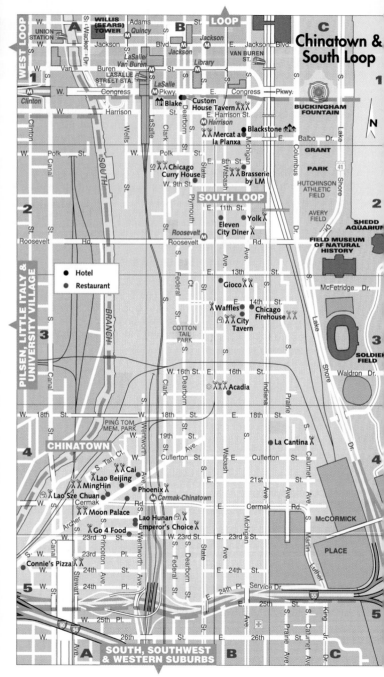

Acadia ⁕

Contemporary ❌❌❌

B3

1639 S. Wabash Ave., Ste. 2F (bet. 16th & 18th Sts.)

Phone:	312-360-9500
Web:	www.acadiachicago.com
Prices:	$$$

Dinner Wed – Sun

Anthony Tahier

The old chestnut of not judging a book by its cover could have been written for Acadia, which hides out in a modest office building next to an overgrown lot in the South Loop. Inside, however, nature is artfully restrained with dark maple tables, pine planks, and cedar accents against bare walls. These add a pastoral counterpoint to the urbane glossy black concrete bar, delicate egg-shaped light bulbs, and rich charcoal gray crushed velvet banquettes. Men take to the occasion with collared shirts and a sport coat or two.

Chef Ryan McCaskey adds inventive features to contemporary American fare, but the slow build of ingredients never detract from the flavor. Expertly seasoned, bacon-wrapped rabbit loin and sausage drizzled with vanilla-apricot jus and dotted with nasturtiums, rest on Dijon-eggplant purée. Meanwhile, *plancha*-grilled Deer Isle shrimp are enhanced, never overpowered, by a chili-lemon marinade and frothy Marcona almond foam.

Diners can create five- and eight-course prix-fixe menus from the à la carte selection, and sommelier Jason Prah offers thoughtful, descriptive wine pairings. End with a poppy seed cake frilled with hibiscus relish, white chocolate powder, and lemon gel.

Brasserie by LM

B2

French

800 S. Michigan Ave. (bet. 8th & 9th Sts.)

Phone: 312-431-1788

Web: www.brasseriebylm.com

Prices: $$

Lunch & dinner daily

Harrison

Elegant but unpretentious, Brasserie by LM–the casual sibling of LM, the long-loved and relocated Lincoln Square darling– aims to comfort and please. Traditional bistro décor goes modern here with persimmon walls, stylized chalkboard wall menus, and curvaceous Cherner chairs that echo mid-century and art deco lineage. The bistro sport of people-watching is A+ with windows facing Michigan Avenue and Grant Park.

Brasserie classics populate the all-day menu: hanger steak frites, *salade Lyonnaise*, mussels, breakfast crêpes, and quiches. Duck rillettes get the full brasserie presentation in a lidded glass jar served with cornichons and baguette croutons; while moist roast chicken arrives golden and crispy thanks to its time cooked under a brick.

Cai

A4

Chinese

2100 S. Archer Ave. (at Wentworth Ave.)

Phone: 312-326-6888

Web: www.caichicago.com

Prices:

Lunch & dinner Tue – Sun

Cermak-Chinatown

Cai rolls out the red carpet for a lavish dim sum banquet on the second floor of Chinatown Square. Under crystal chandeliers, tuxedoed servers navigate carts through a sea of silk-covered chairs and round banquet tables. With almost 100 choices of rolled, steamed, fried, crimped, and folded dim sum illustrated neatly on a single menu page, simply pointing to an order makes sense.

Bamboo steamers may contain a bevy of dumplings and buns like *xiao long bao* soup dumplings; crisply baked green chive puffs; tender shrimp-filled *har gow* dumplings; or fluffy dessert buns with creamy, sweet egg yolks inside. When the dim sum parade ends at 4:00 P.M., the menu shifts to Cantonese specialties and entrée choices nearly as numerous as the earlier menu options.

Chicago Curry House

B2

Indian ☓☓

899 S. Plymouth Ct. (at 9th St.)

Phone: 312-362-9999   Lunch & dinner daily
Web: www.curryhouseonline.com
Prices: ☺☺   🚇 Harrison

If you've got curry on your mind but not a lot of money in your wallet, make your way to Chicago Curry House for an affordable and satisfyingly spicy Indian and Nepali lunch buffet in a white tablecloth setting, just a few blocks west of Grant Park.

The buffet boasts boldly flavored dishes like goat stewed on the bone in a tender, cardamom-inflected curry; and creamy *dal makhani*, black lentils and kidney beans dancing in a fragrant chili sauce. Not into buffets? The roster of dishes on the lunch and dinner menus runs the gamut from Indian favorites like fish *tikka masala* and vegetable samosas, to lesser-known Nepali specialties like *bhuteko kali*, spiced cauliflower with onion and tomato, and abundant combination plates known as *bhojan*.

Chicago Firehouse

B3

American ☓☓

1401 S. Michigan Ave. (at 14th St.)

Phone: 312-786-1401   Lunch & dinner daily
Web: www.chicagofirehouse.com
Prices: $$ 🚇 Roosevelt

The shiny brass fire pole is your second clue (after the restaurant name) that this location was first built as a working firehouse in 1905. Since becoming a restaurant in 2000, the overall vibe has remained more romantic: cherrywood, leather, subway tiles, and other vintage decorative elements echo with 1940s sophistication.

But firefighters are known for appreciating a good meal, and what is better than tasty updates to American classics? Expect the likes of crab-crusted red snapper with sweet and sour eggplant, bok choy, and basil-lime sauce; barbecued pork chop with sweet potato purée and dried cherry pan sauce; or blue cheese-coated ribeye. Bring surf to your turf by adding lobster tail, Alaskan crab legs, or shrimp to their steakhouse entrées.

Chinatown & South Loop

City Tavern

Gastropub XX

1416 S. Michigan Ave. (bet 14th & 16th Sts.)

Phone: 312-663-1278   Dinner nightly
Web: www.citytavernchicago.com
Prices: $$ 🚇 Roosevelt

Gaslight lanterns at the entrance and a prominent wood-and-mirrored bar set the old-world tone inside this throwback tavern, minimally accented by deep blue damask wallpaper, spindle back chairs, and solid bare wood tables. No self-respecting saloon would open its doors without a fireplace to warm the public, and City Tavern hews to this tradition proudly.

The décor is pure 18th century, but the food is modern: Chef Kendal Duque and team deliver upscale global pub cuisine without the sticker shock. Grass-fed grilled ribeye napped with blue cheese-bacon butter; or a seafood shepherd's pie stuffed with salmon, shrimp, and scallops are feasts for the budget-minded gourmand. Pair this with a brew or two from the beer list, and feel a little more communal.

Connie's Pizza

Pizza XX

2373 S. Archer Ave. (at Normal Ave.)

Phone: 312-326-3443   Lunch & dinner daily
Web: www.conniespizza.com
Prices: $$ 🚇 Halsted

Back in 1962, a building with a sign that read "Connie's" was purchased by Jim Stolfe; the name stuck, and in '85, the whole operation moved to its current residence—the huge Archer Avenue spot. Churning out mouthwatering pies for the masses, this Chicago mainstay does most of its biz outside its brick walls, providing catering for professional sporting events (Connie's is the official pizza of the White Sox).

Delish deep-dish is a total Chi-town fave. Bursting with fillings of your choice (try the tender Italian sausage), these stuffed pies are sealed with a buttery bread-like crust and topped with garlicky tomato sauce (also available sans sauce). Call ahead to avoid cooking wait times, and pick up your pizza at the drive-through window.

Custom House Tavern

American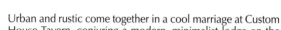

B1

500 S. Dearborn St. (at Congress Pkwy.)

Phone: 312-523-0200
Web: www.customhouse.cc
Prices: $$

Lunch Sun – Fri
Dinner nightly
Library

Urban and rustic come together in a cool marriage at Custom House Tavern, conjuring a modern, minimalist lodge on the ground floor of the Hotel Blake in the South Loop. Stacked gray stone, multiple levels of banquette seating, and polished woods create a sleek and calming neutral palette, while diners get a sneak peek at the kitchen's bustling activity through a long pane of glass.

As one would expect, this pub fare is hearty and satisfying, yet gently tweaks familiar American cuisine, as in braised beef short ribs with potato purée, *cipollini*, greens, and tomato jam; or roasted duck breast with rye berries, beer-braised onions, spinach, and fresh fig mustard. Desserts might include chocolate-hazelnut crunch cake with coffee-cardamom ice cream.

Eleven City Diner

Deli

B2

1112 S. Wabash Ave. (bet. 11th St. & Roosevelt Rd.)

Phone: 312-212-1112
Web: www.elevencitydiner.com
Prices:

Lunch & dinner daily

Roosevelt

What's old is new again at this reprise of the classic Jewish deli. The candy counter is stocked with sweets of yore, like Bazooka Joe, while another counter tempts with hanging salamis, smoked fish, and cured meats ready to eat or to-go.

The extensive menu features ample servings of exactly what should be on a diner menu: big salads, burgers, and thick sandwiches piled high. Many dishes are a twist on the regulars, like the "Shappy" sandwich, which features thick-cut salami grilled and served on challah. The beef and pastrami is served grilled with mozzarella cheese on a French roll, making it clear that this is a Jewish-style deli and not a kosher joint.

Revisit your youth with thick malts, phosphates, and other drinks from the soda jerk.

Emperor's Choice

Chinese Chinese

2238 Wentworth Ave. (bet. Alexander St. & 22nd Pl.)

Phone: 312-225-8800 Lunch & dinner daily
Web: N/A
Prices: Cermak-Chinatown

This striking Quasi-Chinese building–rife with decorative columns alongside ornamental lions–dates back to 1928 and often draws a crowd for being one of the most haunted areas in Chicago (a funeral parlor resides next door). The inside pales in comparison to the façade.

The menu leans Cantonese, but has a few westernized dishes like egg *foo yung*, chicken fried rice, and a pleasant rendition of hot and sour soup. The spicy dry-fried lamb is a delicious surprise, with thin slices of meat lightly coated and fried until tender-crisp and finished with jalapeños lending an addictively sweet heat. With a day's notice they'll prepare Peking duck the right way. Some may suggest that it's too western, so there is also a separate village menu for the Chinese purist.

Gioco

Italian

1312 S. Wabash Ave. (bet. 13th & 14th Sts.)

Phone: 312-939-3870 Lunch Mon – Fri
Web: www.gioco-chicago.com Dinner nightly
Prices: $$ Roosevelt

Gioco offers a new definition of Italian-American—within original brick and plaster walls crafted in the 19th century, a wood-fired pizza oven and crimson Berkel meat slicer share space with a walk-in cooler and wall safe used by infamous city gangster Al Capone. Warmly lit cubbies and tasseled golden pendant lamps infuse contemporary elements to this historic room.

A brief but hearty menu of traditional Tuscan and Umbrian food stars in this incongruously charming arena, and is deliciously supplemented by daily specials like grilled Kurobuta pork chops and a three-course lunch prix-fixe. *Bistecca alla Fiorentina*, *saltimbocca di vitello*, and ricotta gnocchi are pleasant standbys. Also classic yet delightfully charming is tiramisu served in a teacup.

Go 4 Food

A4

Chinese

212 W. 23rd St. (bet. Princeton & Wentworth Aves.)

Phone: 312-842-8688
Web: www.go4foodusa.com
Prices:

Lunch & dinner Wed – Mon

Cermak-Chinatown

Stop by to pick up a fresh, flavorful lunch to-go, or stay awhile at one of the few places in Chinatown where it's actually pleasant to have a sit-down meal. Brilliant red walls offset by dark, sleek furniture and a gleaming stainless kitchen make this a clean, modern neighborhood oasis. With afternoon tea and prix-fixe family-style dinner menus, it's a destination for more than just a quick lunch.

Well-priced and well-portioned Chinese plates like *ma po tofu*, Cantonese-style lobster, and seafood congee back up friendly service. The hundred-spiced chicken in a fiery ginger and garlic sauce is a standout. Are there literally 100 spices in the flavorful gravy? Contemplate it while using a slice of the wok stir-fried chicken breast to sop it up.

La Cantina

Mexican

C4

1911 S. Michigan Ave. (bet. Cullerton & 18th Sts.)

Phone: 312-842-1911
Web: www.lacantinagrill.com
Prices:

Lunch & dinner daily

Cermak-Chinatown

With a chalkboard menu of margaritas at the front bar, a lengthy list of tequilas, and more than a dozen types of martinis, La Cantina certainly lives up to its name. Meanwhile its slender dining room lends itself to hours of relaxation, dimly decked in soft pendant lights and warm terra-cotta walls.

Appetizers like mini *chimichangas* stuffed with steak and dolloped with zesty *pico de gallo* are enough for a meal. Pair them with fragile freshly fried chips, addictively spicy salsa, and an icy, citrusy margarita and you're good to go. But, for a truly filling meal, pick from a large selection of tacos, fajitas, burritos, Mexican, and Tex-Mex specialties like steak tinga, pork carnitas, Michoacan *pollo mole*, and Veracruz seafood treats.

Lao Beijing

Chinese Chinese

A4

2138 S. Archer Ave. (in Chinatown Sq.)

Phone: 312-881-0168
Web: www.tonygourmetgroup.com
Prices:

Lunch & dinner daily

 Cermak-Chinatown

Bringing bold flavors and pungent spices to the ginkgo tree-lined Chinatown Square, Lao Beijing offers great deals and enormous variety to groups large and small. The room may seem no frills, with little more than a colorful quintet of *fuwa* (Beijing Olympic mascot dolls) to perk up the space, and the tuxedo-topped waitstaff are often untucked and rough around the edges. However, let the room's deep-red hues remind you of the aromatic chili oil sure to enhance the many good things to come.

The menu is thick with over 100 choices and color photos of dishes from China's spicier southern regions: Hunan, Yunnan, and Sichuan (home to these wonderfully spiced dumplings). Cheap lunch specials with a soup, main course, and rice can be had for around six dollars.

Lao Hunan

 Chinese

A4

2230 S. Wentworth Ave. (bet. Alexander St. & 22nd Pl.)

Phone: 312-842-7888
Web: www.tonygourmetgroup.com
Prices:

Lunch & dinner daily

 Cermak-Chinatown

The Communist propaganda blanketing Lao Hunan ain't just a clever design scheme. Owner Tony Hu is an unapologetic fan of the Chairman and Maoism, and no matter what locals think of his politics, one thing is for certain—he takes the tenet of "serving the people" to heart with this homage to Hunan cuisine.

Hot, spicy, and aromatic dishes are cardinal here and reveal an authentic creeping heat that gets more addictive with each bite. There are numerous items across the menu to suit just about every palate like roasted green chilies in black bean sauce; Sichuan pepper-laced chicken tossed with ginger and garlic; or lamb sautéed with cilantro. If the heat overwhelms, a smoothie-ologist offering several semi-frozen concoctions is more than happy to soothe.

Lao Sze Chuan

Chinatown & South Loop

Chinese ✗

A4

2172 S. Archer Ave. (at Princeton Ave.)

Phone: 312-326-5040
Web: www.tonygourmetgroup.com
Prices:

Lunch & dinner daily

 Cermak-Chinatown

 Devotees of the deliciously lip-blistering, tongue-numbing, sweat-inducing flavors of Sichuan cuisine know where to go: they're all at Lao Sze Chuan, sitting elbow to elbow in the bright red restaurant adorned with images of that crimson pepper.

The entire menu seems to be marinated in chili paste: the floral, lingering spices of Sichuan peppercorns in richly stewed *ma po* tofu make the dish an addictive choice, but just as spicy and an equally crave-worthy contender is the flash-fried dry chili chicken, piled high with fried sliced garlic and handfuls of red chilies. Vegetarians have a place at the table too, as sliced, crunchy cabbage marinated in chili paste gets the same hit of heat as the meaty morsels in the boiled beef with spicy Sichuan sauce.

Mercat a la Planxa

Spanish ✗✗

B1

638 S. Michigan Ave. (at Balbo Ave.)

Phone: 312-765-0524
Web: www.mercatchicago.com
Prices: $$

Lunch & dinner daily

 Harrison

Inside the Blackstone Hotel, find this colorful Catalan eatery. The sweeping dining space features orange banquettes, mosaics, a brightly tiled open kitchen, and tables facing large windows that bring Grant Park views by day, sultry twilight by night. Friendly service keeps things efficient.

Yet even the room's towering ceilings are not enough to contain the bold flavors of Chef Jose Garces. While respecting the parameters of traditional Catalan cooking with its sexy Bar*th*elona lisp, this cuisine shows delicious ambition in the likes of flatbreads topped with shrimp, chorizo, and garbanzo bean purée; paella; cured meats; and (with advance notice) suckling pig for a group.

The budget-minded stay downstairs for Spanish street food at Bodega N.5.

MingHin

Chinese

A4

2168 S. Archer Ave. (at Princeton Ave.)

Phone: 312-808-1999
Web: www.minghincuisine.com
Prices:

Lunch & dinner daily

Cermak-Chinatown

Get dim sum done right at this Chinatown newcomer that's quickly picking up steam with a hipper crowd than you'd typically see noshing on steamed buns in the neighborhood. Banquet tables of twenty-somethings fill the chic, airy space that gives an understated nod to traditional Chinese décor, with pops of red accents against a neutral, wood- and stone-trimmed dining room.

Piping hot beef noodle rolls; *har gow* with fresh, plump shrimp; and steamed lotus-paste buns are tasty dim sum standouts, offered alongside a multi-page à la carte menu that may include Macau-style roast pork belly; Beijing duck; and live (fresh) seafood. Catering further to its hip and happening patrons, MingHin serves up a late night menu of dim sum and hot pots until 2:00 A.M.

Moon Palace

Chinese

A4

216 W. Cermak Rd. (bet. Princeton & Wentworth Aves.)

Phone: 312-225-4081
Web: www.moonpalacerestaurant.com
Prices:

Lunch & dinner daily

Cermak-Chinatown

More stylish than your average Chinatown restaurant, Moon Palace also boasts particularly friendly, attentive service, and unexpectedly authentic food. Walk into a room of dark wood furnishings and wainscoting juxtaposed with buttery yellow walls, contemporary paintings, and a modern bar.

While the décor is updated, this Chinese menu has not been adjusted to suit the Western palate. The *kung pao* dishes are seriously spicy—tender pieces of chicken are deeply caramelized in a soy-chili oil glaze with peppers, roasted peanuts, and plenty of fried red chilis. Clearly, hand-made soup dumplings (*xiao long bao*) filled with ground pork, ginger, scallions, and rich broth add to the charm here. The noodle soups are as delicious as they are authentic.

Phoenix

A4

Chinese

2131 S. Archer Ave. (bet. Princeton & Wentworth Aves.)

Phone: 312-328-0848   Lunch & dinner daily
Web: www.chinatownphoenix.com
Prices:

 Cermak-Chinatown

Come to Phoenix armed with an appetite and a fun mix of people. This banquet-style dining room in the heart of Chinatown might lack an inspiring décor, and service may be efficient to the point of feeling rushed, but any shortfalls are forgotten over this tasty dim sum.

The requisite carts can be seen winding their way through the dining room, but a menu rife with photographs documents the made-to-order items. Get ready for a smorgasbord of Cantonese classics, from barbecue pork crêpes bursting with smoky and tasty meat; steamed shrimp and cilantro dumplings packed with flavor; melt-in-your-mouth spareribs; and crispy fried rice balls coated in toasted sesame seeds. The á la carte menu offered in the evening showcases tasty traditional Chinese dishes.

Waffles

B3

American

1400 S. Michigan Ave. (at 14th St.)

Phone: 312-854-8572   Lunch daily
Web: www.waffleschicago.com
Prices:

 Roosevelt

As the name implies, this peppy breakfast spot specializes in all things gridded and griddled, serving ten Belgian waffle choices along with a roster of egg dishes, salads, and sandwiches—which come with, of course, house waffle fries. Solo diners bring laptops and groups spread out across picnic bench-style communal seats in this industrial haven shaded in gray.

Apart from classic Brussels and Liège waffles, unorthodox versions like cheddar cheese with braised short ribs; or Waffles Benedict, a pile of pulled pork, poached eggs, and Hollandaise atop a dense Liège waffle, are attention-grabbing. Options without nooks and crannies like rich mini red velvet cupcakes or banana-walnut muffins with real chunks of fruit are scarfed up by the grab-and-go set.

Yolk

American ✗

1120 S. Michigan Ave. (bet. 11th St. & Roosevelt Rd.)

Phone: 312-789-9655

Lunch daily

Web: www.eatyolk.com

Prices: ⊖⊖

🚇 Roosevelt

If walking south through Grant Park works up your appetite, try Yolk for a solid, budget-friendly breakfast or lunch (until 3:00 P.M. daily). This bright, whimsical diner, with its sunny yellow awnings, sits just across from the park, serving up substantial daytime meals as well as carb-loaded desserts.

Just about everything on the menu comes in ample portions alongside abundant diced red potatoes and fresh fruit. Favorites may include the "Irish Bennie," a toasted English muffin topped with sautéed tomatoes, griddled corned beef hash, and poached eggs with tangy hollandaise sauce. Nutella fans and newbies alike should order the chocolate-hazelnut nirvana that is a Nutella crêpe, served folded in quarters with powdered sugar, strawberries, or bananas.

The sun is out – let's eat alfresco! Look for 🏠.

Gold Coast

Glitz and Glamour

What's in a name? When it comes to the Gold Coast, the name says it all. After all, this posh neighborhood is Chicago's wealthiest and most affluent. From the numerous swanky high-rises dotting Lake Shore Drive, to the glittering boutiques of Michigan Avenue, the Gold Coast is luxury defined.

Whoever said money can't buy happiness certainly hadn't strolled through The Magnificent Mile, because this strip presents a serious challenge to that adage. This "magnificent" stretch of shopping, where millionaires mingle over Manolos and heiresses rummage for handbags, is one of the worlds best and most well known. Oak Street, with boutiques from Barneys to Yves Saint Laurent, runs a close second. If in the market for new wheels, take your pick from billionaire boy toys like Bentleys and Bugattis—both of which have dealerships here.

Historical Homes

It's not just about the glitz and glamour though. This neighborhood, listed on the National Register of Historic Places, is also the perfect canvas for architecture buffs. The mansions and buildings crafted in regal Queen Anne, Georgian Revival, and Richardsonian Romanesque styles are just breathtaking. They're all glorious to simply see, even if you're not in the market for a new home.

Applauding the Arts

The stunning Gold Coast takes its history quite seriously, and following this philosophy, area residents host a series of annual events, including the block party extraordinaire, Evening on Astor. This immense event also helps raise money and awareness for preservation. It is home to the Museum of Contemporary Art and the Newberry Library, one of the world's leading research libraries. So it should be of no surprise that this neighborhood celebrates the arts in a big way. The annual Gold Coast River North Art Fair is a must-see celebration of art, music, culture, and food. Whether you're an artist or have constantly dreamed of being one, this is a don't-miss celebration of the visual arts. Culture vultures should rest assured as they are bound to find something edgy and unique at A Red Orchid Theater. Here, an ensemble of artists perform a variety of stunning shows throughout the year.

Boisterous Nights

Just because the Gold Coast is sophisticated doesn't mean this area doesn't know how to party. Visit any of the pubs, clubs, and restaurants along Rush and Division streets to get a sense of how the other half lives it up. Cold winter winds got you down? Find a perch at **Lawry's Prime Rib** for some soulful steakhouse fare. This second outpost (the original is in Los Angeles) features a rather opulent dining room with a few signs of wear and tear. Expensive steakhouse classics like shrimp cocktail, prime rib, and lobster tail are favorites among the regulars seated within this regal room dressed in old tapestries, framed portraits, and gilded chandeliers. For a more rootin'-tootin' good time, stop by the well-liked **Underground Wonder Bar**, where live jazz tunes have been played nightly until the wee hours of the morning for over two decades now. The bar takes up most of the front room at this intimate jazz lair—after sipping a stellar cocktail, make your way to the back where the stage is jammed with musicians of all genres including singers, bassists, guitarists, percussionists, and horn players.

Fast (and Fresh) Food

The stylish Gold Coast is a capital of white-glove restaurants, but don't think that means there isn't good junk food available here as well. **Mr. Kite's Chocolate** will have you flying on a sugar high with its tempting array of goodies including chocolate-covered smores and the like. Get your fill of gefilte while keeping kosher at no-frills **Ashkenaz Deli**. Other delicacies include belly lox, smoked sable, and smoked white fish. It's been here since the 1970s and certainly isn't fancy, but it's just the spot for bagels with lox.

Dog Delights

Up for a double dog dare or merely a hot dog fanatic? Stop by **Gold Coast Dogs** for one or several of its delicious char dogs. These are made even better and more decadent when topped with creamy cheddar cheese. Speaking of crowning hot dogs, famed **Downtown Dogs** carries an equally savory spectrum of traditional varieties. Regulars, tourists, and others gather here for char-grilled dogs, sumptuous street eats, and juicy hamburgers galore. Need to calm and come down from your hot dog high? Duck into **TeaGschwender**, a lovely boutique where you can lose yourself in the world of exotic teas. And if you don't feel like steeping it on your own, snag a seat at **Argo Tea**. From hot tea drinks topped with whipped cream, to flavorful iced drinks, it's like Starbucks without the coffee.

Heaven on Earth

The idiom says that God is in the details, and this is most definitely apparent at the famed **Goddess & Grocer**, a neighborhood gourmet store where you can stock up on foods like soups, salads, chillis, gourmet cupcakes, and other tantalizing desserts, just like Mom would make. Homemade in an haute kind of way, this haven is all about cupcakes, cheeses, and chocolates galore. To add to the glory, they also cater, so you can pretend like you made those divine and delicate hors d'oevres at the baby's christening all on your own. For some quintessential old-world elegance, don your Grandmother's pearls for afternoon tea at the refined and resplendent **Drake's Palm Court**. Sip (not slurp!) your tea while listening to the gentle strains of a harp. Also on the agenda is a delish selection of sandwiches, pastries, fruit breads, and scones. If it's good enough for Queen Elizabeth, it will certainly do.

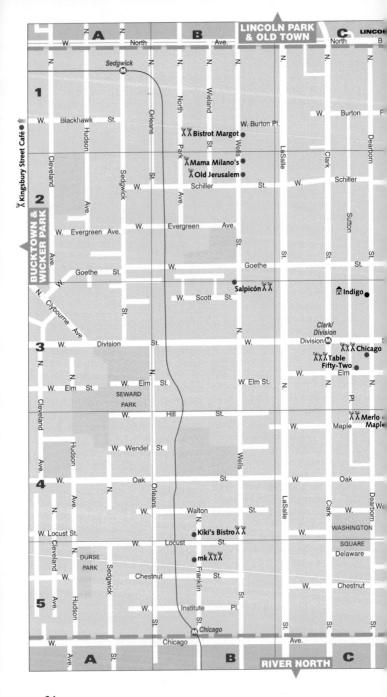

Gold Coast

N

- ● Hotel
- ● Restaurant

LAKE MICHIGAN

PARK

LINCOLN

North Ave.

E. Burton Pl.

E. Schiller St.

E. Banks St.

● Pump Room

E. Goethe St.

GOUDY SQ. PARK

E. Scott St.

E. Division St.

E. Elm St.

● RA Sushi

● Bistrot Zinc

E. Cedar St.

Original Pancake House

● Hugo's Frog Bar & Fish House

E. Bellevue Pl.

E. Oak St.

The Drawing Room

Spiaggia

● Cafe Spiaggia

E. Lake Shore Dr.

● Waldorf Astoria

● Balsan

● Gaylord

● The Drake

Walton

● Talbott

Four Seasons Chicago

● Allium

The Grill on the Alley

Pelago

● Whitehall

Signature Room at the 95th

JOHN HANCOCK CENTER

Raffaello

Delaware

● Sofitel

Café des Architectes

● Mike Ditka's

WATER TOWER PLACE

Chestnut

● Bistronomic

● Bar Toma

● deca

Pearson

The Ritz-Carlton Chicago

● NoMI Kitchen

● Park Hyatt

WATER TOWER

SENECA PARK

LAKE SHORE PARK

MUSEUM OF CONTEMPORARY ART

Chicago Ave.

STREETERVILLE

NORTHWESTERN UNIV. CHICAGO CAMPUS

Allium

D4

120 E. Delaware Pl. (bet. Michigan Ave. & Rush St.)

Phone: 312-799-4900

Web: www.alliumchicago.com

Prices: $$

Lunch & dinner daily

 Chicago (Red)

Executive Chef Kevin Hickey serves a delightful range of American-themed plates to share (or not) at the Four Seasons hotel's new seventh-floor dining entry. The setting feels relaxed yet appropriately sumptuous with thick carpeting, deep-toned polished woods, and a bright punch from vivid artwork. In addition to traditional table seating, find comfortable armchairs and rows of sofas that inspire lounging. Buoyant potato gnocchi stocked with briny clams, bits of pork cheeks, and haunting black garlic; or crisp-skinned striped bass sauced with posole-inspired lobster stew are just two options from the untethered menu that also includes a Chicago-style hot dog with house-made everything. Regional ingredients are a highlight throughout the menu.

Balsan

D4

11 E. Walton St. (bet. Rush & State Sts.)

Phone: 312-646-1400

Web: www.balsanrestaurant.com

Prices: $$

Lunch & dinner daily

 Chicago (Red)

Though the Elysian Hotel has shifted ownership to the Waldorf Astoria, fortunately Balsan remains the same—a casually upbeat bistro, but beautifully befitting the hotel's elegant environs and upscale ambience. Warm, masculine leather and wood elements act as a counterpoint to cool marble floors and a long, inviting bar, while simple wood tables keep the vibe approachable, offsetting the ritziness for average Joes.

Here, bistro classics abound in raw bar offerings and small plates like bass *goujonettes*–buttery, panko-coated fish sticks with parsley rémoulade–in turn lead the way to heftier meals like pappardelle swirled with rich lobster. Grilled ribeye with a melting pat of spinach butter and sea salt-flecked hand-cut fries is another worthy standout.

Bar Toma

D5

Italian ✕✕

110 E. Pearson St. (bet. Michigan Ave. & Rush St.)

Phone: 312-266-3110
Web: www.bartomachicago.com
Prices: $$

Lunch & dinner daily

🚇 Chicago (Red)

In the space formerly graced by Bistro 110, Spiaggia chef Tony Mantuano premieres this ambitious ode to Italian food as seen through the filter of hearty (read: heavy) Midwestern cooking. Stations throughout the food hall-style room showcase a revolving menu of pizza, gelato, Roman *fritti*, and more. But, it's best just to take a seat amid the bustling confusion and let the staff come to you.

Family-style is the way to tackle their carte, especially when confronted with specials on tableside blackboards. Food arrives in stages, so be prepared to share the likes of Tuscan chicken liver spread; or the signature pizza Mantuano with *guanciale* and rapini. For a quick pit stop among the Mag Mile gawkers, breeze by for a glass off the smartly chosen wine list.

Bistronomic

D5

French ✕✕

840 N. Wabash Ave. (bet. Chestnut & Pearson Sts.)

Phone: 312-944-8400
Web: www.bistronomic.net
Prices: $$

Lunch Wed – Sun
Dinner nightly
🚇 Chicago (Red)

Attention menu hounds: even if you like to pre-plan every bite before arriving at a spot, you might do well to wait it out at Bistronomic. After settling in to this richly decorated room beautified with snugly spaced seats and warm crimson walls, pick a cocktail from the brief but well-selected list and peruse their abundant and tempting daily specials—courtesy of Chef Martial Nouguier and team.

Packed with visitors, foodies are certainly missing out on Bistronomic's simple presentations that do not detract from quality. One could make a meal out of smaller items like cheese, charcuterie, or a creamy fish soup with whole mussels. Others may opt to fill up on succulent Amish chicken or a side of hearty white bean-and-bacon cassoulet.

Bistrot Margot

B1

1437 N. Wells St. (at Burton Pl.)

Phone: 312-587-3660
Web: www.bistrotmargot.com
Prices: $$

Lunch & dinner daily

 Sedgwick

Maybe it's the exposed brick walls and the intimate bistro tables spilling onto the sidewalk, or the feeling that comes from a place named after the Chef/owner's daughter, but there's something particularly charming about Bistrot Margot. This group-friendly Gold Coast spot simply offers amiable service and reasonable prices for quality food. Special promotions are abundant, from half-price wines to lunch and dinner specials. While the menu focuses on French standards like duck confit and steak frites, it caters to the Chicago palate with tasty interpretations. Highlights may include the silky fennel and carrot soup or *pomme de terre farci*, a potato shell stuffed with scrambled eggs, cheese, and bacon topped with horseradish crème fraîche.

Bistrot Zinc

French

D3

1131 N. State St. (bet. Elm & Cedar Sts.)

Phone: 312-337-1131
Web: www.bistrotzinc.com
Prices: $$

Lunch & dinner daily

Clark/Division

Tin ceilings, mosaic tiled floors, peppy yellow walls with framed French posters—it's a whiff of Paris in the heart of the Gold Coast. Bistrot Zinc, named for its handcrafted zinc bar, has that lovable neighborhood restaurant thing down pat. From its décor to its delicacies, it's all very classic French bistro. Even the top-shelf staff (sporting bow ties and rolled up sleeves) smell of charm. Just subtract the fussy accents and frosty demeanors here and you're smack dab in the middle of Paris.

Flavorful French comfort food is the house specialty: *croque monsieur*, steak frites, French onion soup, and omelets. The compositions are unfussy, but it's exactly what you wanted. Plus, you can still save some pennies for your piggy bank after a meal here.

Café des Architectes

Contemporary ✗✗✗

D5

20 E. Chestnut St. (at Wabash Ave.)

Phone: 312-324-4063

Web: www.cafedesarchitectes.com

Prices: $$$

Lunch & dinner daily

🚇 Chicago (Red)

Though ensconced in the lobby of the Sofitel Hotel Water Tower, Café des Architectes is more than a hangout for corporate road warriors. Steel and glass shimmer under striking, column-like lightshades, while couples and intimate groups murmur to each other on red banquettes.

Contemporary French cuisine aims skyscraper-high but often only makes it to mid-rise levels. Seared diver scallops and halibut can verge on over-cooked, while vegetables like tender smoked potato ragout fare much better. A three-course prix-fixe dinner menu of the "chef's market selections" certainly allows some flexibility and is prettily priced at $39. Despite frequent gyrations in the pastry department, the end results are consistently creative and harmonious.

Cafe Spiaggia

Italian ✗✗

E4

980 N. Michigan Ave. (at Oak St.)

Phone: 312-280-2750

Web: www.spiaggiarestaurant.com/cafe

Prices: $$

Lunch & dinner daily

🚇 Chicago (Red)

Looking to see what all of the fuss is about without dropping a ton of cash? Visit Cafe Spiaggia, the less pricey and more casual sister of Michelin-starred, and very serious, Spiaggia. Located in the same massive office building overlooking the lake and Michigan Avenue, they don't serve the same rave-worthy food, but you can still sense the style.

The narrow room feels close, in that charming café way, but the suits and ladies who don't bat a false eyelash at 3-hour lunches seem nonetheless contented. Cozy and elegant, the ambience is the reason to come here, since the food can be overreaching, though tasty as in asparagus with *Prosciutto di Parma* and duck egg. Just sit back, savor a nice glass of Italian wine or a beer, and drink in the scene.

Chicago Q

🍴🍴🍴

C3

1160 N. Dearborn St. (bet. Division & Elm Sts.)

Phone: 312-642-1160 Lunch & dinner daily
Web: www.chicagoqrestaurant.com
Prices: $$ 🚇 Clark/Division

Barbecue goes upscale at this ambitious restaurant in a posh setting. The spacious dining room plays against expectations with industrial lighting, a subway-tiled kitchen, glass enclosures, and surprising moneyed Rush Street guests anticipating a traditional Southern picnic experience.

Start at the bar with small-batch American Bourbons and whiskies or a Q Martini adorned with smoked olives. Rich and bold flavors define the menu: silk-tender smoked chicken expertly balances aroma, texture, and spot-on taste in each bite. Braised greens—a trio of mustard, Swiss chard, and collard—simultaneously feel rich and light. Even the baby greens with smoked grape tomatoes and cornbread croutons carry the tastes and textures that make the meal playfully elegant.

deca 😊

🍴🍴

E5

160 E. Pearson St. (at Water Tower Place)

Phone: 312-573-5160 Lunch & dinner daily
Web: www.decarestaurant.com
Prices: $$ 🚇 Chicago (Red)

With deca, The Ritz-Carlton Chicago declares that luxury need not be stuffy. The hotel's product-driven brasserie is actually a come-as-you-are respite, sequestered off the 12th floor lobby. It's situated amid rich carpeting and grand artwork further beautified by a soaring skylight and the soothing sounds of a gently gurgling fountain.

This all-day café features a concise lunch offering that revolves around the bento box-inspired DLT (deca lunch trio) such as French onion soup, grilled tuna sandwich with avocado and black-olive tapenade, and a slice of cake. Other treats include *plats du jour* like Wednesday night's rabbit *moutard*, or entrées such as plump seared scallops over corn bread gnocchi, sautéed with wild mushrooms and peppery watercress.

The Drawing Room

Contemporary

D4

937 N. Rush St. (bet. Oak & Walton Sts.)

Phone: 312-266-2694
Web: www.thedrchicago.com
Prices: $$$

Dinner Tue – Sat

Clark/Division

Slide past the doorman guarding the narrow entry to this subterranean lair, only to discover new heights of culinary cocktail appreciation. Teardrop chandeliers cast a soft glow onto the pretty young things. Find them sitting atop low-slung velvet chairs and leaning across blond wood tables, sipping from coupes and sharing punchbowls. A gadget-laden rack behind the bar is put to constant use by the mixologists.

Though drinks are the draw, a concise menu offers nibbles à la carte or a three-course prix-fixe selection that's just as carefully crafted. Hamachi crudo is drizzled with Arbequina olive oil; juicy *poussin* rests on fregola dressed with Wisconsin cheddar mornay; and plump scallops wrapped in ham play well with a pickled pineapple garnish.

Gaylord

Indian

D4

100 E. Walton St. (bet. Michigan Ave. & Rush St.)

Phone: 312-664-1700
Web: www.gaylordil.com
Prices: $$

Lunch & dinner daily

Chicago (Red)

Among the Euro-chic boutiques of Magnificent Mile, Gaylord looms large. The massive à la carte menu at this subterranean lair features a host of Northern Indian dishes served family-style together with numerous varieties of *roti*. Yet most seem smitten by the fragrant allure of the steaming buffet and its standout lunch items.

Pile a plate with flaky naan; or for a street snack, try the *behl* station teeming with crunchy *sev*, puffed rice, and an array of condiments. Newbies to Indian cuisine will appreciate the buffet labels elaborating on mainstays like *daal*, tandoori chicken, and *pappadam*.

Free bar bites during happy hour draw a crowd—those looking to duck off the street for a quiet drink will always find a bar stool and affable service here.

Gibson's

Steakhouse ✗✗

D4

1028 N. Rush St. (at Bellevue Pl.)

Phone: 312-266-8999   Lunch & dinner daily
Web: www.gibsonssteakhouse.com
Prices: $$$ Clark/Division

There is no better paean to old-school masculinity than Gibson's. Located in the heart of what some call "the Viagra Triangle," this expense account staple is where the power players schmooze, eat, and drink amid dark tables and large portions.

Evoking a sense of the Old World, autographed photos of celebs who have dined here line the walls, and servers in white jackets deliver what is expected: over a dozen different steaks and chops (including W.R.'s Chicago cut ribeye) cooked to order, with classic sides like creamed spinach, asparagus with Hollandaise, and double-baked potatoes. Also sating appetites is a spicy lobster cobb salad and ample desserts. A medley of half-order sizes will keep those lipo'd figures svelte.

The Grill on the Alley

American ✗✗

E4

909 N. Michigan Ave. (at Delaware Pl.)

Phone: 312-255-9009   Lunch & dinner daily
Web: www.thegrill.com
Prices: $$$ Chicago (Red)

Dark and masculine with polished woods, leather booths, and walls cramped with framed sketches and portraits, this maze of rooms is a corporate power house set near the foot of the John Hancock building just off the Westin lobby. Its locale often results in herds of executives that migrate from the conference rooms to the dining rooms for classic American food in a suitably nostalgic setting.

Big lunchtime salads–like the chopped Greek with poached shrimp, a tangy vinaigrette, and generous hunk of feta–are popular at the long wood bar near the entry. Other favorites include starters like the creamy and cheesy spinach-artichoke dip, or the golden brown and flaky chicken pot pie with a light velouté coating tender chicken and vegetables.

Hugo's Frog Bar & Fish House

American

 D4

1024 N. Rush St. (bet. Bellevue Pl. & Oak St.)

Phone: 312-640-0999　　　　　　　　　　Lunch & dinner daily
Web: www.hugosfrogbar.com
Prices: $$　　　　　　　　　　　　　　　 Clark/Division

Housed in a sprawling setting adjacent to big brother Gibson's, Hugo's always seems packed. The vast dining room sets white linen-topped tables amidst dark polished wood and pale walls decorated with a mounted swordfish, fish prints, and model ships. Hugo's bar draws its own crowds with abundant counter seating.

The menu focuses on a selection of fish preparations as well as steaks and chops. These are supplemented by stone crab claws, oysters, crab cakes, chowders, and sautéed frog's legs. Speaking of frog's legs, the restaurant takes its name from the nickname of owner Hugo Ralli's grandfather, General Bruce Hay of Her Majesty's Imperial Forces.

Bring a football team to share a slice of the Muddy Bottom Pie, a decadent (and enormous) ice cream cake.

Kiki's Bistro

French

B4

900 N. Franklin St. (at Locust St.)

Phone: 312-335-5454　　　　　　　　　　Lunch Mon – Fri
Web: www.kikisbistro.com　　　　　　　　Dinner Mon – Sat
Prices: $$　　　　　　　　　　　　　　　 Chicago (Brown)

This French cuisine mainstay had been attracting locals and tourists long before the new condos and other construction cropped up. Regulars and newcomers are warmly greeted into the dining room, decorated with candles, fresh flowers, natural light, and rustic wood beams.

The kitchen turns out solid French fare. The French onion soup uses top-notch Gruyère cheese, which is glistening and charred on top. Showing off the chef's skill is the texture of the duck confit with green peppercorn sauce—the meat just falls off the bone and is accompanied by the lip-licking sauce. Also rich and silky is a lime mousse cake with crème anglaise. Owner Kiki himself was once the sommelier at Maxim's of Chicago, so wines are well-paired, although not particularly rare.

Kingsbury Street Café

Coast

Gold Coast

Contemporary ✗

A1

1523 N. Kingsbury St. (bet. Blackhawk & Weed Sts.)

Phone: 312-280-1718   Lunch daily
Web: www.kingsburystreetcafe.com   Dinner Wed – Sat
Prices: 💰💰   North/Clybourn

Chef Rose Duong and her family ran Work of Art Cakes on Halsted for more than two decades. Having now relocated to an airy and modern loft, they've expanded their repertoire to three meals a day, along with cocktails. Families and young professionals use the high-ceilinged space as their personal food court, crowding around blond butcher block tables.

Big breakfast dishes like the "piggy moo cluck" sandwich piled with bacon, ham, and over-easy eggs on freshly baked bread, take care of hearty appetites; while colorful salads could be tossed with golden and purple beets, pistachios, edamame, and a red wine vinaigrette. Hours for lunch and cocktail service vary, but the pastry counter is always chockablock with *kuchens*, scones, and pavlovas to-go.

Mama Milano's

Pizza ✗

B2

1419 N. Wells St. (bet. North Ave. & Schiller St.)

Phone: 312-787-3710   Lunch & dinner daily
Web: www.mamamilano.com
Prices: $$ Sedgwick

Though the owners are great-grandsons of one of Chicago's early restaurateurs, Mama Milano's is a newcomer to Old Town. Outside, it feels like a Venetian hideaway—easy to miss and tucked off a stone-tiled courtyard. The smartly decorated interior offers zebra-print banquettes, vintage posters, and exposed bricks that lend a boutique feel to the casual but stylish pizza bar.

Neapolitan-esque pizzas are wafer-thin with crisp, chewy crusts that hold up to the weight of tangy tomato sauce and hearty toppings like sausage, pancetta, ricotta, and eggs. Salads and sandwiches round out the menu, but a must for every table is an order of the family's signature spinach bread—an oozing, caramelized, and stromboli-esque combo of mozzarella, Romano, and spinach.

Merlo on Maple

C4

Italian XX

16 W. Maple St. (bet. Dearborn & State Sts.)

Phone:	312-335-8200	Dinner nightly
Web:	www.merlochicago.com	
Prices:	$$$	Clark/Division

This *ristorante* houses many floors, but no matter where you sit, the multi-level beauty boasts Victorian touches (hand-carved banisters and leather banquettes), and an informed waitstaff, who deliver the tastes of Emilia-Romagna. Of course, if you're here on date-night, make sure to carve out a corner on their lower level, which—albeit a few feet below—is the most romantic space.

Red sauce isn't exactly their signature, but the amiable kitchen is happy to please a lady. So if you crave the typical tomato sauce, order away. The homemade pastas are lovely, but dishes like *stricchetti verdi* tossed with rabbit ragù; or the *imprigionata alla Petroniana* use top-notch ingredients from Italy's culinary epicenter and are definitely their more unique items.

Mike Ditka's

D5

American XXX

100 E. Chestnut St. (at Rush St.)

Phone:	312-587-8989	Lunch & dinner daily
Web:	www.mikeditkaschicago.com	
Prices:	$$	Chicago (Red)

Chicago sports legends have a way of becoming restaurateurs at some point, and former Bears coach Mike Ditka is no exception.

However, what is an exception is that locals come here not just because of his 1985 Super Bowl win, but because the food is actually quite good (though lighter appetites might be encouraged to man up). Come very hungry and start with Coach's pot roast nachos. Then, move on to the insurmountable meatloaf stack—layered with jalapeño corn bread, meatloaf, mashed potatoes, and fried onion straws. Doggy bags are de rigueur here, but do try to save room for some banana cream pie.

The space is masculine, comfortable, and lined with sports memorabilia—souvenirs are available for purchase on your way out.

mk

 B5

868 N. Franklin St. (bet. Chestnut & Locust Sts.)

Phone: 312-482-9179   Dinner nightly
Web: www.mkchicago.com
Prices: $$$ Chicago (Brown)

Local darling Michael Kornick continues to build on his solid reputation with this long-standing, well-run restaurant that brings its share of regulars to the western end of the glittering Gold Coast. Service is happy to please: go ahead and order dishes from the tasting menu if an item beyond the expansive à la carte menu strikes your eye. Upbeat, professional staffers are ready to offer recommendations on personal favorites.

The modern American cuisine mirrors the warm atmosphere and clean lines of the dining room and lounge. The oft-changing seasonal menu showcases simply prepared fresh market ingredients like roasted rabbit leg with favas, pancetta, glazed carrots, and corn purée. Desserts are creatively presented enticements to end the evening.

NoMI Kitchen

D5

800 N. Michigan Ave. (entrance on Chicago Ave.)

Phone: 312-239-4030   Lunch & dinner daily
Web: www.nomirestaurant.com
Prices: $$$$ Chicago (Red)

Business meetings, hotel guests, and lunching ladies soak up the sun and skyline from the seventh floor of Michigan Avenue's Park Hyatt, where soaring windows offer views of the historic Water Tower and lake beyond. Modern leather chairs, dark maple tables, and marble décor accents are sleek and polished, though the service can be overly saccharine and scripted.

The adjacent lounge and rooftop garden bar offer equally splendid Magnificent Mile views that only improve with a cocktail or selection from the impressive wine list. Avoid the mediocre, overpriced sushi and stick to elegant items like a silky mushroom soup topped with Sofia goat cheese; and ambitiously creative desserts like a crunchy, minty, cookie-crusted take on frozen pudding.

Old Jerusalem

Middle Eastern

1411 N. Wells St. (bet. North Ave. & Schiller St.)

Phone: 312-944-0459 Lunch & dinner daily
Web: www.oldjerusalemchicago.com
Prices: Sedgwick

Set on a charming and centrally located stretch of Old Town, this family-run Middle Eastern favorite has been eagerly accommodating its happy customers since 1976.

The menu focuses on Lebanese-style classics, such as tabbouleh with cracked wheat, scallions, tomatoes, seasoned with lemon, olive oil, and plenty of crisp, green parsley. Hummus arrives rich with tahini, perhaps accompanying the likes of grilled chicken kebabs and traditional flatbreads. Finish with flaky-sweet baklava.

While the décor may not impress, Old Jerusalem manages to make its well-worn looks feel cozy and comfortable for everyone. Very reasonable prices, family-friendly service, and generous portions make this the neighborhood go-to spot, whether dining in or taking out.

Original Pancake House

American

22 E. Bellevue Pl. (bet. Michigan Ave. & Rush St.)

Phone: 312-642-7917 Lunch daily
Web: www.originalpancakehouse.com
Prices: Clark/Division

While the glitz and glamor of the Gold Coast has proliferated outside its doors, this dressed-down diner has maintained its relaxed, slightly frumpy but comforting disposition. Those looking for a no-nonsense break from the stylish affairs all around should head to this minuscule neighborhood spot that is the place to be—with the long lines to prove it. Just don't call it a greasy spoon: everything's sparkling clean.

Along with a variety of sandwiches, homemade soups, and savory crêpes, it's breakfast–and yes, pancakes–that rules at the Pancake House. Exquisitely poached eggs rest atop buttery and crunchy English muffins to soak up hollandaise sauce in eggs Benedict; whereas potato pancakes with sour cream and apple sauce are meltingly light.

Pelago

Italian

E5

201 E. Delaware Pl. (at Seneca St.)

Phone: 312-280-0700
Web: www.pelagorestaurant.com
Prices: $$$

Lunch & dinner daily

 Chicago (Red)

Understated romance is the name of the game at this well-dressed restaurant, located just off the lobby of Hotel Raffaello. In a setting ideal for impressing dates without going overboard, modern splashes of aqua throughout the serene espresso- and cream-toned rooms keep the Italianate décor on the side of contemporary rather than rustic.

Artisan pastas and seafood take center stage in updated renderings of dishes sourced from Italy's tip to toe, such as square *tonnarelli* tossed with spinach, tender shrimp, and diced tomato that gets a savory punch from melted herb butter. Prospective Romeos and Juliets should make reservations for the desirable upper dining room; walk-ins may need to content themselves with a less-than-intimate bar table.

Pizano's

Pizza

D5

864 N. State St. (bet. Chestnut St. & Delaware Pl.)

Phone: 312-751-1766
Web: www.pizanoschicago.com
Prices: ⊖⊖

Lunch & dinner daily

Chicago (Red)

While Chicago may be hailed as home of the deep-dish pizza, the thin-crust pies at Pizano's have justly earned their own devoted following. Of course, the crowds come for the crust—here it is flaky, buttery, thin (by local standards), and perfectly crisp. As unexpected as it sounds, this pizza is truly some of the best in town.

Still, it should be no surprise, as pizza has long been the family calling: owner Rudy Malnati's father founded Pizzeria Uno. The thinner offspring at Pizano's sates its growing fan-base from three locations, and even ships to those who are only Chicagoan at heart. This refreshing and cozy local spot recalls Italo-American style without feeling like a chain-restaurant cliché. The service staff's genuine warmth is palpable.

Pump Room

Contemporary

D2

1301 N. State Pkwy. (at Goethe St.)

Phone: 312-229-6740

Web: www.pumproom.com

Prices: $$

Lunch & dinner daily

Clark/Division

The original Brat Pack's famed Chicago dining spot has received a fabulous makeover courtesy of Ian Schrager as part of his Public Chicago hotel launch. Celebrity loves company, so Schrager has teamed up with Jean-Georges Vongerichten to ensure that the hotel's restaurant is a destination on its own. The plush setting is awash in soothing pale browns beneath planetarium-chic globe lights; grassy green sofas at the bar break up the monochromatic lull.

The menu's seasonal, locally sourced conceit mimics the approach Vongerichten has taken at his NY hot spot, ABC Kitchen. Fresh flavors abound in creations like roasted and paprika-dusted carrots with avocado, pea shoots, and a bright lemon vinaigrette; or house-made tagliatelle slicked with pistachio pesto.

RA Sushi

Japanese

D3

1139 N. State St. (at Elm St.)

Phone: 312-274-0011

Web: www.rasushi.com

Prices: $$

Lunch & dinner daily

Clark/Division

Benihana's rollicking sushi offshoot, one of 25 locations nationwide, is glitzy enough that the fish should wear sequins instead of scales. Crimson globe lights bounce to the beat of pumping music in this red- and black-accented room dotted with wood furnishings and tile work. Behind the double-height sushi counter with seating for more than a dozen, hangs the stylized silhouette of a whole fish, dramatically sliced.

The playful menu may verge on gimmicky with variations on the restaurant's name popping up repeatedly, as in the crispy "RA"ckin' shrimp or sashimi choices labeled "RA Tapas." Use golf pencils to mark such sushi selections as a *gojira* roll with spicy tuna, shrimp tempura, and *kani kama* crab; or chili ponzu yellowtail with sautéed cashews.

Salpicón

Mexican

B3

1252 N. Wells St. (bet. Division & Goethe Sts.)

Phone: 312-988-7811
Web: www.salpicon.com
Prices: $$

Lunch Sun
Dinner nightly

Salpicón has serious pedigree but it's certainly not too solemn a place. Under the cerulean awning and past a striking glass façade, color reigns in the form of lime green chairs and Schiaparelli-pink tablecloths played against vibrant paintings on yellow walls. The tequila list is similarly eye-opening, boasting more than 100 choices available neat, over ice, or in a margarita.

As one of Chicago's pioneers of upscale Mexican food, Chef/owner Priscilla Satkoff turns out a sophisticated, dramatically flavored mix of classic techniques in modern presentations. Begin with pleasantly earthy *crêpes de huitlacoche* filled with serranos and a trickle of poblano crème; while a deep-red honey and ancho chile paste glazes smoky, garlicky butterflied quail.

Signature Room at the 95th

Contemporary

E5

875 N. Michigan Ave. (bet. Chestnut St. & Delaware Ave.)

Phone: 312-787-9596
Web: www.signatureroom.com
Prices: $$$

Lunch & dinner daily

 Chicago (Red)

First-time tourists and longtime Chicago residents alike take the elevator up, up, up to the 95th Floor of the landmark John Hancock Center for a bird's-eye view of the Windy City. Request a seat in the east-facing main dining room to glimpse gorgeous Lake Michigan through floor-to-ceiling windows, while the west-facing room gets the heart racing with views of the stellar skyline and further west.

Though the memorable setting (minus the slightly dated décor) is the main draw, contemporary American classics aiming to please a wide swath of appetites do yeoman's work throughout the menu. Featured selections have uncovered a modern version of meatloaf with braised duck and buttery whipped potatoes; or a trio of fruit sorbets that cool the palate.

Spiaggia ❀

Italian 🍴🍴🍴🍴

E4

980 N. Michigan Ave. (at Oak St.)

Phone: 312-280-2750   Dinner nightly
Web: www.spiaggiarestaurant.com
Prices: $$$$ 🚇 Chicago (Red)

Jeff Kauck

Mounting floor-to-ceiling windows overlooking the tony intersection of Michigan Avenue and Oak Street sweep guests out of the everyday and into the hushed and gracious world of Spiaggia. Here, modern Italian elegance reigns as jacketed gentlemen talk shop and couples celebrate anniversaries in the intimate u-shaped banquettes. It is the perfect setting for a sumptuous feast of countless courses.

Under starburst chandeliers, guests inspect an extensive wine list spanning the appellations of Italy. These varietals match beautifully with the sophisticated regional cooking courtesy of Chef/owner Tony Mantuano and Executive Chef Sarah Grueneberg.

Imported items from Italian artisan manufacturers mingle with quality products from small American farmers for a rustic-meets-refined melting pot on the plate. Fresh black truffle shavings accentuate but never dominate finely diced Wisconsin lamb tartare; while Quinault River steelhead trout flanked by abalone mushrooms pops with tiny basil-fed snails and *bottarga* atop creamy polenta. First-rate ingredients also take center stage on prix-fixe menus, spotlighting a roster of seasonal elements that may include white and black truffles or aged vinegars.

111

Table Fifty-Two

52 W. Elm St. (bet. Clark & Dearborn Sts.)

Phone: 312-573-4000
Web: www.tablefifty-two.com
Prices: $$$

Lunch Sun
Dinner nightly
Clark/Division

Chef Art Smith's drawl floats overhead like a warm breeze as he chats up guests inside Table Fifty-Two's cozy white row house, a stately survivor of the Great Chicago Fire. Southern charm permeates every inch of the room, from the pressed copper ceiling to the white sideboards to a wood-burning oven churning out the restaurant's signature biscuits.

The meal might get started with an amuse-bouche of deviled eggs topped with pickled mustard seeds, and if it's a Sunday or Monday, the famous fried chicken will be making an appearance on many plates. Plump fried green tomatoes and thick pork chops are on order, but for a true down-home taste, get a tall wedge of hummingbird cake, fragrant with banana and pineapple and slathered in cream cheese frosting.

Look for our symbol 🍸,
spotlighting restaurants
with a notable
cocktail list.

Humboldt Park & Logan Square

Albany Park · Irving Park

This alluring collection of vibrant north side neighborhoods is the heart and soul of where locals live and eat. While the area may live a few blocks off the beaten path, it is great for anyone seeking that perfect dessert, ethnic grocer, hidden bodega, or quick falafel. Plus, any trip through these up-and-coming neighborhoods is sure to be heavenly with tree-lined streets, quaint architecture, and affordable, trendy shops. Begin your adventure in Chicago's prized Koreatown, a commercial thoroughfare spanning miles along Lawrence Avenue, from Cicero to California Avenue.

HUMBOLDT PARK

The core of the city's Puerto Rican community is found here. If there's any confusion as to exactly where it begins, just look for the Paseo Boricua, the flag-shaped steel gateway demarcating the district along Division Street. These storefronts are as much a celebration of the diaspora as the homeland, with their impressive and enticing selection of traditional foods, hard-to-find ingredients, and authentic, slow-cooked *pernil*.

LOGAN SQUARE

An eclectic mix of cuisines (from Cuban and Mexican, to Italian) combined with historic buildings and boulevards, attract a crowd of hipsters, working-class locals, artists, and students to this quarter. Within this community, locally minded at-home cooks and foodies flock to the **Dill Pickle Food Co-op** for bulk groceries. Visitors opt for Sunday's **Logan Square Farmer's Market** on Logan Boulevard, with stalls hawking everything from artisanal soaps and raw honey to organic zucchini. Adults and kids have been saving their allowances for a trip to **Margie's Candies**, for its homemade chocolates, toffees, and rich hot fudge sundaes. A melting pot of global foods, Albany Park offers every gastronomic delight at budget-friendly prices. Highlights may include **Al Khayyam Bakery**, a Middle Eastern grocery with cheeses, olive oils, and flatbreads. For dessert, lull at **Nazareth Sweets** and bite into brittles and pastries like walnut baklava. **Charcoal Delights** is a time-tested, unique burger favorite with such treasures as chicken delight, cheesesteak, and hot dogs with "the works" rounding out the menu. You will be in good hands at **Wellfleet** whose dining counter is perfect for patrons in the mood for a lineup of first-rate fish. This market also supplies restaurants and home cooks with pristine seafood and service. The nearby **Independence Park Farmer's Market** is also worth a trip. This fast-growing market will sate with its medley of produce, plants, and baked goods.

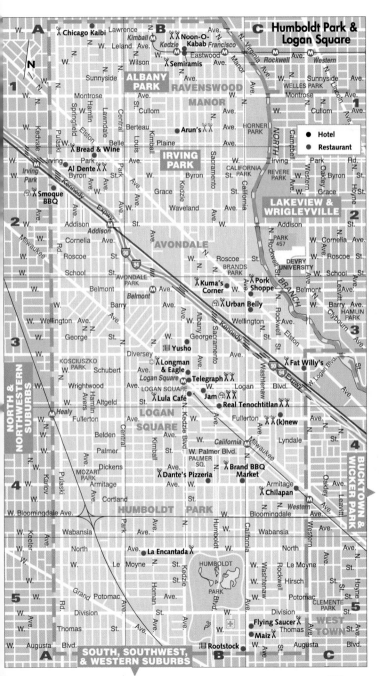

Humboldt Park & Logan Square

Legend:
- ● Hotel
- ● Restaurant

Neighborhoods/Areas:
- ALBANY PARK
- RAVENSWOOD MANOR
- IRVING PARK
- HORNER PARK
- AVONDALE
- LAKEVIEW & WRIGLEYVILLE
- DEVRY UNIVERSITY
- LOGAN SQUARE
- KOSCIUSZKO PARK
- NORTH & NORTHWESTERN SUBURBS
- MOZART PARK
- HUMBOLDT PARK
- BUCKTOWN & WICKER PARK
- WEST TOWN
- CLEMENTE PARK
- PALMER SQ.
- BRANDS PARK
- AVONDALE PARK
- HAMLIN PARK
- WELLES PARK
- REVERE PARK
- CALIFORNIA PARK
- PARK 457

Restaurants/Hotels labeled on map:
- Chicago Kalbi
- Kimball
- Noon-O-Kabab
- Semiramis
- Arun's
- Bread & Wine
- Al Dente
- Smoque BBQ
- Kuma's Corner
- Pork Shoppe
- Urban Belly
- Yusho
- Longman & Eagle
- Telegraph
- Lula Café
- Jam
- Real Tenochtitlan
- Fat Willy's
- (k)new
- Dante's Pizzeria
- Brand BBQ Market
- Chilapan
- La Encantada
- Flying Saucer
- Maiz
- Rootstock

Al Dente

A2

Contemporary ❌❌

3939 W. Irving Park Rd. (bet. Pulaski Rd. & Springfield Ave.)

Phone:	773-208-9539	Lunch Tue – Sat
Web:	www.aldentechicago.com	Dinner Tue – Sun
Prices:	$$	🚇 North/Clybourn

"Al Verde" may be a more apt name for this spirited destination where the dining room is decked with avocado-rich greens and browns. A wall of leafy cutouts delineates the bar area, and Chef/owner Javier Perez sports a lime green coat as he welcomes guests, works in the open kitchen, and serves tables alongside his wife Maria.

The vibe may be green, but the menu is a veritable exhibition of Chef Perez's pedigree—he's worked in many of the city's finest dining establishments over the past two decades. Latin-American flavors do the tango with French and Italian influences in dishes like a *guajillo*-marinated calamari with buttery wild mushrooms adeptly balanced by habanero aïoli; or fork-tender short ribs set atop *mole Poblano* and garlic mashed potatoes.

Arun's

B1

Thai ❌❌

4156 N. Kedzie Ave. (at Berteau Ave.)

Phone:	773-539-1909	Dinner Tue – Sun
Web:	www.arunsthai.com	
Prices:	$$$$	🚇 Kedzie (Brown)

Chef/owner Arun Sampanthavivat oversees every detail at this culinary mainstay, which has been serving a well-dressed and moneyed crowd since 1985.

No need to bring your reading glasses, since you won't need to fuss with a menu at Arun's. Instead, this upscale Thai restaurant treats its visitors to a 12-course prix-fixe of six appetizers, four entrées (served family-style), and two desserts. The dishes change regularly, but expect creations like diced spicy pork served inside a grilled sweet pepper; or Panang beef curry in coconut milk. Carved vegetables shaped like butterflies and fish are memorable flourishes.

From the elegant setting and white-jacketed servers to the bountiful feast, it's no wonder people return so often for the princely experience.

Brand BBQ Market

Barbecue

2824 W. Armitage Ave. (at Mozart St.)

Phone: 773-687-8148
Web: www.brandbbqmarket.com
Prices:

Lunch Fri – Sun
Dinner nightly
 Western (Blue)

Tender pulled duck sandwich with a side of Bourbon creamed corn? Check. Venison sausage stuffed with Gorgonzola and wrapped in bacon atop fried onions and brandy cherry sauce? Check. Old-fashioned barbecue getting a mouthwatering makeover? Double check. Amp up those 'cue cravings and step into this wooden oasis where wood banquettes and thick varnished tables adorn the space; while aromatic woods like apple and hickory, smoke those juicy meats. A retail area selling chunks of wood entices the ambitious to recreate the experience at home.

Sample the selection of savory sauces on the table, from smoky chipotle to tangy-sweet brown sugar-cayenne. Vegetarians, you won't feel left out with meaty smoked tofu and portobello mushrooms, but don't forget to BYOB.

Bread & Wine

International

3732 W. Irving Park Rd. (at Ridgeway Ave.)

Phone: 773-866-5266
Web: www.breadandwinechicago.com
Prices: $$

Lunch Sun
Dinner nightly
 Irving Park (Blue)

What Irving Park lost in a neighborhood Laundromat, it more than makes up for with this mod, casual bistro—boasting its own parking lot, no less. The smooth white bar or kitchen counter is ideal for snacking on fries with malt aïoli, or homemade Cajun cashews. Alternatively, relax at a table made of reclaimed wood for more substantial fare.

Thin slices of scallop crudo are simply dressed with corn, lime, and Fresno chile rings; and pea tendril cavatelli is rich with Guinea hog belly lardons. Ambitious diners will choose from the "5th Quarter" section of the menu featuring lesser-used cuts like crisp-fried chicken feet.

A shop near the exit offers take-home treats, including the kitchen's popular nut varieties, with 10 percent discounts for dinner guests.

Chicago Kalbi

A1

3752 W. Lawrence Ave. (bet. Hamlin & Lawndale Aves.)

Phone: 773-604-8183 Dinner Wed – Mon
Web: www.chicago-kalbi.com
Prices: $$

Take me out to the ballgame—or the Korean barbecue joint where a ballplayer would feel right at home, as the case may be at this quirky spot. Autographed baseballs line walls and shelves, while photographs and posters of ballplayers paper the walls; but the cluttered décor doesn't deter locals from frequenting this modest but welcoming space.

Gas grills at each table give off an intoxicatingly savory perfume as patrons take their time searing their choice of well-marbled marinated beef, including the always-popular *bulgogi* or *kalbi*, and cool their mouths with a traditional array of *banchan*. For those who prefer their meat off the grill, a beef tartare takes an interesting twist of flavor when folded with Asian pears, sesame seeds, and sesame oil.

Chilapan

C4

2459 W. Armitage Ave. (at Campbell Ave.)

Phone: 773-697-4374 Dinner Mon – Sat
Web: www.tenangrypitbulls.com/chilapan
Prices: $$ Western (Blue)

A newer and even bluer Chilapan has opened in Ravenswood, but this original neon-painted Mexican spot keeps on trucking under the rumble of the Blue Line. Its snug dining room has fewer seats than an El car, but Chef/owner Jorge Miranda's food brings a crowd that spills out onto the sidewalk tables. Salmon-colored walls and Aztec-inspired art keep the space lively.

The focused menu showcases brightly flavored Mexican dishes, including *taquitos conchita* filled with slow-roasted pork and topped with mango guacamole and *chiltomate*; or *rollito de espinaca* with *chihuahua* cheese and spinach-stuffed grilled skirt steak. Desserts may include roasted pineapple upside-down cake with piña colada salsa and homemade sour cream ice cream with strawberry sauce.

Dante's Pizzeria

B4

Pizza ✗

3028 W. Armitage St. (at Whipple St.)

Phone: 773-342-0002

Web: www.dantespizzeriachicago.com

Prices: $$

Lunch & dinner daily

 California (Blue)

 Brush up on your knowledge of classic literature before heading to Dante's, where the Divine Comedy serves as inspiration. The no-frills décor, basic counter service, and metal soundtrack may seem like purgatory, but stay awhile as the pricey pies are pure paradise.

Each of the 20-inch pizzas–floppy and foldable in the classic New York-style–reference characters from this famous Italian epic. Try the Beatrice with garlic sauce and mushrooms; or the signature Inferno pie with nine rings of toppings like *giardiniera*, jalapeños, and pepperoni. It would be a sin not to share a starter of deep-fried poblano poppers oozing with cream cheese, bacon, and red onion; or sumptuously rich mozzarella sticks. Not ready for such gluttony? Simply order by the slice.

Fat Willy's

C3

Barbecue ✗

2416 W. Schubert St. (at Artesian Ave.)

Phone: 773-782-1800

Web: www.fatwillys.com

Prices: $$

Lunch & dinner daily

 Fat Willy's telegraphs an authentic and messy barbecue experience by luring all with its wafting scent of smoke, hickory, and apple wood piles stacked at the entrance. This is only further teased by homemade sauces and paper towel rolls poised atop kraft paper-protected tables. With customers' doodles from the tables plastering the walls, it's a sign everyone comes and leaves happy here.

Crack through the charred surface on baby back and St. Louis-style rib slabs to devour the pink-tinged center, an indication of superior smoking. Brisket might verge on the dry side, but pulled pork sandwiches are juicy, while corn dogs are hand-dipped and fried. Root beer from Milwaukee's Sprecher Brewery adds a little Midwest taste to the bona fide Southern flavor.

Flying Saucer

C5

American

1123 N. California Ave. (at Haddon Ave.)

Phone:	773-342-9076	Lunch daily
Web:	www.flyingsaucerchicago.com	
Prices:		

The Flying Saucer may look retro, like a 1950s-esque diner complete with a Formica counter, but there's nothing "Leave It To Beaver" about this anti-establishment gathering place. A well-pierced and tattooed crowd enjoys breakfast all day and the walls are lined with local artists' work.

The kitchen created a homey diner menu with a twist, that is popular with vegetarians and locavores. Try the *huevos volando*, two eggs (organic for a few cents more) cooked your way and smothered in a homemade, spicy and smoky salsa, *guajillo* sauce, and *chihuahua* cheese over warm corn tortillas. A side of organic black beans accompanies, and bright cilantro and sweet chopped onion finish the dish. Wash it all down with a Flying Saucer blend coffee.

Jam

B3

American

3057 W. Logan Blvd. (at Albany Ave.)

Phone:	773-292-6011	Lunch daily
Web:	www.jamrestaurant.com	
Prices:		

Relocated from its old Ukrainian Village digs, Jam has made its way to Logan Square with more moxie than ever. Formerly a breakfast-and-lunch-only operation, this bohemian lime- and charcoal-accented spot has expanded its kitchen to proffer dinners and prix-fixe menus highlighting produce from the Logan Square farmer's market.

But regulars still return for breakfast favorites that are big on flavor but manageable in size—perhaps German chocolate pancakes, or malted custard French toast that's cooked sous vide to make sure the malt-spiked vanilla cream infuses every inch of brioche? Savory dishes like *guisado verde* gild the lily by nestling braised beef in tender risotto before topping the pile with fresh corn, tangy tomato *crema*, and a sunny-side up egg.

(k)new

Contemporary XX

C4

2556 W. Fullerton Ave. (at Rockwell St.)

Phone: 773-772-7721   Dinner Mon – Sat
Web: www.knewrestaurant.com
Prices: $$

Though its nondescript façade on a busy stretch of West Fullerton might give you pause, a dreamy setting awaits through the doors of (k)new. Blonde wood furniture and white linens set off by veneered aqua blue walls and exposed ceiling beams whisper "cozy-romantic-casual," a feeling that's amplified by accommodating service.

Chef/owner Omar Rodriguez presents an eclectic menu that builds on unexpected flavor pairings and smartly done glazes and reductions. The rack of two succulent, generously cut venison chops, drizzled with a red wine-fig reduction over sweet mashed potatoes, is straightforward and deliciously executed. *Cavatappi* with lobster, shrimp, and mascarpone sparks with a bold combo of tarragon, mint, and basil for a pleasantly novel dish.

Kuma's Corner

American X

B3

2900 W. Belmont Ave. (at Francisco Ave.)

Phone: 773-604-8769   Lunch & dinner daily
Web: www.kumascorner.com
Prices:

Dig out your old Metallica t-shirt and you'll fit right in at this heavy metal-themed burger joint and dive bar serving locally made beers. It's racy and raucous with head-banging music, so leave Grandma and the kids behind. Forget about any conversation, since Iron Maiden will be pounding in your ears, but in a place with burgers this good, your mouth will be otherwise engaged.

Keeping with the unconventional theme, each burger is named for a heavy metal band from Megadeth to Black Sabbath. Juicy and delicious, these heavenly burgers are the clear draw, as in the Lair of the Minotaur, served on a pretzel roll piled high with caramelized onions, pancetta, creamy Brie, and Bourbon-soaked pears.

La Encantada

Mexican ✗

B5

3437 W. North Ave. (bet. Homan & St. Louis Aves.)

Phone: 773-489-5026   Lunch & dinner Tue – Sun
Web: www.laencantadarestaurant.com
Prices: ⊗⊗

Run by the gracious Enriquez family, this *encantada* (enchanted) spot lives up to its name. Inside, royal blue, golden yellow, and exposed brick walls are hung with bright, gallery-style artwork (much of it for sale), while contemporary Latino tunes waft through the air, creating a quixotic vibe. Culinary inspiration begins in the family's hometown, Zacatecas, but pulls from all around the country, with seriously delectable results.

Dig into the rich and cheesy *quesadilla de huitlacoche*; or the divine *chile en Nogada*, poblano peppers stuffed with ground beef, squash, fruit, and walnuts, topped with a creamy walnut sauce and pomegranate seeds. Pair these delicacies with such decadent sides as chipotle whipped potatoes.

Lula Café

American ✗

B3

2537 N. Kedzie Ave. (off Logan Blvd.)

Phone: 773-489-9554   Lunch & dinner Wed – Mon
Web: www.lulacafe.com
Prices: $$ 🚇 Logan Square

♿

The music industry's loss is the Chicago food scene's gain—if the band Tallulah had hit the big time, co-owner Amalea Tshilds would be rocking out at Red Rocks, and Logan Square would be minus this precious, upscale, cozy haunt. And judging from the always-crammed room of hip regulars (squeezing even more in after a 2011 revamp), many others would be missing out as well.

🍴 Seasonal, organic, and sustainable ingredients are co-owners' Tschilds and Jason Hammel's passion, and their commitment carries through from breakfast to dinner. Dishes as varied as butter-braised chanterelles on house-made crackers, or sweet potato ice cream showcase the full flavors generated from simple components. A nightly six-course vegetarian tasting menu is an established hit.

Longman & Eagle

B3

Gastropub

2657 N. Kedzie Ave. (at Schubert Ave.)

Phone: 773-276-7110
Web: www.longmanandeagle.com
Prices: $$

Lunch & dinner daily

Logan Square

Clayton Hauck

Now that the secret's out about Longman & Eagle's high-end gastropub pleasures, the frenetic mobs of truffle-loving hipsters have moved on to the next underground discovery, while the rest of us are free to enjoy a more mellow dining experience. Make no mistake; this is still a tavern at heart, a rough-and-tumble room kept in check by haute cuisine. A Wurlitzer jukebox blares rock and roll; Scotch, rye, and Bourbon listings escalate into the triple digits; and servers in flannel shirts and jeans keep the cool quotient turned to 11.

The maturity of the menu brings a hush of gravitas to the cooking. A thick slice of seared foie gras terrine layered with roasted portobellos and drizzled with ham hock-truffle vinaigrette would never find a home at a down 'n dirty dive. Follow that with delicious porcini agnolotti with diced braised veal heart and huckleberries; or Gruyère donuts licked with fig jam and you know what the fuss is all about.

If you want to impress your cohorts even further, tell them how this haven was named after the artist who sculpted the eagle atop the Illinois Centennial Monument in Logan Square. That'll keep your beatnik cred in the black for a few more weeks, eh?

Maiz

Mexican

C5

1041 N. California Ave. (bet. Cortez & Thomas Sts.)

Phone:	773-276-3149	Dinner Tue – Sun
Web:	www.maizchicago.com	
Prices:	☒☒	

An authentic Mexican restaurant in the heart of Humboldt Park isn't a surprise. Faithful Mexican-American life is what this area is all about. But even here, Maiz Antojitos Y Bebidas is a standout.

The menu is a celebration of corn and its common variations found as Mexican snacks, as the name suggests. Try anything corn-heavy like the *elote*, served street-style slathered with butter, mayo, cheese and chile powder; or the *tamal de elote*, two uniquely corn-flavored tamales served simply with lettuce and tomato. The *corundas*, a heavenly street food from Michoacan, are a delightful find here bathed in a dark *mole* with onions, crumbled cheese, and *crema*. Get a little green mixed in with your yellow by adding the *nopales*, a salad of diced cactus paddles.

Noon-O-Kabab

Persian

B1

4661 N. Kedzie Ave. (at Leland Ave.)

Phone:	773-279-9309	Lunch Mon – Fri
Web:	www.noonokabab.com	Dinner nightly
Prices:	☒☒	🚇 Kedzie (Brown)

Noon-O-Kabab is that great little neighborhood spot you hit up for its good food, reasonable prices, and über friendly service. Tucked into arched alcoves, the tile floors and wood furnishings may be simple, but its walls are adorned with beautiful tile murals of dancing figurines.

Delightful Persian specialties are the order of the day. Swing by for a comforting bowl of *ghormeh sabzi*—a stew of lamb, red beans, spinach, fenugreek, and cilantro; or *joujeh koubideh*—skewers of juicy, saffron-flavored ground chicken, served with dill-lima bean basmati rice, and the traditional charbroiled whole tomato. Their bustling catering business a few doors down (also the spot for pick-up and delivery), sells the best *bastani* (Persian gelato) in sunnier months.

Pork Shoppe

C3

Barbecue

2755 W. Belmont Ave. (bet. California & Washtenaw Aves.)

Phone: 773-961-7654   Lunch & dinner Tue – Sun
Web: www.porkshoppechicago.com
Prices:

 Belmont (Blue)

Step into this den of macho–boasting boutique barbecue– and thank your stars the men are brilliant behind the smokers, as they certainly make for dull decorators. The stoic dining room (imagine wood floors, a rusted communal bar, tables, and chairs) is barely enriched by framed mirrors and relics of old farming equipment.

But, pork is Prada here and shoppers have perfected the routine: place an order, take a number, a wad of brown towels, and sauce (sweet, tangy, and wicked) up! A sammy with smoked pork belly pastrami may steal the show, but window-shop your way through other items like Texas brisket tacos, crunchy and fragrant with onion and cilantro; and oversized chocolate chip cookies. Best with your barbecue is beer, wine, and...Bourbon.

Real Tenochtitlan

B3

Mexican

2451 N. Milwaukee Ave. (bet. Richmond St. & Sacramento Ave.)

Phone: 773-227-1050   Lunch & dinner Tue – Sun
Web: www.realtenochtitlan.com
Prices: **$$**

 California (Blue)

Memorable *mole* awaits at Real Tenochtitlan, which delivers a polished take on the Mexican fine-dining experience. Details like a wood-coffered ceiling and draped red fabric give the large room an inviting and elegant hacienda feel that's nothing like the typical mom-and-pop joint.

Moles are justifiably the house specialty: the stunningly complex *mole blanco*, with white chocolate, roasted almonds, pine nuts, and chiles, is a revelation; but those who want to sample more sauces have their work cut out for them with *verde*, *chichilo*, *rojo coloradito*, *negro*, and *manchamanteles* variations. For a simpler but no less satisfying dish, homemade tortillas, wood-grilled onions, and woodland mushrooms take the *enchiladas de hongos* far beyond run-of-the-mill.

Rootstock

Contemporary

B5

954 N. California Ave. (bet. Augusta Blvd. & Walton St.)

Phone: 773-292-1616
Web: www.rootstockbar.com
Prices: $$

Lunch Sun
Dinner Mon – Sat

This vibrant, funky wine bar gaining a steady following on the western edge of un-touristy Humboldt Park makes its focus known at first glance: patrons sit down to a bare table, laid only with the wine list—actually a thick, bound book with meticulous descriptions of each well-chosen selection.

Agreeable staffers know their way around the wines and the small plates menu, which showcases house-made charcuterie. Highlights may include an alluringly rustic presentation of silky rabbit rillettes with pickled vegetables and blackberry verjus; or sublimely tender confit duck sporting a chewy, crispy skin. A small but friendly bar makes an appealing option for solo dining, while sizeable portions and a low-key vibe are perfect for catching up with friends.

Semiramis

Lebanese

B1

4639 N. Kedzie Ave. (bet. Eastwood & Leland Aves.)

Phone: 773-279-8900
Web: www.semiramisrestaurant.com
Prices: ⊖⊖

Lunch & dinner daily

Kedzie (Brown)

This Lebanese café outshines the competition in an ethnically diverse area filled with Middle Eastern eateries, Korean restaurants, and halal meat shops.

Inside the pleasant space, where colorful tapestries brighten the walls as art, Semiramis offers tasty takes on standards, from refreshing salads to golden brown falafel patties with hints of garlic, sesame oil, and parsley, wrapped in warm and tender flatbread. Have that alongside French fries topped with sumac and garlic for a serious non-burger-and-fries treat. With its focus on good, simple, fresh Lebanese food made from top ingredients, Semiramis does it right, while providing a warm place to sit and eat. You have to BYOB, but both eat-in and to-go orders are filled quickly by the friendly staff.

Smoque BBQ

Barbecue ✗

3800 N. Pulaski Rd. (at Grace St.)

Phone: 773-545-7427

Web: www.smoquebbq.com

Prices:

Lunch & dinner Tue – Sun

Irving Park (Blue)

At this unassuming barbecue joint set upon a dull corner in Irving Park, the focus is on food and not as much the ambience. This may be a take-a-number counter service, but one forkful of meltingly tender brisket, smoked for 15 hours, and find that you won't need to muse on anything else around.

Beyond brisket, the meats–by the pound, on platters, or in sandwiches–are the main draw. Pulled pork, smoked chicken, saucy-slick ribs, and peppery Texas sausage weigh down plates, accompanied by piles of sides like cider vinegar slaw, crisp fresh-cut fries, or macaroni and cheese. There's only one dessert option and it's peach cobbler. But, place your trust with the geniuses in the kitchen, and it's all one needs to end a meal here.

Telegraph

Contemporary ✗✗

2601 N. Milwaukee Ave. (at Logan Blvd.)

Phone: 773-292-9463

Web: www.telegraphwinebar.com

Prices: $$

Dinner nightly

Logan Square

Sipping and staring are equally relaxing pursuits at this urbane, stylish wine bar with banks of expansive windows facing Logan Square Park. Charcoal and deep teal walls and dark, chunky wood tables throughout the restaurant let intimate moments unfold among the industrial fixtures.

Slink onto a tawny leather barstool and leaf through the compact but well-chosen wine list, stocked with wines by the glass from all corners of the world. To go with that *vino*, nibbles range from petite to hearty plates in bold flavor combinations, and might include a creamy cannellini bean tartine with ribbons of summer squash, decked out with a fried squash blossom for good measure; or a daring combination of grilled lamb saddle with oysters and cherries.

Urban Belly

C3

3053 N. California Ave. (bet. Barry Ave. & Nelson St.)

Phone: 773-583-0500
Web: www.urbanbellychicago.com
Prices:

Lunch & dinner Tue – Sun

Belmont (Blue)

Chef Bill Kim's fiery Asian cuisine is easily the liveliest thing on this otherwise dreary stretch of California Avenue. Speedy ordering from laminated menus at the counter and even more rapid delivery to your seat at one of four communal tables means you can dig in to the fragrant food as quickly as possible.

Duck and *pho*-spiced dumplings perk up ravenous taste buds with cinnamon, star anise, and cardamom. Flavorful bowls of udon with tender shrimp in a sweet chili-lime broth; or rice piled with pork belly and sweet pineapple get even zestier with a few shakes of *nanami togarashi* and Belly Fire sauces placed upon every table. Can't snag a chunky wood stool? Rest easy—even though Urban Belly doesn't take reservations, they definitely do takeout.

Yusho

B3

2853 N. Kedzie Ave. (bet. Diversey Pkwy & George St.)

Phone: 773-904-8558
Web: www.yusho-chicago.com
Prices: $$

Lunch Sun
Dinner nightly

Logan Square

 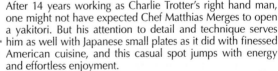

After 14 years working as Charlie Trotter's right hand man, one might not have expected Chef Matthias Merges to open a yakitori. But his attention to detail and technique serves him as well with Japanese small plates as it did with finessed American cuisine, and this casual spot jumps with energy and effortless enjoyment.

Divided between birds, land, and sea, the menu offers variation for grazers and snackers. Dishes combine intriguing textures and flavors, as in grilled tofu topped with puréed chrysanthemum, pineapple, walnuts, and a drizzle of *umeboshi* vinaigrette; or tempura-battered cod with creamy *chawan mushi* and crispy ginkgo nuts. As with most yakitori, beer is a must, and dozens of domestic and international craft brews do Yusho's food proud.

Lakeview & Wrigleyville
Roscoe Village

"Peanuts! Get your peanuts!" When the Cubs are playing, expect to hear the call of salty ball-game snacks through the north side's best-known neighborhood, though locals may actually be stopping into **Nuts on Clark** for some pre-game caramel corn. Lakeview is the umbrella term for the area north of Lincoln Park, including Wrigleyville (named after its iconic ball field) and Roscoe Village.

Enter Eastern Europe

Even when the beloved Cubs finish their season at Wrigley Field (as sadly happens each October), American summertime classics continue to shape the area's cuisine, yet for historic reasons. Thanks to their large Eastern European immigrant population, an abundant variety of sausages and wursts can be found in casual eateries and markets located along a number of blocks. Showcasing these juicy and tender specialties is the reputed **Paulina Market**, where expected items like corned beef, lamb, veal, and turkey are offered beside more novel offerings like ground venison, loin chops, and "baseball bat summer sausages." The local Swedish population knows to come here for tried and true favorites such as pickled Christmas hams and cardamom-infused sausages. Paulina's incredible growth and steadfast commitment to quality makes this not just a local institution, but also one of Chicago's biggest and most popular meat markets.

Classic Chicago

Equally important and comparably carnivorous is the Windy City's love for the humble hot dog. Here, chefs, foodies, and touristas stand in lines that may wraparound the block at **Hot Doug's**, the lunch-only purveyor of creatively encased meats in combinations named either to celebrate sultry starlets (like the spicy "Keira Knightly"), or maybe to immortalize their friends. Fridays and Saturdays are particularly crowded, because that's when Doug (the bespeckled gentleman at the counter) serves duck fat fries. **Byron's Hot Dog Haus** isn't as gourmet, but both their hot dogs and burgers are classic Chicago and very tasty. Note that the location near Wrigley only has outdoor picnic tables and no inside seating.

Baking in Bavaria

Even Chicagoans can't live on hot dogs alone. When they hunger for something else, they have their choice in Lakeview. Bavarian baked goods have been a mainstay of **Dinkel's Bakery** since 1922 (and in its current locale since 1932). Originally opened by a master baker who hailed from Southern Bavaria, the business is still family run and remains famous for its traditional renditions of strudels, butter kuchen, and, stollen (items can be purchased fresh, but are also available frozen for shipping). Also praiseworthy is Dinkel's Burglaur (a big breakfast sandwich), and their decadent donut selection is addictive and all the rage.

Sweet Indulgences

For a different type of sweet, stopover for the globally-influenced, Chicago-based **Mayana Chocolates** in flavors as accessible as cookies n' cream and raspberry-dark chocolate, or the more exotic Turkish coffee and hazelnut and coriander praline. At her **Bittersweet Pastry Shop**, Chef/owner Judy Contino is well-known for her wedding cakes, pastries, and other delights like breakfast breads, cheesecakes, brownies, and cupcakes. She's been sculpting these sweet treats for almost two decades now. Those seeking a more local, sustainable, and classic American experience should head to **Fritz Pastry** for breakfast items or vast bakery offerings like banana bread, cinnamon rolls, hand pies, and macarons. Another laudation (even if they come in sinful buttery and sugary packages) to Chicago's neighborhoods is **City Caramels**. Walk in to this sanctum of sweet to be greeted by simple, lip-smacking treats. Eat your way through Bucktown (think coffee-inspired caramels with chocolate-covered espresso beans); Lincoln Square (toasted hazelnuts anybody?), and Pilsen (Mexican drinking chocolate with ancho chili, cinnamon and *pepitas*) with their respective caramel and candy cuts. However, Chicagoans who prefer to end their meals with more of a bite should linger at **Pastoral**—hailed as one of the country's top spots for cheese. Their selection of classic and farmstead cheeses as well as fresh breads and olives is a local favorite, as are their weekend classes and tastings.

Fascinating Food Finds

An offbeat, quirky vibe is part of what makes Lakeview thrive. Testament to this is **The Flower Flat**, which cooks up a comforting breakfast and brunch in an actual flower shop. Meanwhile, **Uncommon Ground** is as much a restaurant serving three meals a day, as it is a coffee shop known for its musical acts. During the months between June through September, stop by on Friday evenings to tour America's first certified organic rooftop garden before tasting its bounty on your plate downstairs. Aspiring young chefs with big dreams proudly present a wholesome grab-n-go restaurant called **Real Kitchen** that features home-style dishes like baked Amish chicken paired alongside some unique, crusty sandwiches like a salty and heart-warming pork belly BLT.

ROSCOE VILLAGE

The Landshark Lager Oyster Festival attracts folks to Roscoe Village each September with Irish and American music, plenty of beer, and a certain mollusk believed to have aphrodisiac qualities. Homesick New Yorkers and transplants take note: This neighborhood is also home to **Apart Pizza**, Chicago's very own homage to the thin-crust pie, though you might be wise to refrain from admitting how much you enjoyed it. Remember, this is a true find and guilty pleasure in deep-dish land.

Lakeview & Wrigleyville

A   B   C

WELLES PARK

Sunnyside

W. Montrose Ave.

W. Pensacola Ave.

Royal Thai

Chalkboard

Roong Petch   Glenn's Diner

Montrose

Mixteco G

Cullom

Cullom

Berteau

Cho Sun Ok

Berteau

Warner   Ave.

Browntrout

Plaine

Belle

Thai Room

Belle

Sticky Rice

Irving

Park

Irving Park Rd.

Always Thai

REVERE PARK

Byron

sola

Grace

Grace

Waveland   Ave.

LAKEVIEW

Addison St.

Addison

Cornelia   Ave.

Paulina

El Tinajon

Roscoe

Frasca

School

Wishbone

DEVRY UNIVERSITY

457 St.

FELLGER PARK

Belmont

Bakin' & Eggs

Barry

HAMLIN PARK

Wellington

George St.

Diversey

Diversey

Pkwy.

Clybourn

Wolfran

Kennedy Expwy.

W. Logan Blvd.

NORTH

BRANCH

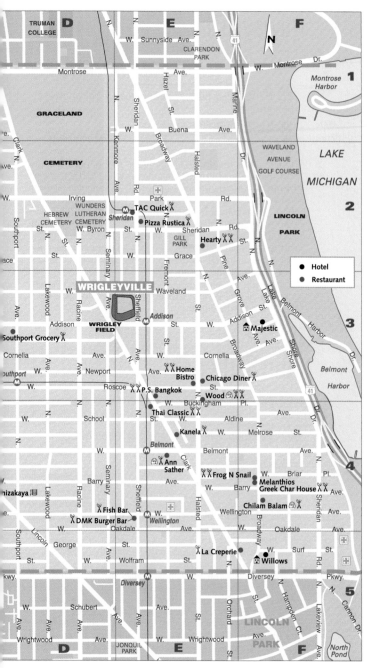

Always Thai

C2

1825 W. Irving Park Rd. (bet. Ravenswood & Wolcott Aves.)

Phone: 773-929-0100   Lunch & dinner daily
Web: www.alwaysthaichicago.com
Prices: 💰💰   🚇 Irving Park (Brown)

Nestled under the Brown Line, Always Thai is more than just Thai. With *satay*, curries, edamame, tempura, and *shu mai* on the menu, it is a pan-Asian eatery, with a substantial take-out business for neighborhood residents. The room which seats about 40 isn't fancy, but a colorful mural brightens the scene. *Nam sod* (ginger salad) is served in a fun footed bowl, with a slightly sweetened lime dressing and is a light, unexpected start to the meal. *Pad kee mao* needs an extra kick from the chili sauce on the table but is a tasty dish of drunken noodles, served with plump shrimp. There isn't a specific regional focus to the menu here, but there aren't many missteps either—making Always Thai a good choice for post-Cubs games or a casual dinner.

Ann Sather 😍

E4

909 W. Belmont Ave. (bet. Clark St. & Wilton Ave.)

Phone: 773-348-2378   Lunch daily
Web: www.annsather.com
Prices: 💰💰   🚇 Belmont (Brown/Red)

The cinnamon rolls served at this Swedish bakery and restaurant could rival deep-dish pizza as the iconic Chicago food—that's how strongly locals feel about them.

But those hot, fresh rolls glazed with sugar aren't the only reason breakfast-goers flock here. Despite the large volume of business Ann Sather does, the kitchen still pays attention to every detail. The roast duck comes out greaseless, and topped with the traditional sweet yet tart lingonberry sauce. Meats, pickled herring, Swedish meatballs, homemade sauerkraut with caraway seeds, and excellent spaetzle are all cooked to perfection, so a sampler plate is a good choice for the indecisive. The bottomless cups of coffee are an added bonus, as are a few more of those cinnamon rolls to-go.

Bakin' & Eggs

C4

American

3120 N. Lincoln Ave. (bet. Barry & Belmont Aves.)

Phone: 773-525-7005

Web: www.bakinandeggschicago.com

Prices:

Lunch daily

Paulina

Three words (flight of bacon) might be the only enticement needed for a meal at Bakin' & Eggs. But if the likes of maple- pepper- jalapeño- mesquite- or cherry-smoked bacon isn't enough, the easygoing café has a full menu of breakfast and lunch treats for sweet and savory appetites...including pastries from Lovely Bake Shop.

Seated atop brushed aluminum chairs, bleary-eyed regulars sip Intelligentsia coffee and pots of Rare Tea Cellar tea; while families pile into old whitewashed church pews to chow on such creative sandwiches as chicken sausage, fried eggs, and cheddar drizzled with maple syrup on cinnamon-raisin bread. Fresh-baked muffins like vanilla cupcake and peanut butter brownie; or buttermilk pancakes with whipped cream smile for the kids.

Browntrout

B2

American

4111 N. Lincoln Ave. (bet. Belle Plaine & Warner Aves.)

Phone: 773-472-4111

Web: www.browntroutchicago.com

Prices: $$

Lunch Sun

Dinner Wed – Sun

Irving Park (Brown)

The natural beauty of a fish caught by Chef Sean Sanders during his New Zealand honeymoon inspired this pleasant neighborhood spot. Front windows swing wide open in warmer months and bring a breeze to the mocha dining room. The neatly sketched chalkboard displays nightly specials and a list of their favorite (often organic) farmers— sources used in addition to their own rooftop garden.

The menu is broken down into "Smalls" like the whitefish brandade or smoked crappie and "Bigs" like Texas Bandera quail with almond, pineapple, and sage *pistou*. Brunch is a hit with the likes of blueberry beignets and cured salmon with a soft-cooked duck egg.

Kids eat free during the week and Wednesdays allow you to create your own three-course bargain menu for $35.

Chalkboard

A m e r i c a n ✗✗

B1

4343 N. Lincoln Ave. (bet. Montrose & Pensacola Aves.)

Phone: 773-477-7144
Web: www.chalkboardrestaurant.com
Prices: $$

Lunch Sat – Sun
Dinner Wed – Mon
🚇 Montrose (Brown)

When your roster of dishes changes daily, why not ditch the paper menu entirely and just write it all up on a giant chalkboard? That's the premise of Chalkboard, so fittingly named for its wall-spanning display of daily items. Recalling a European tearoom, brightly striped banquettes, framed mirrors, and shelves of knickknacks fill the rest of this cozy space.

The night's offerings may unveil such diverse dishes as escargot with garlic confit; fried chicken served atop buttermilk mashed potatoes; or Dover sole. The signature cookie dough spring roll is one of the few constants; house-made biscuits are another, though even their flavors change subtly with the season.

Pick your seat wisely—if posted beneath the blackboard, ordering can be a challenge.

Chicago Diner

V e g e t a r i a n ✗

E3

3411 N. Halsted St. (at Roscoe St.)

Phone: 773-935-6696
Web: www.veggiediner.com
Prices: ⊜⊗

Lunch & dinner daily
🚇 Addison (Red)

This small, tightly packed dining room features retro red tables lined with stainless steel, black vinyl chairs, and rustic pine booths. When the weather behaves, not only is the large garden luscious, but the neighborhood is convenient to Wrigley Field and all manner of North Side attractions.

But people come here for the ample vegetarian menu. Since 1983, the kitchen has specialized in dishes with faux meats. This is where former carnivores come to satisfy a craving, such as the gyros seasoned like lamb, filled with shredded romaine, diced tomatoes, and served with a cool, vegan-friendly *tzatziki*. Other favorites have included the Fib Rib and Radical Reuben sandwiches. The Chicago Diner's sumptuous baked goods are available around town.

Chilam Balam

 Mexican

F4

3023 N. Broadway (bet. Barry & Wellington Aves.)

Phone: 773-296-6901 Dinner Tue – Sat
Web: www.chilambalamchicago.com
Prices: $$ Wellington

If the world ends in December 2012 as the Mayans predicted, go out with a bang and make sure at least one of your last meals is at Chilam Balam. This clandestine no-reservations spot, named after the book foretelling the doomsday prophecy, quickly gets packed to the brick walls. A stool at the small four-seat bar offers a peek into the semi-open kitchen and a place to mix your bevy (BYOB) or sip with a lip-smacking virgin sangria while waiting for a table.

Though ostensibly a Mexican restaurant, the dishes are hardly predictable and may unveil crispy frog's legs with sour orange aïoli; or smoky chorizo meatloaf. Duck enchiladas with fried lemon and tomatillo sauce spotlight unorthodox flavor combinations and seasonal ingredients from local farms.

Chizakaya

 Japanese

D4

3056 N. Lincoln Ave. (bet. Barry & Wellington Aves.)

Phone: 773-697-4725 Dinner Tue – Sat
Web: www.chizakaya.com
Prices: Paulina

What reads like a standard ramen joint at lunch turns into a hopping *izakaya* at sundown, where an upbeat soundtrack sways the hanging light bulbs and fresh-faced Chicagoans pass small plates up and down the communal tables in the back room. Tilted ceiling panels in the main dining room boast murals featuring modern interpretations of classic Japanese art and iconography, a fitting comparison given the contemporary twists on faithful *izakaya* fare.

Dishes showcase a range of flavors and textures: *takoyaki* with tender octopus meld with spicy mayo and bonito flakes; and skewered *kushi yaki* like chicken gizzards, beef tongue, and Wagyu with wasabi and lime go quickly. Refreshment comes with a tangy strawberry-yuzu sorbet that nicely finishes the savory fare.

Cho Sun Ok

Korean ✗

B1

4200 N. Lincoln Ave. (at Berteau Ave.)

Phone: 773-549-5555   Lunch & dinner daily
Web: www.chosunokrestaurant.com
Prices: 🚇 Irving Park (Brown)

Cho Sun Ok is not just OK, it's one of those places you either love or hate. The lovers are here for their flavorfully authentic Korean food, while haters can't get past the gruff service. But really, who cares when you can grill your own meat and pair it with the best of their *banchan*, like spicy kimchi, seawood salad, and glazed roasted potatoes?

Honey-toned floors and furnishings impart a cozy feel and couple harmoniously with their highly regarded soups and stews. Between the small smattering of tables, find big flavors in delicacies like *maduguk*, a peppery beef soup bobbing with tender *mandu*, dried seaweed, and scallions; *suhn dubu*, a soft tofu stew with mixed seafood; and *nakji bokkeum*, octopus stir-fried with vegetables in a fiery sauce.

DMK Burger Bar

American ✗

E4

2954 N. Sheffield Ave. (at Wellington Ave.)

Phone: 773-360-8686   Lunch & dinner daily
Web: www.dmkburgerbar.com
Prices: 🚇 Wellington

Want a stellar burger? Hit DMK Burger Bar, brainchild of David Morton (of steakhouse fame) and Michael Kornick (mk). Grab a seat at the lengthy bar or cop a squat on an old church pew and admire concrete floors, exposed pale brick, and weathered wood borders contrasting chocolaty-purple pressed-tin ceilings. What this place lacks in comfort, it makes up for in comfort food.

Follow the locals, and order by number. Perhaps #11: a dolled-up gyro featuring the likes of sheep's milk feta, olive tapenade, and *tzatziki* atop a grass-fed lamb patty; or go for #3: beef topped with pastrami, Gruyère, sauerkraut, and remoulade. Cross over to the bad side and pair your sammie with hand-cut gourmet fries. And for a fine finale, slurp up a cold brew or homemade soda.

El Tinajon

 B3

Guatemalan

2054 W. Roscoe St. (bet. Hoyne & Seeley Aves.)

Phone: 773-525-8455   Lunch & dinner daily
Web: N/A
Prices: 💰💰

🚉 Paulina

A mainstay of the residential Roscoe Village neighborhood, El Tinajon offers authentic Guatemalan dishes. The bright, friendly décor includes Mayan handicrafts throughout the storefront. Bring an appetite and focus on the well-made dishes. Perhaps start with the *yucca con ajo*, tender cassava in a rich garlic butter sauce. Do not skip the *jocon cobanero*, a soulful and tart green chicken and potato stew with elegant tomatillo flavor. Each element of the stew is cooked perfectly and sided with colorful rice; it's a positively lovely dish. *Rellenitos* make a unique and enjoyable finish of rich plantains stuffed with cinnamon and chocolate sweetened black beans.

The appealing breakfast menu provides a promising start to any gray, winter day.

Fish Bar

 E4

Seafood

2956 Sheffield Ave. (at Wellington Ave.)

Phone: 773-687-8177   Lunch & dinner Tue – Sun
Web: www.fishbarchicago.com
Prices: $$

🚉 Wellington

Sidled up next to its sibling, DMK Burger Bar, this good-time seafood shack does it up right. The atmosphere is light and casual: old metal stools line a long wooden bar, strips of weathered wood panel the walls, and a table is set beneath the polished hull of a canoe.

Daily seafood dishes come raw (tartares, ceviches, and carpaccio), grilled, and fried; while soups, bisques, and chowders warm the belly. Tasty sandwiches run the gamut from lobster roll and fried oysters to crab cake. Dive into a plate of crispy rock shrimp, lightly breaded and tossed in spicy *sriracha* mayo and fresh *tobiko*. Alternatively, a Ball jar loaded with a ceviche of corvina, pineapple, Serrano chilies, avocado, lime, and cilantro, served with crackers is super refreshing.

Frasca

C3

Italian

3358 N. Paulina St. (at Roscoe St.)

Phone: 773-248-5222
Web: www.frascapizzeria.com
Prices: $$

Lunch Sat – Sun
Dinner nightly
 Paulina

Like stepping into a warm, aromatic wine barrel, Frasca embraces its name (Italian for "branch") with a wraparound wooden bar flanking the wood-fired pizza oven, tables fashioned from tree trunks, planked walls, and forest-motif wallpaper.

As denoted by the brick oven, Frasca's pizzas with fresh, flavorful toppings (perhaps the *rustica* with fennel sausage?) are the heart of the operation, though seasonal pastas and entrées are also available. An "Old World Farmer's Table" menu lets diners check off items from a list of bruschetta, cheeses with homemade jams, and cured meats for a choose-your-own *antipasto* adventure. Sharing plates is encouraged, down to the list of wines by the glass that allows for mixing and matching with other menu components.

Frog N Snail

F4

American

3124 N. Broadway (bet. Barry Ave. & Briar Pl.)

Phone: 773-661-9166
Web: www.frognsnail.com
Prices: $$

Lunch & dinner Tue – Sun

 Belmont (Brown/Red)

Dale Levitski, chef of Lincoln Park's Sprout, takes a more approachable and less conceptual–though not simplistic–tact with his new venture that aims to please from noon through night. A long wooden bar gives way to a coffee and crêpe station, while a mix of low booths, high tables and stools, and SRO counters keep it casual with earthy décor throughout.

The signature Frog N Snail dish shows off the restaurant's mix of refined and homey: kale, leek, and green peppercorn ragout is tossed with snails and topped with crispy frog's legs. Dishes gravitate to kid-friendly inspiration and familiar dishes get sassy garnishes like pigs in a blanket wrapped in croissants with piquillo piperade, or *croque monsieur* with rosemary ham and golden raisin mustard.

Glenn's Diner

American

1820 W. Montrose Ave. (bet. Ravenswood & Wolcott Aves.)

Phone: 773-506-1720
Web: www.glennsdiner.com
Prices: $$

Lunch & dinner daily

 Montrose (Brown)

A seafaring menu that would sate the likes of Captain Ahab meets an "anytime breakfast" including Cap'n Crunch in one of the area's quirkier spots. With over 16 varieties of fresh fish on any given day and a blackboard menu that makes Egyptian tombs look brief, there is surely something here for everyone.

This is food that strives to please, as in the cargo shrimp cooked in garlicky butter and blanketed in a bubbling veil of provolone and Parmesan cheese with a comparably cheesy toasted French roll. The country-fried Dover sole is a hearty treatment of delicate fish, alongside sautéed zucchini, red onions, and a potato cake.

And if none of this suits you, there are plenty of savory egg dishes and 30 types of cereal—yes, this is a Seinfeld kind of place.

Hearty

American

3819 N. Broadway (bet. Grace St. & Sheridan Rd.)

Phone: 773-868-9866
Web: www.heartyboys.com
Prices: $$

Lunch Sun
Dinner Wed – Sun

 Sheridan

Like the clever pun in their name, the playful food from Hearty Boys Dan Smith and Steve MacDonagh takes American comfort classics and gives them a spin. The whimsy begins in a mod room that mixes exposed brick with burnt orange and aquamarine accents at tables bedecked with "flower" bouquets made from soda cans.

Lavender-buttermilk fried chicken; *beefaroni* with braised short ribs; and state fair-worthy corndogs that may be filled with rabbit or bacon all transform childhood favorites into adult delicacies. More elegant dishes like a savory Parmesan cheesecake with black walnut shortbread and smoked beef brisket with carrot and fig tzimmes also might appear on a menu that changes quarterly, enhanced by herbs grown in the restaurant's rooftop garden.

Home Bistro

American XX

3404 N. Halsted St. (at Roscoe St.)

Phone:	773-661-0299
Web:	www.homebistrochicago.com
Prices:	$$

Dinner Tue – Sun

Belmont (Brown/Red)

Home Bistro (HB for those in the know) is a chipper American bistro fixed up with orange faux-finished walls cradling framed mirrors, artwork, and painted quotes. In keeping with this ideal, the staff is particularly hospitable and kind. The tight-knit team is proud of their bistro, and loyal fans keep returning to this delicious den where everybody knows your name—as well as the names of servers and kitchen staff, all printed on the menu.

Here, comfort foods may have Euro flair but translate into all-American dishes like white anchovies atop a mound of arugula with creamy Yukon Golds; handmade fettuccine ribbons woven around deliciously seasoned duck sausage and Parmesan sprinkles; and a piping hot fruit bread pudding trickled with whipped cream.

Kanela

American X

3231 N. Clark St. (bet. Belmont Ave. & School St.)

Phone:	773-248-1622
Web:	www.kanelachicago.com
Prices:	⬭⬭

Lunch daily
Dinner Thu – Sat

Belmont (Brown/Red)

With an array of options devoted to the most important meal of the day, Kanela helps its Lakeview neighbors break the fast every morning and afternoon. Its mellow java brown interior is a haven for the unhurried, but speedy patrons can grab a quick jolt at the tiled bar in the corner, proudly pouring Austria's Julius Meinl coffee.

Whether starving for savory bites like freshly griddled homemade chicken sausage flecked with herbs and spices, or sweeter plates like banana split crêpes with strawberries, bananas, and Nutella–or a little of both–Kanela delivers. A double stack of French toast stuffed with blueberry-studded Greek yogurt and topped with apple-jalapeño chutney simultaneously sates every craving with just the right amount of heat.

La Creperie

F5

French

2845 N. Clark St. (bet. Diversey Pkwy. & Surf St.)

Phone: 773-528-9050   Lunch & dinner Tue – Sun
Web: www.lacreperieusa.com
Prices:

🚇 Diversey

Since 1972, La Creperie has been churning out countless lacy crêpes at this miniscule family-run bistro, charmingly evocative of a French pastoral home replete with weathered plank flooring and lived-in furniture. The tiny front bar with its copper hood was once the restaurant's kitchen and its original *bilig*, the traditional round griddle on which crêpes are cooked, hangs proudly on the wall.

The paper-thin Breton crêpes–buckwheat versions filled with savory ingredients and wheat rounds packed with sweet fare–are the star attraction, though sandwiches and brunch are served daily till 4:00 P.M. *La complète* is truly a breakfast in itself, bursting with wafer-thin ham, cheese, and scrambled eggs alongside pan-fried potatoes and bacon. *Quel* Grand Slam!

Melanthios Greek Char House

F4

Greek

3116 N. Broadway (bet. Barry Ave. & Briar Pl.)

Phone: 773-360-8572   Lunch & dinner daily
Web: www.melanthiosgreekcharhouse.com
Prices: $$

You won't have any trouble finding such an anchor on this stretch of Broadway—just look for the stucco and beam-embellished façade that appears to be transplanted from Greece. It's an all-around good time at Melanthios, where high spirits reign and the staff makes you feel like family. Brace for a gleeful affair, whether you dine outside or retire indoors, where whitewashed walls, ceiling fans, and a brick fireplace exude a rustic air.

One glance at this menu is enough to bring tears to your *yia yia's* eyes. Expect oldies but goodies like bubbling casseroles of pastitsio, layering hollow noodles, ground beef, and seasoned tomato sauce beneath a thick blanket of rich, fluffy, and custardy béchamel sauce. Come on weekends for whole roasted lamb or pig.

Mixteco Grill

C1

1601 W. Montrose Ave. (at Ashland Ave.)

Phone: 773-868-1601
Web: www.mixtecogrill.com
Prices:

Lunch Sat – Sun
Dinner Tue – Sun
Montrose (Brown)

Set on a stretch of Montrose that houses everything from a retro electronics store to a pilates studio, Mixteco lives up to its name, offering a delightful mix of Mexican specialties. This grill isn't about burritos and quesadillas. Instead, Mixteco dishes up fab regional Mexican cooking that hungry diners lap up as if it were going out of fashion.

The easygoing 'tude and warm flavor make this resto a favorite of neighborhood denizens and deal seekers. Choose from a plethora of deliciousness including *cochinita pibil*—slow-roasted pork with achiote and sour orange juice; *sopes di pollo*, corn masa boats with chicken, *mole*, and crunchy sesame seeds; or sinful *crepas de cajeta*...that is if you haven't already gorged on the tortilla chips.

Pizza Rustica

E2

3908 N. Sheridan Rd. (bet. Byron & Dakin Sts.)

Phone: 773-404-8955
Web: www.pizzarustica.co
Prices:

Lunch & dinner
Wed – Mon
Sheridan

A few blocks north but worlds away from the chaotic fandom of Wrigleyville, Chef/owner Stefano Romano plies his pies on this quiet block of Sheridan. The pizzas pulled from his oven are alternately described as Roman- or Venetian-style, but rest assured as these rectangular pies with creative toppings on flaky, buttery crust are a delectable departure from the stuffed varieties of Chicagoland.

Order by the piece to try specialties like the *patate rosmarino* with rosemary and paper-thin potato slices; *tropicale* with ham, pineapple, and spicy *giardiniera*; or go simple with the classic Margherita. Half and whole pizzas amply feed tables willing to share, with pastas and nightly specials such as *maiale tonnato* and *linguini al granchio* rounding out the menu.

P.S. Bangkok

E3   Thai ✗✗

3345 N. Clark St. (bet. Buckingham Pl. & Roscoe St.)

Phone: 773-871-7777   Lunch & dinner Tue – Sun
Web: www.psbangkok.com
Prices: ⊜⊜   🚇 Belmont (Brown/Red)

♿ Carved wood artwork, a faint ring of wind chimes, and engaging service makes even first-time visitors feel like they're being graciously welcomed to a private home instead of ducking into a Thai respite on one of Lakeview's busiest drags. P.S. Bangkok's simple but polished setting sets the tone for the carefully prepared and sumptuous dishes served here. The menu runs the gamut through rolls, dumplings, noodles, and rice dishes. "Dreamy, creamy, crispy crab" lives up to its description as a luxurious take on the ubiquitous crab Rangoon. While other esoteric specialties like red curry with stir-fried corn and tomatoes; *rama* curry with peanuts, coconut, and tamarind; or duck marinated in Chinese spices and served on rice noodles are equally satisfying.

Roong Petch

C1   Asian ✗

1828 W. Montrose Ave. (bet. Ravenswood & Wolcott Aves.)

Phone: 773-989-0818   Lunch & dinner Mon – Sat
Web: www.roongpetch.com
Prices: ⊜⊜   🚇 Montrose (Brown)

♿ The décor may not have changed since Roong Petch opened its doors over a decade ago, but that's not why Ravenswood
🛋 regulars have been wearing down the carpet at this Thai standby. Beyond delivery and takeout, sit-down customers toting BYOB bags from the nearby wine store are warmly welcomed by mellow tunes, even if they're just stopping by for the $5.95 lunch special.

Dishes might take a few extra minutes to arrive, but rest assured each accompaniment is fresh and unique. Double 00 chicken gets its name from the "top-secret" chili sauce that blankets tender cubes of poultry with sweet heat, while cumin, turmeric, and coconut milk penetrate deeply to flavor chicken *satay*. Noodle staples like spicy basil and pad Thai are sprightly rather than rote.

Royal Thai

Thai 𝕏

B1

2209 W. Montrose Ave. (bet. Bell Ave. & Leavitt St.)

Phone: 773-509-0007   Lunch & dinner Wed – Mon
Web: www.royalthaichicago.com
Prices: Western (Brown)

Royal Thai has long been a family-run standby that is inviting, cordial, well maintained, and very friendly. Glass-topped tables are dressed with silk runners embroidered with elephants and padded menu binders—their orangey hues match the assortment of plump goldfish swimming through the room's towering fish tank.

The cooking here sticks to the classics, and although the menu does not reveal uncommon regional specialties, it is all tasty and spiced to your liking. *Som tum* arrives as a fresh and crunchy green papaya salad that is mouthwateringly sweet, tart, and pungent; *tom yum* soup is bracingly seasoned with lemongrass, lime, and chili; and a crisped and golden brown deep-fried fillet of Idaho trout is dressed with a brightly flavored tamarind sauce.

sola

Contemporary 𝕏𝕏

B2

3868 N. Lincoln Ave. (at Byron St.)

Phone: 773-327-3868   Lunch Sat – Sun
Web: www.sola-restaurant.com   Dinner nightly
Prices: **$$**   Irving Park (Brown)

This is a place that feels alive and warm—even before you've started on one of their seasonal cocktails, like The Great Pumpkin. The bar is a nice stop for a solo meal, while high-backed striped banquettes, orange fabric panels, and a boxy motif lend a contemporary feel to the dining space.

The very eclectic, Asian-influenced menu offers a sense of border-crossing and island-hopping adventure. Expect a colorful rendition of wasabi-crusted scallops with plump peas, roasted carrots, ginger-carrot butter, and a dark soy-based sauce. Weekend brunch may offer *huevos benedictos* with chorizo, corn bread, and salsa hollandaise. Tropical desserts might feature juicy circles of warm, braised pineapple with creamy coconut sorbet and macadamia shortbread cookies.

Southport Grocery

 D3

American

3552 N. Southport Ave. (bet. Addison St. & Cornelia Ave.)

Phone:	773-665-0100	Lunch daily
Web:	www.southportgrocery.com	
Prices:		Southport

Open for breakfast and lunch, this sleek neighborhood bistro also offers (as the name suggests) enough homey dishes for take-away and extensive top-of-the-line ingredients to keep even the most finicky foodie happy. Locals love this place, which occasionally leads to long lines on weekends and lots of high-energy conversations inside.

The made-from-scratch vibe is apparent in all the dishes, providing a welcome alternative to greasy spoon breakfasts. The chopped salad with herbed buttermilk dressing is a meal unto itself. Sandwiches may include the roast beef melt, with pickled vegetables, smoked Swiss, and crispy shallots. Save room for the grilled coffee cake, stuffed with cream cheese and grilled until gooey—it's as decadent as it sounds.

Sticky Rice

A2

Thai

4018 N. Western Ave. (at Cuyler Ave.)

Phone:	773-588-0133	Lunch & dinner daily
Web:	www.stickyricethai.com	
Prices:		Irving Park (Blue)

Lots of heart went into decorating this hipster hangout, focused on the regional cuisine of Northern Thailand. Bright yellow and orange paint, huge wood carved flowers and screens make it the brightest Thai joint around. The same degree of heart goes into the food, prepared lovingly (and slowly) by the kitchen.

The menu stands out, and as one would hope given the name, the sticky rice is fantastic. A daily special might include super-tender baby cuttlefish with crispy tentacles accented by Thai basil, onions, ginger, and lemongrass. Their *larb* is piquant, made here with ground pork instead of the more commonly found chicken. Save room for desserts featuring guess what–more sticky rice–perhaps accompanied by some funkadelic durian.

TAC Quick

E2

Thai ✗

3930 N. Sheridan Rd. (at Dakin St.)

Phone: 773-327-5253
Web: www.tacquick.net
Prices: ⊝⊜

Lunch & dinner Wed – Mon

🚇 Sheridan

It's a two-menu operation here at TAC Quick. One lists all the familiar Westernized favorites from beefy *nam tok* to soups, noodles, and spicy Chinese broccoli with slices of crispy pork belly, jalapeño, and garlic. And the second...well, it's a secret (sort of, given that it's posted on the website), but this is where Chef Itti really struts his stuff and garners a loyal following. Fiery, wonderfully traditional, and infinitely adventurous dishes like Thai beef jerky; Issan fermented pork and rice sausage; "mouse ear" salad; and Kari curry with squid, shrimp, onions, and coconut milk are whipped up with aplomb. The word is out, so hop off the train one stop shy of Wrigley and join the heat-seekers for some Thai Authentic Cuisine.

Thai Classic

E4

Thai ✗✗

3332 N. Clark St. (bet. Buckingham Pl. & Roscoe St.)

Phone: 773-404-2000
Web: www.thaiclassicrestaurant.com
Prices: ⊝⊜

Lunch & dinner daily

🚇 Belmont (Brown/Red)

Spotless and pristine, Thai Classic has remained a staple of this vibrant area of Lakeview for over 20 years now. Large windows anchor the dining room allowing for streams of natural night, and of course, plenty of people-watching opportunities. The menu chronicles not just Thai typicals like spring rolls, *satay*, salads, curries, rice and noodle dishes, but ventures beyond the classics with an array of special entrées. *Gai yaang* is a house specialty made with boneless Thai barbecued chicken, pounded flat and marinated in coconut milk and an enticing reserve of herbs and spices.

Another home run is the jungle curry, bathing with chicken, crisp vegetables, and spicy chili oil. The weekend offers an afternoon buffet perfect for bodies on a budget.

Thai Room

A2

Thai

4022 N. Western Ave. (at Cuyler Ave.)

Phone: 773-539-6150
Web: www.thairoomchicago.com
Prices:

Lunch & dinner Tue – Sun

 Irving Park (Blue)

Despite her old age, this Thai fixture is still pretty, prim, and proper. With such vibrant frills (burgundy carpets, dark wood-panels, and intricate woodwork), it is only fitting that the "room" tones it down with white-clothed tables topped with woven fabric and clear glass.

Upon entering, notice a sign (warning?) on the front door announcing a limited availability of mango sticky rice. Make a dash for it, and pray that the elderly entourage saved some for you. To the hum of soft music, glide through tasty Thai food like *sai gioong e-san*, sausages filled with ginger and cashews; *luuk chin tod*, meatballs licked with sweet 'n spicy sauce; and the house specialty, Thai Room catfish, flaky and fried, crowned with sautéed vegetables and green curry.

Wishbone

C4

American

3300 N. Lincoln Ave. (at School St.)

Phone: 773-549-2663
Web: www.wishbonechicago.com
Prices:

Lunch daily
Dinner Wed – Sun

 Paulina

From the wraparound counter with glimpses of a bustling kitchen to the booths and ample tables topped with comforting, all-American food, this place is just plain fun. Competence and comfort extend to the lightning-fast service, making it a favorite for larger groups and families.

Walls adorned with unusual artwork and a vast collection of chickens and roosters gives the place a quirky vibe. It's Southern with a twist and unique takes on American favorites. The counter is filled with regulars on a first-name basis, enjoying a limited all-day breakfast menu. Dinner offerings may include specials like smoky and spicy Cajun salmon served alongside perfect collard greens with smoked turkey. Or, get your Southern on with some shrimp and grits.

Wood

Contemporary ✗✗

E3

3335 N. Halstead St. (at Buckingham Pl.)

Phone: 773-935-9663
Web: www.woodchicago.com
Prices: $$

Lunch Sat – Sun
Dinner nightly
🚇 Belmont (Brown/Red)

Lest you wonder if there might be a connection between a spot so named and its litany of treats, it's true there is a wood-fired oven in the kitchen. But the double entendre is very much intentional, played up with cheekily named cocktails like "a stiff one" and "rough rider" to be sipped in the warm wood plank-lined room decked with handsome furnishings. Affordably priced small plates match the cocktails at this Boystown setting, focusing on contemporary American classics like a delicate soft shell crab atop summer vegetable succotash; or squares of wood-grilled flatbread topped with country ham, charred kale, and raclette. Belgian frites off the "Backwoods" late night menu, offered with a choice of 12 sauces, are near-legendary for local night owls.

Red=Particularly Pleasant.
Look for the red ✗ and 🏠 symbols.

Lincoln Park & Old Town

LINCOLN PARK

History, commerce, and nature come together in these iconic Chicago districts. The eponymous park, running along the Lake Michigan shore, offers winter-weary Chicagoans an excuse to get outside. And to add to the outdoor fun, famed Lincoln Park keeps its patrons happy and frolicking with a splendid spectrum of outdoor cafés, restaurants ranging from quick bites to the city's most exclusive reservations, and takeout spots perfect for assembling a picnic.

Populated by post-college roommates, young families, and affluent yuppies, Lincoln Park is a favorite amongst locals and visitors, no matter the time of the year. It includes more than a handful of designated historic districts, pre-Great Chicago Fire buildings, museums, shopping, music venues, and the famous (and free) Lincoln Park Zoo.

Delicious Dining

Well-heeled foodies make reservations to come here for some of the most exclusive restaurants in town (including legendary though now sadly shuttered **Charlie Trotter's**, **Alinea**, and **L2O** to name a few). During the weekend, the area is hopping, thanks to a combination of the theater, bar scene, and scores of apartment buildings that cater to the twenty- and thirty-somethings crowd. On summer Wednesdays and Saturdays,

the south end of the park is transformed into hipster-chef-foodie central during the **Green City Market**. With the objective to elevate the availability of top-notch produce, and to improve the connect between farmers and local producers with restaurants and food organizations, this market aims to educate the masses about high-quality food sourcing. (In winter it is held inside the Peggy Notebaert Nature Museum). Additionally, the market draws long lines largely by dint of its fresh meats, cheeses, and fluffy crêpes.

Best of Bakeries

Fans of the sweets made from local ingredients at **Floriole Café & Bakery** have reason to rejoice—Floriole also has a Lincoln Park storefront that showcases a lunch menu alongside daily specials. Also luring a pack of visitors are their perfect pastries, breakfast delights, sandwiches, salads, cookies, and sweet treats. Those with an affinity (or addiction) for all things baked can now get them even when Green City is closed. For other stomach-filling options outside of the market, try the heartwarming **Meatloaf Bakery**, where meat loaf and mashed potatoes are crafted into all manner of dishes, such as a cupcake-shaped "loaf" (with mashed potato icing). Other treats may include the *mother loaf, a wing and a prayer loaf, loaf-a-roma,* and the *no buns about it burger* *loaf.* Don't let the quirky titles fool you, because this may just be some of the best and most gratifying food in town. This expanse is also a great place in which to satisfy that Chicago hot dog craving. Like many foods (Juicy Fruit, Cracker Jack, and Shredded Wheat, for example), it is said that the Chicago-style dog may have originated at the Chicago World's Fair and Columbian Exhibition (in 1893), although that provenance is not definitive. Others credit the Great Depression for its birth. One newcomer is the chef-driven **Franks 'n' Dawgs**. Bustling at most hours, this Lincoln Park gem employs fresh and locally sourced ingredients featured in their fun food. Look forward to hand-crafted, juicy hot dogs, homey artisan breads, and gourmet sausages. Speaking of meat, **Butcher & the Burger** is doing its part to say at the helm of the burger chain. **The Wieners Circle** is as known for its late hours (as late as 5:00 A.M.) and purposefully rude service, as for its tasty repertoire of dogs and fries. Lincoln Park is one of the dog-friendliest areas around, but then what else would you expect from a neighborhood named after a park? Bold foodies and college grads are forever flocking to **Etno Village Grill** whose flavorful Balkan-style sandwiches are bound to sate Fido's appetite as well as your own. Chase this down with a stop at **Three Dog Bakery**, where the chef caters to canine customers.

A Perfect Quench

Wash down all that tasty grease at **Goose Island Brewery**, makers of the city's favorite local beers. Loop the Goose Canoe Tours (offered during the summer) gives you a view of the Chicago River Island for which the brew is named. If you're still parched, visit the friendly and casual relaxed **Webster's Wine Bar**. Nab a seat on their streetfront patio, where you can enjoy a glass or two from their winning and expansive wine selection. It is a whole different ballgame at **Karyn's Fresh Corner and Raw Café**, a restaurant with a full vegan and raw menu. The adjacent **Fresh Corner Market** sells meals to-go, plus fresh juices and supplements. "Meatballs" are made from lentils, and "sloppy Joes" from soy protein, and the raw food experience is unlike anything else you've seen.

OLD TOWN

The Old Town quarter sports a few quaint cobblestoned streets that house the Second City comedy scene (now with a Zanies, too, for even more laughs); June's annual must-see (and must-shop) Old Town Art Fair; the Wells Street Art Fair; and places to rest with beers and a groovy jukebox like the **Old Town Ale House**. Wells Street is the neighborhood's main drag, and is where browsing should begin. Any epicurean shopping trip should also include the **Old Town Oil** for fab hostess gifts like infused oils and aged vinegars. Prefer a sweeter vice? **The Fudge Pot** tempts passersby with windows full of toffee, fudge, and other chocolaty goodness. Whether you smoke or not, the **Up Down Cigar** is worth a peek for its real cigar store Indian carving.

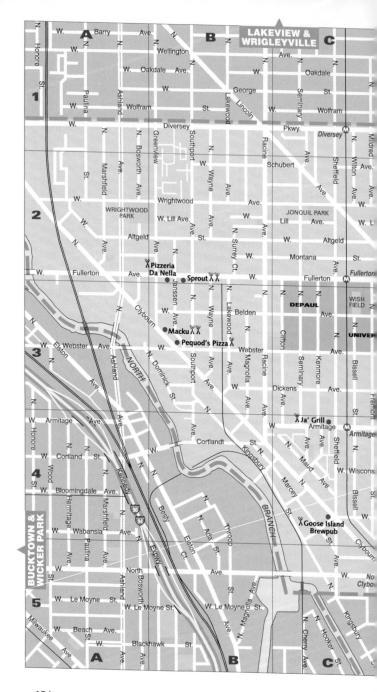

Map labels:

A B C

N. Honore St.

W. Barry Ave.
W. Wellington Ave.
W. Oakdale Ave.
N. Paulina St.
N. Ashland Ave.
W. Wolfram St.
W. George St.
N. Seminary
N. Lakewood
N. Racine Ave.
N. Sheffield Ave.
W. Wolfram St.

Diversey Pkwy.
Diversey (M)

N. Marshfield Ave.
N. Bosworth Ave.
N. Greenview Ave.
N. Southport Ave.
N. Wayne Ave.
W. Schubert Ave.
N. Racine Ave.
N. Wilton Ave.
N. Mildred Ave.

WRIGHTWOOD PARK
W. Wrightwood Ave.
W. Lill Ave.
W. Altgeld St.
N. Surrey Ct.
JONQUIL PARK
W. Lill Ave.
W. Altgeld St.
W. Montana St.
W. Fullerton Ave.
Fullerton (M)

✗ Pizzeria Da Nella
✗✗ Sprout
N. Janssen Ave.
N. Wayne
N. Lakewood
W. Belden Ave.
DEPAUL
WISH FIELD
UNIVER

N. Clybourn
● Macku ✗✗
● Pequod's Pizza ✗
N. Dominick St.
N. Southport Ave.
N. Magnolia Ave.
N. Racine Ave.
W. Webster Ave.
N. Clifton
N. Seminary
N. Kenmore
N. Bissell

W. Elston Ave.
W. Webster Ave.
N. Ashland
W. Dickens Ave.
N. Fremont St.

W. Armitage Ave.
✗ Ja' Grill ●
Armitage (M)
N. Honore
N. Wood St.
W. Cortland St.
Cortlandt St.
N. Kingsbury
N. Maud Ave.
N. Sheffield Ave.
N. Clybourn

W. Bloomingdale Ave.
N. Kennedy
N. Hermitage
N. Marshfield Ave.
N. Ada St.
N. Throop St.
N. Elston Ave.
BRANCH
N. Marcey St.
W. Wiscons
N. Bissell

BUCKTOWN & WICKER PARK

W. Wabansia Ave.
N. Paulina
N. Besly
✗ Goose Island Brewpub ●
N. Clybour

W. North Ave.
N. Bosworth
N. No Clybo

W. Le Moyne St.
W. Le Moyne St.
N. Magnolia Ave.
N. Kingsbury

W. Beach Ave.
N. Milwaukee Ave.
W. Blackhawk St.
N. Cherry Ave.
N. Hooker St.

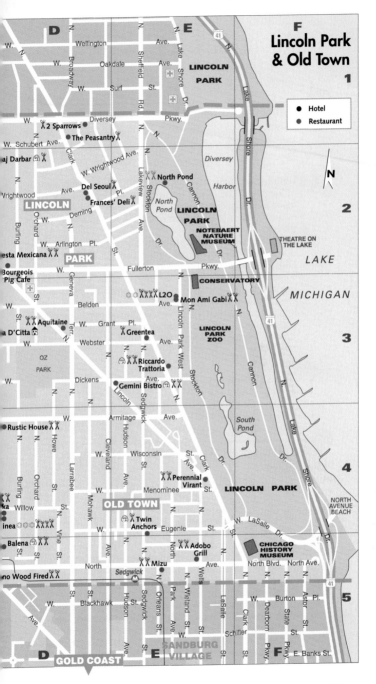

Lincoln Park & Old Town

● Hotel
● Restaurant

LINCOLN PARK

LAKE MICHIGAN

LINCOLN PARK ZOO

OLD TOWN

GOLD COAST

SANDBURG VILLAGE

2 Sparrows
The Peasantry
Raj Darbar
Del Seoul
Frances' Deli
North Pond
Fiesta Mexicana
Bourgeois Pig Cafe
L2O
Mon Ami Gabi
Aquitaine
Pasta D'Citta
Greentea
Riccardo Trattoria
Gemini Bistro
Rustic House
Perennial Virant
Twin Anchors
inea
Topolobampo / Balena
Adobo Grill
Mizu
Wood Fired

NOTEBAERT NATURE MUSEUM
THEATRE ON THE LAKE
CONSERVATORY
CHICAGO HISTORY MUSEUM
NORTH AVENUE BEACH

Diversey Harbor
North Pond
South Pond

155

Adobo Grill

E5

Mexican ✕✕

1610 N. Wells St. (bet. Eugenie St. & North Ave.)

Phone:	312-266-7999
Web:	www.adobogrill.com
Prices:	$$

Lunch Sat – Sun
Dinner nightly
🚇 Sedgwick

Fun, festive, and flavorful, Adobo Grill is celebrated as a longtime Old Town crowd-pleaser. Housed within a meandering building, it is at once cozy and lively with everyone from local denizens and families to solo diners at the bar.

First, order a lip-smacking margarita with fresh lime, then flag down one of the roving guacamole carts for a wildly popular tableside rendition. The solid Mexican bill of fare offers something for everyone, like little tostadas with anchiote-marinated chicken, pickled onions, black beans, and sour cream; and *arrachera adobado*—grilled flank steak with a rich adobo, smoky *frijoles puercos*, grilled tomatoes, onions, and their unique house-made tortillas.

Brunch brings signature starters, small plates, and *huevos rancheros*.

Aquitaine

D3

American ✕✕

2221 N. Lincoln Ave. (bet. Belder & Webster Aves.)

Phone:	773-698-8456
Web:	www.aquitainerestaurant.com
Prices:	$$

Lunch Sun
Dinner nightly
🚇 Fullerton

According to Chef/partner Holly Willoughby, this elegant spot inherits its name from Eleanor of Aquitaine, queen consort of England and France in the 12th century. French-influenced dishes spruce up the mostly American, seasonally changing menu. The brooding, sexy interior is styled in charcoals and reds, with ornately designed wallpaper and a large, welcoming bar.

Get started with a *petite tarte*—a fluffy egg quiche loaded with portobello mushroom, sun-dried tomato, and goat cheese tucked into a crisp, buttery shell; and then dig into a pretzel roll, stuffed with roasted chicken, tomato, arugula, and truffle-lemon dressing. End with a tantalizing dessert like amber cake, layers of lemon madeleines and custard topped with caramel and pistachio.

Alinea ✿ ✿ ✿

D4

Contemporary ❌❌❌❌

1723 N. Halsted St. (bet. North Ave. & Willow St.)

Phone: 312-867-0110   Dinner Wed – Sun
Web: www.alinea-restaurant.com
Prices: $$$$ 🚇 North/Clybourn

Lara Kastner

You may as well be approaching the outside of Willy Wonka's chocolate factory—the only sign is an easel next to the valet. Once inside, the metaphor continues with a fuschia-lit hallway that tapers and actually constricts as you walk. However, the contemporary space becomes supremely comfortable and even luxurious as you settle into a yellow leather chair for the meal of a lifetime.

Shakespeare wrote his plays in three acts. Alinea captivates diners for nearly 20 moving, transformative courses that often require their participation and humor—"Eat with your fingers here...Use nothing here." Neptune would approve of an extraordinary series of seafood courses, like mussels with saffron-chorizo broth or oyster mignonette, strategically placed on driftwood and kelp. A pane of glass displaying 60 condiment options is the star of a braised shank, belly roulade, and roasted loin of lamb course.

Dessert is theatre here, starring Chef Grant Achatz who may personally deliver that white chocolate orb with pansies, strawberries, English pea powders and pearls to your table, then smash it like a cotton-candy, beignet, and sherry gastrique-filled piñata. Eccentric? Intense? Extraordinary? Absolutely.

Balena

Italian

1633 N Halstead St. (bet. North Ave. & Willow St.)

Phone: 312-867-3888
Web: www.balenachicago.com
Prices: **$$**

Dinner nightly

 North/Clybourn

Just a few steps from the Steppenwolf and Royal George theaters, pre-show crowds fill their bellies with Italian-inspired cuisine infused with a few global tweaks at Balena. Rustic rafters hung with twinkling orbital lights crisscross the towering ceiling in this barn-like space, but dark oak floors help warm things up. Primo spots at the chef's counter get a first-hand view of the action.

You'll pay a few bucks if you want the bread basket, but it's worth it given the ever-changing selection that might unveil lemon pepper challah or ramp crostini. Simple and shareable plates have featured salt-and-pepper chicken thighs set over a hash of green garlic and topped with mustard greens; or spicy grilled "Korean cut" short ribs with charred orange and basil.

Bourgeois Pig Cafe

Deli

738 W. Fullerton Pkwy. (at Burling St.)

Phone: 773-883-5282
Web: www.bpigcafe.com
Prices:

Lunch & dinner daily

 Fullerton

This old brownstone is a bookish coffee house and cozy, lived-in feeling café. Seats are available downstairs, but a trek upstairs brings added character with shabby-chic chandeliers, straw baskets, and a fireplace surrounded by young kids wearing vintage clothes. Despite the antiques and bookcases, this is a place for Kindles.

Excellent bread is paramount to every cleverly named sandwich and panini. *The Great Gatsby* is a riff on the club, *The Catcher in the Rye* means Reuben here, and *The Old Man and the Sea* is their tuna salad. *The Hobbit* is a triple-decker BLT panini on good sourdough with sun-dried tomato pesto, mayo, bacon crumbles, tomatoes, avocado, and alfalfa sprouts—a combination so outrageously good that you will be sad when it is gone.

Boka

D4

Contemporary 🍴🍴🍴

1729 N. Halsted St. (bet. North Ave. & Willow St.)

Phone: 312-337-6070

Web: www.bokachicago.com

Prices: $$$

Dinner nightly

🚇 North/Clybourn

Eric Kleinberg

An undercurrent of romance buzzes through Boka, from the airy patio to the remodeled lounge, and through the tented ceiling of the chic dining room. What's decidedly missing from the modern, appealing space is any hint of stuffiness or pretense. Though many guests are giddily celebrating special occasions under the billowing white fabrics, the restaurant is classy but casual. Their playlist might even spin the occasional Hendrix tune.

Mediterranean touches and fresh seafood dominate the contemporary American menu. Sample the likes of plump Atlantic salmon with grilled cantaloupe, cherry tomatoes, chorizo crumbles, and tart gazpacho poured tableside; or silky Maine diver scallops paired with Wagyu beef and fiddlehead fern-studded ramp risotto. A selection of raw seafood may arrive in a bento box featuring snapper carpaccio with tangy plum sauce, kelp noodles, or yellowfin tuna with finger limes and *sriracha* "pearls" to dazzle and intrigue.

Go with hungry dining companions to try the four- six- or nine-course tasting menus that offer a broad sampling of the kitchen's talents. Chef Giuseppe Tentori may even toss in a few of his all-time favorite dishes, often not available à la carte.

Del Seoul

Korean ✗

2568-2570 N. Clark St. (bet. Deming Pl. & Wrightwood Ave.)

Phone: 773-248-4227   Lunch & dinner daily
Web: www.delseoul.com
Prices: 🍜

 Diversey

The Korean "street" food craze has hit the nation, but Del Seoul's moan-worthy delights are far beyond some passing fad. Thank the Jeon family for whipping up those intoxicating flavors into a menu of addictive fusion specialties, as well as *bulgogi* and *bahn mi*. Savory "Seoul style" dumplings are made from a 100-year old recipe, and *gamja* fries are smothered in kimchi, pork belly, and melted cheese.

And the tacos... oh, the tacos. Grilled white corn tortillas stuffed with chicken, spicy pork, braised beef *kalbi*, or sesame-chili shrimp, then crowned with cilantro-onion relish, chili-garlic salsa, and a secret slaw. Luckily, tacos are not too big, so try a variety. Order at the counter from the overhead video screen, take a number and grab a seat.

Fiesta Mexicana

Mexican ✗✗

2423 N. Lincoln Ave. (bet. Fullerton Ave. & Halsted St.)

Phone: 773-348-4144   Lunch & dinner daily
Web: www.fiestamexicanachicago.com
Prices: 🍜

 Fullerton

A long-time hangout for the twenty-somethings and young families living in Lincoln Park, Fiesta Mexicana lives up to the party-style atmosphere its moniker promises. The brick-lined space features a high ceiling, separate bar, and a number of dining rooms, with a large mural of a colorful mountain scene welcoming diners.

Guests are greeted with tasty chips and salsa and an expansive menu offering a cross-section of Tex-Mex, traditional Mexican, and Mexican-inspired fare. The combination platters are a solid way to sample the Tex-Mex choices; while chile poblano-spinach and artichoke *fundido* shows off the kitchen's creative juices. Opt for a starter rather than a dessert, as these are the weakest link.

Good value specials are offered at lunch.

Frances' Deli

Deli

D2

2552 N. Clark St. (bet. Deming Pl. & Wrightwood Ave.)

Phone: 773-248-4580
Web: www.francesdeli.com
Prices: 💲💲

Lunch daily
Dinner Sat – Sun

Lincoln Parkers love this deli/diner for good reason. Snug and inviting in a well-worn sort of way, Frances' may be short on looks but is long on satisfaction. The line is out the door on weekends with a mix of students, locals, and young professionals.

Everyone flocks here for crowd-pleasing and gut-busting meals. The burgers, triple-decker sandwiches bursting with quality meats, and yummy breakfasts like challah French toast and omelets, could cure any hangover. Potato pancakes and blintzes are better than grandma's. You definitely won't have room, but milkshakes, malts, and sundaes are musts. That thick, icy, and exactly-as-it-should-be chocolate-peanut butter milkshake is seriously the bomb, though you'll need to lie down later.

Gemini Bistro

American

E3

2075 N. Lincoln Ave. (at Dickens Ave.)

Phone: 773-525-2522
Web: www.geminibistrochicago.com
Prices: $$

Dinner Tue – Sun

 Armitage

An unfussy attitude meets a gleamingly chic design in this white-tiled Flat Iron building just off Lincoln Avenue's main drag. Ease a likely wait at the no-reservations spot with a cocktail like the margarita-esque Heater or Gemini lemonade over at the marble bar. Early birds can snag the prix-fixe menu along with a coveted sidewalk patio table.

Loosely inspired by its Mediterranean neighbors, Gemini's menu might unveil a generous fillet of flaky pan-roasted halibut napped in lobster sauce alongside fava bean and corn succotash; or pea-studded risotto accented with mint, black pepper, and a healthy dose of Parmigiano Reggiano.

One tip: consider the reasonable valet instead of risking a parking ticket in this permit-heavy neighborhood.

Goose Island Brewpub

Gastropub

C4

1800 N. Clybourn Ave. (at Willow St.)

Phone: 312-915-0071
Web: www.gooseisland.com
Prices:

Lunch & dinner daily

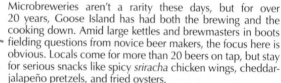 North/Clybourn

Microbreweries aren't a rarity these days, but for over 20 years, Goose Island has had both the brewing and the cooking down. Amid large kettles and brewmasters in boots fielding questions from novice beer makers, the focus here is obvious. Locals come for more than 20 beers on tap, but stay for serious snacks like spicy *sriracha* chicken wings, cheddar-jalapeño pretzels, and fried oysters.

The pork sausage sandwich is prepared with a fun twist, served with German Dusseldorf mustard and caramelized onions on a pretzel roll. That chocolate bark, too, has a surprise: it is made with dark Belgian chocolate, sea salt, bacon, and spent grain from the brewing process.

Dedicated fans may want to grab a Green Line Growler of their favorite brew to-go.

Greentea

Japanese

E3

2206 N. Clark St. (bet. Belden & Webster Aves.)

Phone: 773-883-8812
Web: N/A
Prices: $$

Lunch Tue – Sat
Dinner Tue – Sun

Regulars of this bento box-sized sushi spot are happy that its nondescript façade is easy to miss. They'd rather you walk on by as they keep this soothing space with pristine seafood their little secret. Restful seafoam-tinged walls and soft Japanese music keep the focus on the quiet but busy *itamae* sporting bright red shirts and ace slicing skills.

Those in-the-know flock here for fresh nigiri and sashimi like rich and dusky smoked salmon, creamy *otoro*, pure white hamachi, and silky *maguro*. Even the pickled ginger is perky and crisp. Fried baby crabs are an inventive starter–popcorn for the sushi set–and the maki are creatively prepared yet manageably sized. A lobster and jalapeño roll wrapped with tofu skin is tasty, simple, and without kitsch.

Ja' Grill

C4

Jamaican

1008 W. Armitage Ave. (bet. Kenmore & Sheffield Aves.)

Phone: 773-929-5375
Web: www.jagrill.com
Prices:

Lunch Fri – Sun
Dinner nightly
Armitage

Ja' Grill conveys the Jamaican spirit loud and clear. Patron saint Bob Marley (dreads aglow in red, yellow, and green) kicks out the jams from a large mural set off by a sunset orange back-lit bar. Reggae beats and a bottle of Red Stripe further heighten the mood. A downstairs lounge caters to the drinks-and-DJ crowd, where dancehall, dub, and ska spin live on weekends.

The menu schools the palate on Jamaican classics with rubs and sauces that build with a slow burn. Hearty mains like pork ribs, or jerk shrimp benefit from a healthy slathering of spices. The kitchen smartly offers veggie sides like fried sweet plantains and a warm cabbage salad to cool the heat.

Caveat emptor: ask for the prices of daily specials before ordering or risk sticker shock.

Macku

B3

Japanese

2239 N. Clybourn Ave. (bet. Greenview & Webster Aves.)

Phone: 773-880-8012
Web: www.mackusushi.com
Prices: $$

Dinner nightly

Sushi fans fall into two camps: east and west. There are those who love their westernized maki (spicy tuna anyone?) and those who go the traditional nigiri route. Whether you're a newbie or an aficionado, Macku has you covered.

This contemporary Japanese restaurant literally lays out every option; its neat display of fresh fish at the sushi bar is an enticing sign of what's to come. Start with straightforward favorites like salmon, tuna, and yellowtail; or choose from the nice selection of specialty rolls, like the spicy spider roll with soft shell crab, *kanikami*, chili oil, avocado, and cucumber.

The menu may have it all, but this modern and stylish restaurant is small with just a sprinkling of tables and seats at the pristine counter.

L2O ❀ ❀

Seafood XXXX

E3

2300 N. Lincoln Park West (bet. Belden Ave. & Fullerton Pkwy.)

Phone: 773-868-0002
Dinner Thu – Mon
Web: www.l2orestaurant.com
Prices: $$$$

Katherine Bryant

L2O's classic façade in contrast with the contemporary interior is an upscale and unpretentious reflection of its notable locale. The dining room is inspired by the underside of a boardwalk, though these columns and coral-like sculptures seem immaculate and nearly golden when steeped in the sophisticated romance of velvet alcoves and white leather chairs. The atmosphere is absorbing, service is suave, and intensity is afoot.

À la carte offerings are wonderful, but the range of fixed price menus is a better way to explore this new, brave, and very talented kitchen's skill.

Expect the likes of profoundly anise-like fennel cream layered with basil, lemon, and flaky-sweet Maryland blue crab meat *en gelée* that zings with a speckle of *piment d'Esplette*. Yet each course seems to best the last, when followed by a dish of cubed and creamy vanilla-kissed cauliflower custard topped with explosively briny Black Sea osetra caviar and disks of sweet langoustine tartare. Or, try a slender pigeon breast layered with foie gras and cooked sous vide. The meat is then sliced into coins and stacked among Mandarin segments, bright white turnips, and whipped sweet potato purée enriched with foie gras mousse.

Mizu

E5   J a p a n e s e   ✕✕

315 W. North Ave. (at Orleans St.)

Phone: 312-951-8880   Dinner nightly
Web: www.mizurestaurant.com
Prices: $$ Sedgwick

This Lincoln Park Japanese restaurant is a real find. Chocolate brown banquettes line the walls, while white orb chandeliers cast a soft glow over the beige tiled floors of this contempo-chic gem. For the ultimate *izakaya* experience, visit the tatami room, located behind sliding wooden doors—it's the real McCoy, complete with the shoes-off sensibility, and mats for sitting on the floor.

The extensive menu attracts all by offering a little bit of this (yakitori, their specialty) and a little bit of that (traditional and westernized sushi and sashimi). Oyster shooters, grilled squid, *gyoza*, soba—you name it, and they have it. Maki like the New Mexico with tuna, yellowtail, *tobiko*, avocado, and jalapeño, show the chefs' creative touch.

Mon Ami Gabi

E3   F r e n c h   ✕✕

2300 N. Lincoln Park West (at Belden Ave.)

Phone: 773-348-8886   Dinner nightly
Web: www.monamigabi.com
Prices: $$

Within the historic Belden-Stratford hotel, Mon Ami Gabi offers an instant trip to Lyon by way of Lincoln Park. This appealing brasserie stays lively with the cozy ambience of a French bistro straight from central casting. Leather banquettes, dusky yellow walls, and wooden wine racks set the scene, while old-world tuxedo-clad servers play the part, perfectly.

Chef Gabino Soletino (the "ami" referenced in the restaurant's name) and team turn out faithful renditions of classic brasserie food such as an anchovy-rich Caesar salad with shards of baguette croutons, dusted with black pepper ground at the table; plump and on-point medium-rare filet mignon with a healthy dab of butter and béarnaise sauce; or French onion soup capped with gooey Gruyère.

North Pond

E2

Contemporary

2610 N. Cannon Dr.

Phone: 773-477-5845
Web: www.northpondrestaurant.com
Prices: $$$

Lunch Sun
Dinner Tue – Sun

Built in 1912 as a warming house for ice skaters, this craftsman-style cottage inspired by Frank Lloyd Wright is home to North Pond. Luring guests with an elegant pastoral setting is Chef Bruce Sherman's stellar cooking. Presented amid large windows, flickering votives, soft jazz tunes, and a crackling fireplace, this is a dreamy nook for date-night duos. Centered on its ingredients-first philosophy, the menu highlights a range of sustainable, seasonal produce. Plates like soft shell crab atop a tropical mango-coconut compote and streaked with cashew butter; or an ivory white halibut fillet topped with almonds and coated with a citrus-snap pea purée are commendable examples of the layers of complementary flavor and textural contrast found in each dish.

The Peasantry

D1

Contemporary

2723 N. Clark St. (bet. Diversey Pkwy & W. Drummond Pl.)

Phone: 773-868-4888
Web: www.thepeasantry.com
Prices: $$

Lunch Fri – Sun
Dinner Tue – Sun
 Diversey

The team behind critically acclaimed Franks 'N' Dawgs has expanded beyond hot dogs. They now run a roster of critters including eclectic street food in this cheeky modern-meets-rustic space. A mural running the length of the bare wood banquette features a playful black and white graffiti-ed animal menagerie ranging from cows to an octopus.

Though the food might have familiar names like pigs in a blanket, the ingredients surprise those who might expect standard comfort fare. These are chorizo wrapped in golden puff pastry and served on pancetta-studded white beans. Snacks like truffle fries with a triple hit of aromatic butter, salt, and oil; spicy kimchi popcorn; or a deconstructed *poutine* with duck confit make for unexpectedly tasty eating.

Pequod's Pizza

Pizza

B3

2207 N. Clybourn Ave. (at Webster Ave.)

Phone: 773-327-1512
Web: www.pequodspizza.com
Prices: $$

Lunch & dinner daily

 Armitage

Ditch your diet, grab your fellow Blackhawk fans, and head into this Lincoln Park stalwart for some of the best pie in town. Christened in 1970 for Captain Ahab's whaling ship, Pequod's sails a smooth menu of bar food apps, hearty sandwiches (try the tender Italian beef with melted cheese and hot peppers), and fantastic pizzas.

Crusts range from thin- to deep-dish, but the specialty is the pan pizza, with its cake-like crust and halo of caramelized cheese that sticks to the sides of the pan. Toppings like spicy sausage and pepperoni are heaped on with abandon, as if the pizza makers are whipping up a pie to take home for themselves. Pequod's stays open till 2:00 A.M. most nights, so stop by for a late night nosh and ponder the great white whale.

Perennial Virant

American

E4

1800 N. Lincoln Ave. (at Clark St.)

Phone: 312-981-7070
Web: www.perennialchicago.com
Prices: $$

Lunch Sat – Sun
Dinner nightly

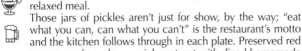

Vie chef Paul Virant brings his signature farmhouse panache to Lincoln Park after taking the helm of Perennial's kitchen in 2011—that means Ball jars as far as the eye can see, preserving various vegetables on shelves and even hanging from light fixtures. A first-come, first-served communal table seats barflies who don't mind eating amongst the cocktail crowd, but reservations for the dining room make for a more relaxed meal.

Those jars of pickles aren't just for show, by the way; "eat what you can, can what you can't" is the restaurant's motto and the kitchen follows through in each plate. Preserved red pepper purée perks up rainbow trout with diced homemade bacon; while *carnaroli* rice cakes come bedecked with pea shoots, pickled peas, and beans.

Pizzeria Da Nella

 B2

1443 W. Fullerton Ave. (bet. Greenview & Janssen Aves.)

Phone:	773-281-6600
Web:	www.pizzeriadanella.com
Prices:	$$

Lunch & dinner daily

🚇 Fullerton

♿
🪑

The tradition, not the pizza, runs deep at this Neapolitan darling on West Fullerton. Naples-born *pizzaiola*, Nella Grassano takes center stage, stretching dough, then judiciously sprinkling toppings on her pies before sliding them into an oven burning with white oak for a mere two minutes. Her husband and brother pitch in to serve salads with fresh *mozzarella di bufala* and *prosciutto di Parma*, homemade pastas, and crusty bread from the same oven.

Despite baking in temperatures that can seriously escalate, pizzas emerge crisp with the perfect char. Diavola pies are dotted with spicy salami rounds and red pepper flakes, washed down with an Italian or Midwest-brewed beer. An expansive brick-paved patio begs for a leisurely Italian lunch; why not indulge?

Raj Darbar

D2

2660 N. Halsted St. (bet. Schubert & Wrightwood Aves.)

Phone:	773-348-1010
Web:	www.rajdarbar.com
Prices:	$$

Dinner nightly

🚇 Diversey

♿

This stretch of Halsted has seen its share of change, from college-kid hangouts to upscale boutiques to what was the world's first two-story Home Depot. Amidst this odd mix of retail you will find Raj Darbar, with its drab décor but seriously talented kitchen.

Alu tikki are a wonderful way to start: smooth and creamy (yet textured) seasoned potatoes create a casing for a chili-rubbed pea filling all dipped in chickpea batter and crisply fried. Tender *jheenga tandoori* is incredible; the shrimp is marinated in a mixture of yogurt, garlic, and ginger with the addition of spices then perfectly roasted in the tandoor. *Biryani*, *pudina paratha*, and *dum ki gobhi* are solid choices while *rasmalai* makes for a competent, creamy ending to a fragrant feast.

Riccardo Trattoria

Italian XX

2119 N. Clark St. (bet. Dickens & Webster Aves.)

Phone: 773-549-0038   Dinner nightly
Web: www.riccardotrattoria.com
Prices: $$

The understated wood and cream décor doesn't look anything like an Italian *nonna*'s kitchen. But, the soulful personality of Chef/owner Riccardo Michi and his cache of family recipes make his eponymous restaurant a second home to half the city, it seems—a go-to spot equally suited to flirty date nights and big, boisterous dinners.

As intimated by the word "trattoria" authentic rustic Italian cooking presides over the menu. One baseball-sized *arancino* would suffice for a hearty appetizer, but in the spirit of *abbondanza*, you get two. Veal roulades, pounded thin, stuffed with sausage and pistachios, and paired with Tuscan fries are standouts among the *secondi*; while a light, fluffy version of tiramisu makes even those who beg off dessert take a second bite.

Rustic House

American XX

1967 N. Halsted St. (bet. Armitage Ave. & Willow St.)

Phone: 312-929-3227   Dinner Tue – Sun
Web: www.rustichousechicago.com
Prices: $$ Armitage

Rustic House takes its name pretty seriously, marking its walls with burlap, building its bar with weathered barn planks, and hanging iron wheel chandeliers lit by pillar candles. But as befits its setting in a historic building, there's an edge of refinement to the rusticity, tweaking familiar tropes with a glamorous update.

The menu follows the same polished comfort food path; you'll find a juicy free-range organic chicken turning on the rotisserie each night, sometimes joined by a rack of veal or suckling pig.

Snack on thin kettle chips and homemade onion dip before spooning up chicken pot pie draped with a fluffy puff pastry blanket. Sauternes-soaked blueberry peach pie in an iron casserole is the perfect marriage of down-home and elegant.

Sono Wood Fired

Pizza ✗✗

D5

Pizza ✗✗

1582 N. Clybourn Ave. (bet. Halsted St. & North Ave.)

Phone: 312-255-1122 Dinner Tue – Sun
Web: www.sonowoodfired.com
Prices: $$ 🚉 North/Clybourn

The harlequin-tiled imported Italian pizza oven blazing away in the corner is not only the focal point of Sono's dining room—it's the reason for their lively crowd continually chowing down at the tightly packed tables and sleek oak bar. Everyone's here for the signature blistered, lightly charred but still chewy Neapolitan-style pizzas, made distinctively creative with fresh, local, and imported artisan ingredients like wild mushrooms, crispy sage, spicy *sopressata*, or *fior di latte* mozzarella.

Antipasti like mussels in a garlicky white wine broth spend some time in the oven for a touch of wood-fired flavor before hitting the table; while flash-fried artichoke hearts or Parmesan-dusted calamari served family-style ease the wait for those precious pies.

Sprout

B2

Contemporary ✗✗

1417 W. Fullerton Ave. (bet. Janssen & Southport Aves.)

Phone: 773-348-0706 Lunch Sun
Web: www.sproutrestaurant.com Dinner Tue – Sat
Prices: $$$ 🚉 Fullerton

Polished marble floors, chunky flagstone walls surrounding a skylit-enclosed patio, and decorative twig accents lend an earthy, natural vibe to complement Chef Dale Levitski's ode to all things organic. In turn, tables and cubby booths provide an intimate and romantic feel to the space, though casually hip servers keep things from getting too precious. The approachable staff is pleased to answer questions about those abstractly described dishes outlined on the à la carte and three-course prix-fixe menus.

The oft-changing items include the chef's inventive take on *pho* with seared ono, sirloin carpaccio, and spicy seaweed broth; or the childhood favorite grilled cheese featuring a white cheddar *fritto* encasing slow-cooked onions and Granny Smith apples.

Twin Anchors

Barbecue 🍴

E4

1655 N. Sedgwick St. (at Eugenie St.)

Phone: 312-266-1616
Web: www.twinanchorsribs.com
Prices: $$

Lunch Sat – Sun
Dinner nightly
🚇 Sedgwick

Chicago was Frank Sinatra's kind of town, and Twin Anchors was his kind of restaurant. This Sinatra sweetheart and easygoing local institution has been dishing out barbecued ribs since 1932, and its owners of thirty years are intent on maintaining its traditions. A no-reservations policy means regulars prefer off-hours and weekend lunch to avoid long waits and take advantage of the chatty service. Come dressed for a mess since the vibe is unfussy.

As for the food, fantastic baked beans, ribs, and barbecue chicken are all a must. Their three sauces (Zesty, Original Mild, and Prohibition) are as great on fries as 'cue. The bar menu brings tasty bites like house-made potato chips or wings; the "Little Piglet" menu has wee ones squealing with delight.

2 Sparrows

American 🍴

D1

553 Diversey Pkwy. (Bet. Cambridge Ave. & Lehmann Ct.)

Phone: 773-234-2320
Web: www.2sparrowschicago.com
Prices: ⊛⊛

Lunch daily

🚇 Diversey

Two Charlie Trotter veterans opened this daytime café—a spot as completely pleasing as it is busy. Fronted by plate glass, the lofty room is warm with sunshine, has a convivial buzz, and boasts a frenetic open kitchen.

The carte includes a breakfast-themed selection of sweets and savories that showcase the likes of "pop tarts." That mass-produced morning pastry of yore may elicit a stronger Proustian effect than madeleines, but the 2 Sparrows version is alike only in name and memorable in its own right. Flavors change daily and may feature caramelized apples tucked into a buttery shell drizzled with lemon and thyme glaze. The fresh baked biscuit slathered with lamb sausage gravy is a heartier option; while the veggie burger is a healthier one.

Loop

The constant hustle and bustle of Chicago's main business district is named after the El train tracks that make a loop around the area. Their clickety-clack noise is an intrinsic part of the soundtrack of the Windy City.

Today's Loop

This neighborhood has a culinary resonance, as well, one that is perpetually evolving with the region. It wasn't that long ago that the Loop locked up at night. When offices, housed in the great iconic Chicago skyscrapers, closed at 5:00 P.M., so did the surrounding businesses, and thus, the area remained quiet and deserted. However, thanks to a revitalized Theater District, new residential living, hotels, and student dorms, there are now renewed restaurants, thrilling wine boutiques, and gorgeous grocery stores open past dusk. Local foodies and visitors with queries can now contact the Chicago Cultural Center's "culinary concierges" with any food tourism-related question.

Sensational Spreads

Start your voyage and begin exploring at Block 37, one of the city's original 58 blocks. It took decades of work, and several political dynasties, but the block is now home to a new five-story atrium with shopping, restaurants, and entrances to public transportation lines. Here, you'll find Japanese cream puff sensation **Beard Papa**, with its *mochi* ice cream, *fondant au chocolat*, mango ice showers, and vanilla-filled baked obsessions. Probiotic **Starfruit Cafe** with a spectrum of delicious frozen yogurts also has an outpost here, as does **Andy's Frozen Custard**, a more decadent choice for travelers thirsty for a treat.

There are also several quick food options on the Pedway level that are popular for office lunches. (The Pedway system of tunnels links crucial downtown buildings underground, which is essential during those cruel Chicago winters.) In the same vein, for a quick grab and go lunch, **Hannah's Bretzel** (131 S. Dearborn St.) is ideal. Lauded as "über sandwich makers," their version of the namesake is fashioned from freshly-baked German bread and features ultra-divine fillings. While their menu may resemble that of an average diner, one bite into their sandwiches (perhaps the grass-fed sirloin special spread with showers of nutty Gruyére, vine tomatoes, field greens, onions, and spicy horseradish aïoli), and find yourself in sandwich nirvana.

Chicago Chocolate Tours gives two-plus hour tastes of downtown's candy and baked icons' sites on Thursdays and Fridays. These delicious walking tours leave from Macy's State Street location. Another popular preference is **Tastebud Tours**, which has a Loop option on its daily tour menu. Stops include hot dogs, pizza, and **The Berghoff**—the city's oldest restaurant. Check out the historic Berghoff bar for lunch, dinner, dessert, and of course, steins of beer. Also terrific is Berghoff's pre-theater, prix-fixe menu that reveals such juicy eats as *sauerbraten*, potato pierogies, and Thai codfish cakes. Their bevy of beers (think: the Berghoff Seasonal Special, Prairie Lager, and Sundown Dark) will keep you quenched; and if you're in the mood for something lighter, root for the root beer. When strolling these grounds, don't miss the range of public art that pops up in many of the government plazas and other open spaces across the Loop. Summer also brings a mélange of musical performances to Millennium Park, Grant Park, and the Petrillo Music Shell, that is just begging for a picnic *en plein air*.

Market Carousing

During warmer months, several farmers' markets cater to the downtown crowd, including the ones at Federal Plaza on Tuesdays and Daley Plaza on Thursdays. Concession carts freckle the streets of various locations in nearby Millennium Park, and are perfect for grabbing a snack whilst sauntering. Some years ago, produce options increased dramatically with the opening of **Chicago's Downtown Farmstand**, a locally focused vegetable purveyor on Randolph Street that showcases a wide selection of colorful produce. Lake Street's **Pastoral Artisan Cheese** (a favorite of both *Saveur* Magazine and locals alike) is the go-to, made-to-order sandwich haven for the Loop's lunch crowd. The city is filled with

caffeine addicts as well as coffee connoisseurs; and sightseeing is tiring, so make sure you get a pick-me-up at **Intelligentsia Coffee**, a local coffee chain with an emphasis on direct trade. Locations can be found all over town, but the **Millennium Park Coffeebar** is particularly convenient and delicious. Outfitted with an industrial-style decor, it reflects the architecture of nearby Millennium Park. Caffeine junkies also appreciate the several **Torrefazione Italia** locations dotting maps of the Loop. And of course, no trip to Chicago, much less the Loop, would be complete without munching on **Garrett Popcorn**. Head to one of their three Loop locations (follow the aroma for directions) for cheese, caramel, pecan, and other enticingly flavored popcorn.

Taste of Chicago

The Taste of Chicago is one of the city's biggest events. This 10-day summer fête in Grant Park draws hordes of hungry diners and food gourmands from near and far. (The park itself was incorporated before the city was founded.) For the last 30 years, local restaurants have set up scores of food booths that feature delicacies from around the globe. The place is packed for the 10-day duration, thanks to the great food and live music, but come July 4th weekend, it's a bit of a madhouse! This ever-beloved festival is now the second-largest attraction in the state; and the revered (local) **Eli's Cheesecake** is the sole remaining original Taste of Chicago exhibitor. In 2010, it celebrated its 30th anniversary with a giant, creamy cheesecake.

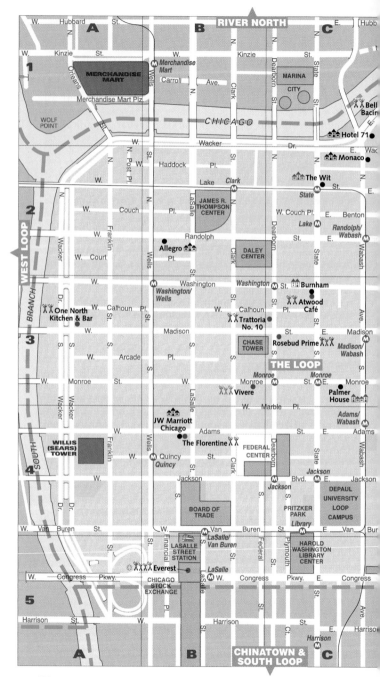

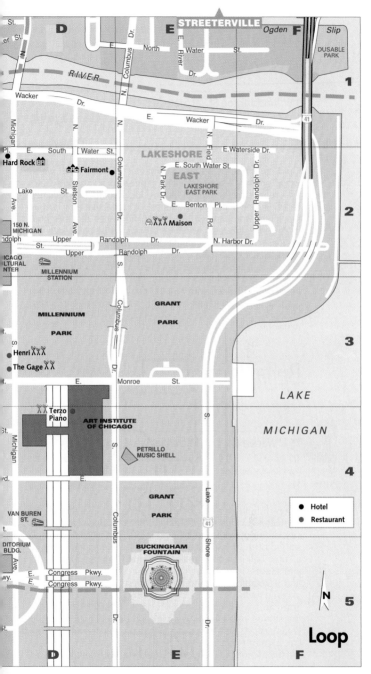

Atwood Café

C3

Contemporary ✗✗

1 W. Washington St. (at State St.)

Phone: 312-368-1900

Web: www.atwoodcafe.com

Prices: $$

Lunch & dinner daily

🚇 Washington

Gold-curtained windows, sculptural sconces, and warm wood accents leave a striking impression at Atwood Café. The refined setting plays up its location in the Reliance Building–one of the first modern skyscrapers that now houses the Hotel Burnham–with art deco flourishes that heighten its historic grandeur. Attentive service keeps pace with the business lunch scene, State Street shoppers, and dinner guests making the most of a prime pre-theater location.

The turn-of-the-century setting gives way to a contemporary Mediterranean-influenced menu that features dishes such as shrimp chowder with feta cheese and crispy tasso ham garnish; pan-roasted lake trout with celery root purée, toasted almonds, and arugula; or slow-roasted rabbit with date *gastrique*.

Bella Bacinos

C1

Italian ✗✗

75 E. Wacker Dr. (bet. Michigan Ave. & State St.)

Phone: 312-263-2350

Web: www.bellabacinos.com

Prices: $$

Lunch & dinner daily

🚇 State/Lake

Deep-dish, thin-crust, or stuffed, Chicagoans love their pizza no matter how it is sliced and Bella Bacinos, one of four in the city, dishes up some fantastic pizza with top ingredients. It all started over 30 years ago when Dan Bacin decided to throw a curve ball into pizza making. No more canned ingredients and sauces. Instead, Bacin used the freshest meats, cheeses, and vegetables he could find. The result? Some of the best pizza in town.

You can have it any way you want it at Bella Bacinos, but the stuffed pizza is always a pleaser. This location, in the landmark Mather Tower, has a swanky décor with a lively bar. It's more than just pizza (hearty pastas and entrées round out the menu), but really, why would you want anything else?

Everest ✿

French 🍴🍴🍴🍴

B5

440 S. LaSalle St. (bet. Congress Pkwy. & Van Buren St.)

Phone: 312-663-8920
Dinner Tue – Sat

Web: www.everestrestaurant.com

Prices: $$$$

🚇 LaSalle/Van Buren

Lettuce Entertain You

The name makes perfect sense, once you have ascended the forty floors of the Chicago Stock Exchange to this dramatic view of the city skyline. But, regardless of how the market performs, Everest is always up. Naturally, on a clear night window tables are prime real estate here. The updated room is not large, though mirrors impart the illusion of space; while billowing fabrics, white columns, and tabletop sculptures fashion a look that, depending on your age and stage, is either timeless or dated. Yet, no one is complaining, as the mood is always just right for celebrations.

Everest's classic Alsatian menu is a pleasant departure from the city's more ubiquitous cuisines. The beautiful and fertile marriage between Franco-Germanic ingredients and flavors is rightly evident in smoked salmon curls and herbaceous *fleischnacka* gently garnished with tangy *melfor aigrelette* and crème fraîche swirls. Take your eyes off the view for a moment to coddle a foie gras terrine which changes regularly but is always a delicious way to start.

And to close, the *baba*–based on an 18th century Alsatian recipe–packs a fantastically boozy punch with fluffy, rum-soaked cake paired with pineapple-raisin ice cream.

The Florentine

Italian   ✗✗

B4

151 W. Adams St. (bet. LaSalle & Wells Sts.)

Phone: 312-660-8866   Lunch & dinner daily
Web: www.the-florentine.net
Prices: **$$**   🚇 Quincy

Forget you're entering a JW Marriott and pretend you're living *la dolce vita* instead, while ascending a grand double spiral staircase to the second floor of the historic Continental & Commercial National Bank Building. A spacious, high-ceilinged room decked out in lush materials—marble bar, walnut flooring, velvet booths, and saddle leather seats—radiates a mien of modern Italian luxury.

Under the chef's watchful eye, the contemporary Italian cuisine is a notch above typical hotel dining. Antipasti like grilled octopus with tomatoes, *ceci*, and salsa verde are faithful renditions with strong flavors. Entrées include delicate pan-fried Lake Superior whitefish with pesto and pine nut relish; or braised short ribs with mascarpone creamed polenta.

The Gage

Gastropub   ✗✗

D3

24 S. Michigan Ave. (bet. Madison & Monroe Sts.)

Phone: 312-372-4243   Lunch & dinner daily
Web: www.thegagechicago.com
Prices: **$$**   🚇 Madison

In a sprawling set of historic buildings directly opposite Millennium Park, The Gage provides refuge from the teeming Michigan Avenue crowds—and has abundant room to hold them all. Clubby leather booths and celadon-tiled columns bring decorum to this bustling space. Sit at the long, curving counter flanked by old posters to get your sports fix, or stake your claim at one of the many tables for a more leisurely meal. The broad menu covers British pub classics like Scotch eggs while appropriating international flavors with flair. Rich and satisfying fondue does rarebit one better with the addition of spinach and baguette slices; and piles of thinly sliced pork belly, pickles, grilled onions, and smoked Gouda comprise a fresh version of the Cuban sandwich.

Henri

D3   French XXX

18 S. Michigan Ave. (bet. Madison & Monroe Sts.)

Phone: 312-578-0763   Lunch Mon – Fri
Web: www.henrichicago.com   Dinner nightly
Prices: $$$ 🚇 Monroe

A restaurant with prime Michigan Avenue real estate likely doesn't need to fuss too much since foot traffic is guaranteed, but Henri has established itself as an elegant and charming hideaway on this otherwise tourist-clogged stretch. Charcoal walls offset breathtaking views of Millennium Park, while pendant chandeliers provide a romantic flush for couples settling into plush seats.

The modern French-inspired dishes are as polished as their surroundings. A quivering quail egg in its shell crowns gently smoked steak tartare; warm root vegetables and rich, lemon-infused, caper-butter sauce offset pristine and pale Dover sole meunière. Finish on a dramatic note with dense but moist spiced-pear Savarin with tart pomegranate "soup" and crème fraîche.

Maison 😊

E2   French XXX

333 E. Randolph St. (bet. Benton Pl. & Randolph St.)

Phone: 312-241-1540   Lunch Mon – Fri
Web: www.maisonbrasserie.com   Dinner nightly
Prices: $$ 🚇 Randolph

Well-heeled business executives and informal tourists flock to this chic and urbane penthouse bistro in the new Lakeshore East development on the north end of Grant Park. Under a pale arched ceiling and dangling lacy black umbrella lampshades, full-length windows look out on park and skyscraper views that show off both the city's architectural curves and natural beauty.

Peek through a tinted glass cutout in a marble wall to watch as the kitchen brings renewed life to brasserie staples served on vibrantly graphic cheese plates. Dishes may include a deboned whole trout *amandine* capped with lemon brown butter and green beans; *salade Lyonnaise* with a warm poached egg and tangy bacon vinaigrette; or profiteroles drizzled tableside with dark chocolate sauce.

One North Kitchen & Bar

American ✕✕

A3

1 N. Wacker Dr. (bet. Madison & Washington Sts.)

Phone:	312-750-9700	Lunch & dinner Mon – Fri
Web:	www.restaurants-america.com	
Prices:	$$	🚇 Washington

Besuited business lunchers–those harried denizens of the FiDi–pile into this corporate echo chamber and hunch around white linen-topped tables to chow down and shrug off work worries for a brief hour. When the weather behaves, the cubicle-bound rush to fill the outdoor seating and soak up the rays in the midst of a busy workday. Arrive early to get the best service before the lunch crowds descend.

The menu accommodates those grabbing a bite on the run with bar food-style plates that span the globe from maki to crispy chicken tacos spiced with roasted corn salsa. Those who have more time appreciate the bulked-up sandwiches loaded with slaw and fries; health-conscious salads; and seafood entrées like ginger-crusted tuna frilled with pearl onions.

Rosebud Prime

Steakhouse ✕✕✕

C3

1 S. Dearborn St. (at Madison St.)

Phone:	312-384-1900	Lunch Mon – Fri
Web:	www.rosebudrestaurants.com	Dinner nightly
Prices:	$$$	🚇 Monroe

Class and elegance drift through the striking bi-level dining space, where luxurious rose banquettes, soaring ceilings, and a gorgeous mezzanine create an air of sophistication. Knowledgeable, tuxedo-clad servers rapidly fire off daily specials, though still maintain passion and sincerity. Thin, crispy, salted raisin bread and fresh rolls with honey butter start things off right, while scrumptious starters like peppercorn ahi tuna with ginger soy, coconut shrimp, and smoked salmon pastrami please the palate.

Slice into a juicy *petit* filet, seared just so and served with a side of jus. Complete the decadence with fresh blueberries, raspberries, and strawberries coupled with velvety sabayon—whipped with a touch of cream and spiked with Grand Marnier.

Terzo Piano

Italian

D4

159 E. Monroe St. (bet. Columbus Dr. & Michigan Ave.)

Phone: 312-443-8650
Web: www.terzopianochicago.com
Prices: $$$

Lunch daily
Dinner Thu
🚇 Monroe

Setting a restaurant within the Art Institute of Chicago's Modern Wing leads to heightened aesthetic expectations, and Terzo Piano meets every one. A bright white room with clean lines befitting a Malevich composition is comfortably scattered with tables offering up Stieglitz-worthy skyline views. Stroll in from the museum or enter via the suspended bridge from Millennium Park.

The kitchen takes pride in making all menu elements from scratch, executing refined and delightful farm-to-table cuisine. Seasonal ingredients from local farms lead to a frequently changing menu, which may include eggy *fettuccini alla chitarra* tossed with spring garlic and almond pesto; or milk chocolate *cremeux* tucked between toasted brioche and placed atop raspberry jam.

Trattoria No. 10

Italian

C3

10 N. Dearborn St. (bet. Madison & Washington Sts.)

Phone: 312-984-1718
Web: www.trattoriaten.com
Prices: $$

Lunch Mon – Fri
Dinner Mon – Sat
🚇 Washington

Pick up the phone before stepping in to Trattoria No. 10, since reservations are an absolute must at this clubby, cozy, and inviting spot. Located below street level, this charming place feels a world away from the hustle and bustle, but take a look around and you'll find Loop lawyers and other business people brokering deals over dishes like grilled calamari or sausage-stuffed ravioli.

The rustic Italian specialties are what keep this spot on the speed dial of so many area power brokers. From house-made ravioli with butternut and acorn squash in sweet walnut butter sauce, and Berkshire pork osso buco with mascarpone mashed potatoes, to farfalle with duck confit, asparagus, mushrooms, pearl onions, and pine nuts, it's gourmet comfort food defined.

Vivere

Italian XXX

B3

71 W. Monroe St. (bet. Clark & Dearborn Sts.)

Phone: 312-332-4040
Web: www.vivere-chicago.com
Prices: $$

Lunch Mon – Fri
Dinner Mon – Sat
Monroe

Within the venerable Italian Village restaurant family, Vivere is the relative spring chicken of the group, with only two decades on the job compared to its sibling's 85 years of tradition. The third-generation owners keep the experience as sparkling as the copper and brass in the dining room, mixing formality with spirited charm in a vibrant and curvaceous wood-toned space.

Italian specialties abound here: tiered layers of smoked *scamorza*, spinach, and San Marzano tomato sauce in *pasticcio affumicato* warm with each forkful; while linguini Calabrese is redolent with jumbo lump crab, shaved garlic, and Calabrian red chili rings. Exceptional pheasant *agnolottini* is justly lauded. Allow the well-informed staff to guide you through the vast wine selection.

Your opinions are important to us. Please write to us directly at: michelin.guides@ us.michelin.com

Pilsen, Little Italy & University Village

This cluster of neighborhoods packs a perfect punch, both in terms of food, spice, and sheer energy level. It lives up to every expectation and reputation, so get ready for a tour packed with literal, acoustic, and visual flavor. The Little Italy moniker applies to one stretch of Taylor Street. While it abuts the University (of Illinois at Chicago) Village neighborhood, Little Italy is bigger and more authentically Italian than it first appears. Make your way through these streets only to find that they are

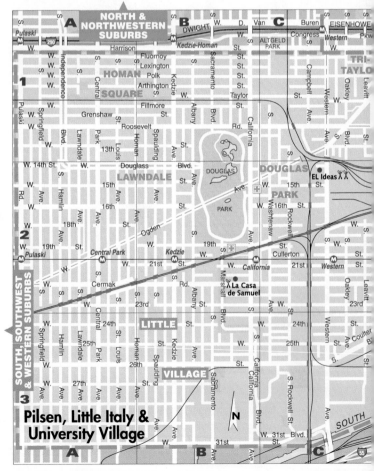

as stuffed with epicurean shops as an Italian beef sandwich is with meat. And, while on the topic, try a prime example of this iconic Chicago sandwich at the aptly named **Al's No. 1 Italian Beef**. When in Little Italy, one must start with **Conte Di Savoia**, an Italian grocery and popular takeout lunch counter. In June, folks flock here for the Oakley Festa Pasta Vino festival. Wash lunch down with a frozen fruit slush from **Mario's Italian Lemonade**. Lemon is the most popular flavor from the cash-only stand, but offbeat varieties like chocolate and banana are also refreshing. On further strolling along these vibrant grounds, make sure you gander the Christopher Columbus statue, which was originally commissioned for the 1893 World's Columbian Exposition.

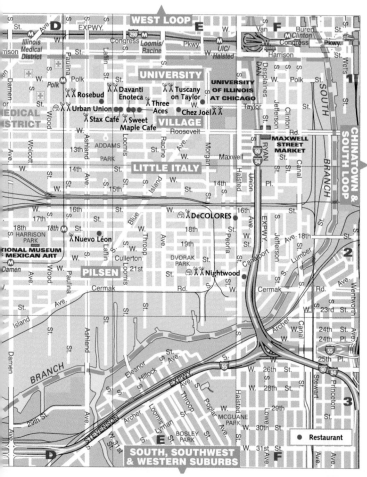

UNIVERSITY VILLAGE

Like any self-respecting college "town," University Village houses a deluge of toasty coffee shops and cafés. A population of doctors, medical students, nurses, and others working in the neighborhood hospital contributes to an always-on-the-move vibe. **Lush Wine & Spirits** sells the expected, plus local obsession **Salted Caramel** is noted for its popcorn, especially the bacon-Bourbon variety.

On Sundays, the destination is the legendary **Maxwell Street Market**. Relocated to Desplaines Street in 2008, this sprawling market welcomes more than 500 vendors selling produce, Mexican street food including tamales and tacos, and non-food miscellanea. Celebrity chef, Rick Bayless and the like shop here for locally grown tomatoes and tomatillos; while others buy ingredients for at-home culinary creations (not to mention tires, tube socks, and other flea market fare). Maxwell Street Market is also *the* choice for authentic Mexican delicacies.

PILSEN AND LITTLE VILLAGE

Chicago's massive Mexican population (more than 500,000 per the last U.S. Census count) has built a patchwork of regional Mexican specialties, many of which are found in the south side's residential Pilsen and Little Village neighborhoods. Pilsen is home to the free National Museum of Mexican Art, the only Latino museum accredited by the American Association of Museums, as well as an abundance of authentic Mexican taquerias, bakeries, and other culturally relevant businesses. Everyone goes all out for Mexican Independence Day in September, including more than 25 participating area restaurants, while the Little Village Arts Festival packs 'em in October.

Stop by sumptuous **Sabinas Food Products** factory for freshly-made tortillas and chips to take home, followed by a trip to the Tuesday farmer's market at the Chicago Community Bank. Much of Pilsen's 26th Street is filled with auto chop shops and other workaday businesses. But the large-scale tortilla factories, where three or four women press and form corn tortillas, are an exception. Since 1950, **El Milagro** has offered a unique taste, with a cafeteria-style restaurant (presenting seven kinds of tamales on the menu) and a store that sells burritos, spiced corn chips, maize, and those locally made tortillas. And while feasting, don't forget to fix your eyes upon the mural on the wall. Environment-conscious fans can't resist the siren call of **Simone's Bar**. They all congregate at this certified green restaurant and place-to-be-seen for some quality beers, stirring cocktails, and first-rate food. Whether you perch on the patio, in "The Lab," or in their front room, the likes of empanadas, portobello fries (complete with a soy dipping sauce), and a black & blue grilled steak (topped with tomatoes, blue cheese, and fresh basil) are bound to have you smitten.

Chez Joël

French 🍴🍴

E1

1119 W. Taylor St. (bet. Aberdeen & May Sts.)

Phone: 312-226-6479
Web: www.chezjoelbistro.com
Prices: $$

Lunch Tue – Sat
Dinner Tue – Sun

A bit of Paris has landed in Little Italy with Chez Joël, the charming, red-brick corner bistro with its Francophile following and tasty fare. Gilded mirrors, pale yellow walls, a stunning crystal-beaded chandelier, and red velvet-draped windows weave an aura of timelessness, while French oldies piping through speakers add to the romance.

Owned and operated by brothers Joël and Ahmed Kazouini, the beloved spot spins out bistro favorites like crocks of French onion soup with a deliciously browned and bubbly lid of cheese; steamed mussels with white wine; crème brûlée; and profiteroles. Cocktails like the Bleu Margarita and the Calvados Royale also have a sexy accent. In warmer weather, snag a seat in the breezy courtyard and dine under the trees.

Davanti Enoteca

Italian 🍴🍴

E1

1359 W. Taylor St. (at Loomis St.)

Phone: 312-226-5550
Web: www.davantichicago.com
Prices: $$

Lunch & dinner daily

With its warming wood-burning oven, brick arches displaying wine, and robust selection of Italian dishes, Davanti Enoteca knows how to combat Chicago's coldest winters. Sunny windows and French doors that open to the outside world on warmer days assure that this is a lovely spot, no matter the time of year.

The kitchen finds inspiration in classic Italian favorites, yet caters to Chicago's tastes. Irresistible mounds of spaghetti *cacio e pepe* are richer than the traditional Roman dish, but this creamier rendition boasts a luscious, pecorino-based sauce that is nonetheless delicious. While dishes are not often complex, they highlight superior ingredients, as in the seared Nantucket Bay scallops in a hearty, delicate, and fresh cauliflower soup.

DeCOLORES ☺

E2

1626 S. Halsted St. (bet. 16th & 17th Sts.)

Phone: 312-226-9886
Web: www.decolor.us
Prices: $$

Lunch Thu – Sun
Dinner nightly

DeCOLORES isn't just a festive family-run Mexican restaurant; it's a *galeria y sabores*, a gallery that fits right into Pilsen's art district showcasing local artists. The often-changing artwork, illuminated by skylights and wide window panes throughout the stylish space, matches the creativity on each plate that comes from recipes passed down through generations.

After homemade corn chips with two salsas (green tomatillo or smoky roasted red pepper), choose from ceviches, grilled meats, shrimp-centric seafood dishes, and specialties like *taquitos de papa*—a vegetarian explosion of shredded beets, chayote, purple cabbage, mashed potatoes, and tart tomato-citrus sauce. Even though it's BYOB, the bar generously offers chilled beer glasses and mixers.

EL Ideas

C2

2419 W. 14th St. (at Western Ave.)

Phone: 312-226-8144
Web: www.elideas.com
Prices: $$$$

Dinner Tue – Sat

Western (Pink)

Hidden on a dead end street, EL Ideas pays homage to the city's train system via elevated ideas in cuisine. Stealing the spotlight is a cadre of male cooks chatting up diners in the wide-open kitchen. Amid this interactive set, finer details like white linens and sparkling crystal for that (BYO) bevy lend a highbrow feel.

High-backed chairs make this multi-course meal a supremely enjoyable affair. Ensuring new heights of intimacy, the "creator" himself may demand you to lick your plate of foie gras mousse with *togarashi* and yuzu-sake. Meanwhile, seared scallops with miso butter and dashi foam; trio of rabbit with chicory-wrapped *rillettes* and tender sausage; or a creamy egg yolk mingled with sturgeon bacon and toasted brioche showcase sublime skill.

La Casa De Samuel

B2

Mexican 🍴

2834 W. Cermak Rd. (bet. California Ave. & Marshall Blvd.)

Phone: 773-376-7474

Lunch & dinner daily

Web: www.lacasadesamuel.com

Prices: 💷

 California (Pink)

This Mexican jewel has been tossing tortillas since 1989, and it's still going strong. Packed with everyone from *familias* to couples, wallet-friendly La Casa de Samuel draws them in with juicy, flavorful dishes topped with aromatic sauces. From the chunky salsa made with toasted chilies to the crêpes flambé prepared tableside and doused with flaming Cointreau for added drama, everything is good from start to finish.

The most exotic offerings can be skipped, but do try the baby eels, venison, or oven-baked goat. The more usual suspects include the *taco de cecina* (a tasty mixture of salty beef and crunchy bits with white onion and cilantro) and *tacos al pastor* with roasted pork, marinated in the spicy-red achiote paste made with annatto seeds.

Nightwood

F2

Contemporary 🍴🍴

2119 S. Halsted St. (at 21st St.)

Phone: 312-526-3385

Lunch Sun

Web: www.nightwoodrestaurant.com

Dinner Mon – Sat

Prices: $$

Despite its ultra-modern, loft-like vibe, a sense of soulfulness pervades Nightwood, bringing to mind warm thoughts of hearth and home. Clearly proud of the restaurant's commitment to farm-sourced, seasonal ingredients, the staff makes every detail testament to their mission, and the steady stream of customers rewards their effort.

An open bar, kitchen, and shelving throughout the space matches the full transparency of the constantly changing menu, which showcases peak-of-the-season ingredients like spring's fiddlehead ferns presented with a wood-grilled Slagel Farm veal chop. Even potentially curious dishes like smoked trout and creamy cheese wrapped in mortadella and dressed in honey mustard turn out to be gorgeously interesting spreads.

Nuevo Léon

Mexican

D2

1515 W. 18th St. (bet. Ashland Ave. & Laflin St.)

Phone: 312-421-1517 Lunch & dinner daily
Web: www.nuevoleonrestaurant.com
Prices: 18th

From the minute your feet step on the clay tiles inside this Mexican eatery, you'll be transported into the cultural ambience for which Pilsen is known. Take in the artifacts like hand-painted plates and murals on the walls, and Mexican music blasting.

Like any good Mexican joint, this local darling has combination platters on the menu, and they're the finest way to get a cross-section of the kitchen's best. The *carne a la Tampiqueña* includes simply-seasoned tender grilled beef, tomato-scented rice, beans, and both a tomatillo-lime salsa verde and smoky red chile salsa, which elevate the taste to something extraordinary. The *horchata* is well-spiced and soups of the day vary by season. Large portion sizes mean leftovers for lunch *mañana*.

Rosebud

Italian

D1

1500 W. Taylor St. (at Laflin St.)

Phone: 312-942-1117 Lunch & dinner daily
Web: www.rosebudrestaurants.com
Prices: $$ Polk

Handsomely appointed and sultry even at lunch, Rosebud evokes those Italian red sauce joints where deals are brokered by wise guys in hushed voices over the likes of a fat pork chop Calabrese. This is the original location that launched a mini-chain of Rosebuds throughout Chicago, and its nostalgic charm still retains its character—as well as the characters who've been coming here for more than 30 years.

Live out your Godfather fantasy in a seat by the leaded glass windows, watched over by a painting of the Chairman of the Board while slurping down *pasta e fagioli*, sausage and peppers, or chicken Vesuvio. And since we're reliving this fantastical classic, leave the gun, as they say, and take the crispy cannoli garnished with pistachios and strawberries.

Stax Café

American ✗

E1

1401 W. Taylor St. (at Loomis St.)

Phone: 312-733-9871
Web: www.staxcafe.com
Prices:

Lunch daily

Comfortable seats, fresh juice, and French toast: the perfect recipe for a classic brunch hangout. At Stax, an airy nook near the UIC campus, staffers in t-shirts with cheeky slogans ("We are Breakfast Poets. Oh, how we love thee") swiftly refill coffee mugs and deliver eggs Benedict and burgers to sleepy-eyed eaters.

Breakfast and lunch options are wide-ranging: omelets like the Spanish Harlem, filled with chorizo, roasted tomatoes, poblanos, and *queso fresco*, are beautifully fluffy and light. Ham and cheese crêpes with honey mustard walk the line between sweet and savory; and heavenly ricotta pancakes with strawberry-rhubarb compote sweeten the morning. Eyeing the mini chocolate Bundt cake? Snag it at the start of your meal—desserts sell out early.

Sweet Maple Cafe

E1

American ✗

1339 W. Taylor St. (bet. Loomis St. & Racine Ave.)

Phone: 312-243-8908
Web: www.sweetmaplecafe.com
Prices:

Lunch daily

You know that neighborhood breakfast spot where locals grab a cup of coffee *en route* to tide them over while they stand in line outside waiting for a table? In Little Italy, Southern-style Sweet Maple Cafe is definitely that place, with a smidge of Southern charm and hospitality mixed in.

Regulars love the large, fluffy pancakes (with honey, applesauce, butter, and syrup); scrambled eggs served with flavorful country-style pork sausage patties; and, requisite at any place that calls itself "Southern," those flaky biscuits and buttery grits. Sweet Maple Cafe also serves lunch, but breakfast is offered through the afternoon; and with such tasty omelets, home fries, plus a range of morning delights, why would you you even bother about lunch?

Three Aces

Gastropub

1321 W. Taylor St. (bet. Loomis & Throop Sts.)

Phone: 312-243-1577 — Lunch & dinner daily
Web: www.threeaceschicago.com
Prices: $$ — Racine

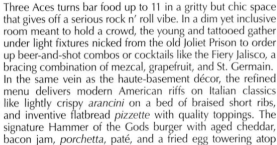

Three Aces turns bar food up to 11 in a gritty but chic space that gives off a serious rock n' roll vibe. In a dim yet inclusive room meant to hold a crowd, the young and tattooed gather under light fixtures nicked from the old Joliet Prison to order up beer-and-shot combos or cocktails like the Fiery Jalisco, a bracing combination of mezcal, grapefruit, and St. Germain.

In the same vein as the haute-basement décor, the refined menu delivers modern American riffs on Italian classics like lightly crispy *arancini* on a bed of braised short ribs, and inventive flatbread *pizzette* with quality toppings. The signature Hammer of the Gods burger with aged cheddar, bacon jam, *porchetta*, paté, and a fried egg towering atop juicy beef is a one-of-kind showstopper.

Tuscany on Taylor

Italian XX

1014 W. Taylor St. (bet. Miller & Morgan Sts.)

Phone: 312-829-1990 — Lunch Mon – Fri
Web: www.tuscanychicago.com — Dinner nightly
Prices: $$ — UIC-Halsted

Gazing down the parchment-lined walls in this airy dining room, hungry visitors can't help but notice (and smell) an open kitchen straight out of a Tuscan culinary brochure. Cooks in chef's toques bustle among polished copper pans and shelves stocked with pasta and San Marzano tomatoes next to a wood-fired oven that sets the stage for a classic *festa Italiana*.

The menu boasts an array of pizzas, but also offers appetizing versions of traditional and modern items like sausage-stuffed agnolotti in a fennel- and tomato-cream sauce, trailed by decadent cocoa-dusted squares of tiramisu. If the values on the wine list don't excite, savants who like to store their own stash can take advantage of the brass nameplate-engraved wine lockers at the entrance.

Urban Union

International XX

1421 W. Taylor St. (bet. Laflin & Loomis Sts.)

Phone: 312-929-4302
Web: www.urbanunionchicago.com
Prices: $$

Dinner nightly

 Polk

Mix-and-match is the name of the game at Urban Union. Counters and communal seating throughout the cavernous space are primo for sipping wine by the glass (ten of which are on tap), and industrial-chic plank tables are scattered with shareable plates arriving from the open kitchen. Prices may match the portions, but the bill, like stacks of dishes, can add up quickly.

The handwritten menu changes often, though the focus remains on seafood—a raw bar teems with oysters and clams, and a wood-burning oven handles mussels, head-on shrimp, and even olives. Meat courses like grilled flank steak with buttered Thumbelina carrots are simple yet delectable, while crispy chocolate "copy kat" cake is so divine, it should be packaged and sold for future snack attacks.

Look for the symbol 🛏
for a brilliant breakfast to
start your day off right.

River North

Art galleries, a hopping nightlife, well-known restaurants and chefs, swanky shopping, great views, even a head-turning fast-food chain: Almost everything that Chicago boasts is offered here. Perhaps because River North offers so much it also attracts so many. From ladies who lunch and office workers, to tour bus-style tourists, most folks who pass through the Windy City make a stop here.

Beyond the Ordinary

River North (which, it stands to reason, is located north of the Chicago River) has no shortage of food and drink attractions. True, as you pull up to Ontario and Clark streets, you might just think, "chain restaurant central," but even the chains in River North have a particular charm. Among them is the **Rock 'n' Roll McDonald's**, a block-long, music-themed outpost of the ubiquitous burger chain. One of the busiest **MickeyD's** in the world, this one has an expanded menu, music memorabilia, and bragging rights to the first two-lane drive-through. (Remember: McDonald's is a local chain, still headquartered in the suburbs.)

The Rainforest Café (with its wild range of flesh, fowl, and fish dishes); the forever hip and boisterous **Hard Rock Café**; and **M Burger** (a noted chain rolled out by the Lettuce Entertain You Enterprise) are all quite the hit, and popular tourist draws. One of *the* most beloved burger joints, M Burger is a Michigan Avenue marvel boasting an array of juicy burgers (try the no meat Nurse Betty) alongside fries and shakes. Speaking of drive-through chains, River North is the flagship location of **Portillo's**, a local, cherished hot dog, burger, and beer chain. Its giant exterior belies its efficient service and better-than-expected food. When it comes to size, few buildings can top the mammoth **Merchandise Mart** (so large it has its own ZIP code). Along with its history, retail stores, boutiques, and drool-worthy kitchen showrooms, it is also home to two great food shops. At **Artisan Cellar**, in addition to boutique wines, paninis, and specialty cheeses, you can also purchase Katherine Anne Confections' fresh cream caramels. Locals also love **The Chopping Block** for its expertly taught and themed cooking courses, well-edited wine selections, and their newly stocked shiny knife lines. (There's another location in Lincoln Square for north side courses.) Nearby, the Cooking Hospitality Institute of Chicago, known as **CHIC**, cradles a student-run restaurant where diners can get a glimpse of the next big thing in Chicago kitchens. Well-tread by locals in the know, CHIC displays a unique blend of elegance and comfort paired with gracious service and a daily-changing bill of fare. Open Books, a used bookstore that relies on its proceeds to fund literacy programs, has plenty of cookbooks on its shelves. Outfit any kitchen with finds from the Bloomingdale's Home store in the 1912 Medinah Temple. You'll smell the **Blommer Chocolate Outlet Store** before you see it. Late at night and early in the morning, the tempting chocolate aroma wafts down the river beckoning city dwellers to its Willy Wonka-esque confines. This is where to stock up on sweets from the 70-plus-year-old-brand. Blommer's also boasts a specialty cocoa collection ranging from such fabulously sinful flavors as black cocoa, cake-based cocoa powders, and Dutch specialty varieties.

Deep-Dish Delights

River North is as good a place as any to indulge in the local phenomenon of Chicago-style, deep-dish pizza. Also called stuffed pizza (referring to the pie, but it could also refer to the way you'll feel after you snarf it down), deep-dish pizza was created in the Windy City in the 1940s. Closer to a casserole (or, as they say in the Midwest, "hot dish,") than an Italian-style pizza, this is a thick, doughy crust, holding abundant cheese, sauce, and tasty toppings.

Some say it is Chicago water in the dough that makes that crust so distinctive. Deep-dish pies take a while to fashion, so be prepared to wait wherever you go. **Pizzeria Uno** (or its sister **Pizzeria Due**), and **Giordano's** are some of the best-known pie makers. If a little indigestion isn't a concern, chase down that priceless pizza with another Chicago-style specialty:

The Italian beef sandwich. Very much like a messy, yet tasty French dip, an Italian beef isn't Italian, but all Chicago. Dating back to the 1930s, it featured thinly-sliced, seasoned beef on a hoagie crowned with either hot or sweet peppers. If you order it "wet," both the meat and the bread will be dipped in pan juices. You could also add cheese, but this isn't Philly! Two of the biggest contenders in the Italian beef wars are in this 'hood: **Al's Italian Beef** and **Mr. Beef**. Both eateries have top-notch sausages and hot dogs on the menu as well.

Get Your Groove On

Nightlife in River North is a big deal with everything from authentic Irish pubs to cocktail lounges, for those who like to see-and-be-seen. Nestled in the landmark Chicago Historical Society Building, **Excalibur** is a multi-floor dance club and is all about velvet ropes, house music, and an epic drink list. **Blue Chicago** is a civilized place where you can sip on a drink and listen to that world-famous Chicago sound, the Blues. **English**, an aptly named British bar, is a popular watering hole for watching soccer and other sports, not usually broadcasted at your typical Chicago sports bar. English is also home to "Top Chef" alumna, Radhika Desai. And finally, don't skip the **Green Door Tavern**, which gets its name from the fact that its colored front told Prohibition-era customers where to enter for a drink. Order their "famous sandwich" or "Green Door Burger" and you will understand what all the fuss is about.

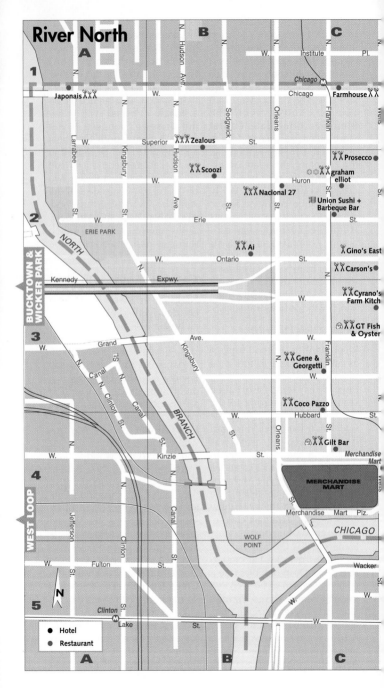

River North

A B C

Japonais ✕✕✕

Farmhouse ✕✕

Zealous ✕✕✕

Scoozi ✕✕

Prosecco ✕✕

graham elliot ✕✕✕

Nacional 27 ✕✕✕

Union Sushi + Barbeque Bar

Ai ✕✕

Gino's East ✕

Carson's ✕✕

Cyrano's Farm Kitch ✕✕

GT Fish & Oyster ✕✕

Gene & Georgetti ✕✕

Coco Pazzo ✕✕

Gilt Bar ✕✕

ERIE PARK

Merchandise Mart

MERCHANDISE MART

WOLF POINT

CHICAGO

BUCKTOWN & WICKER PARK

WEST LOOP

● Hotel
● Restaurant

N

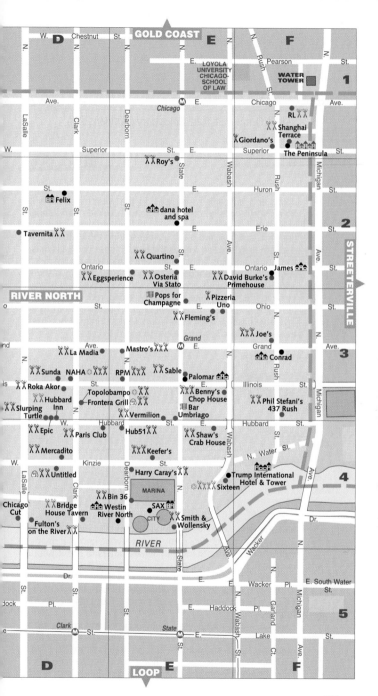

Ai

B2

Japanese

358 W. Ontario St. (bet. Kingsbury & Orleans Sts.)

Phone: 312-335-9888
Web: www.aichicago.us
Prices: $$

Lunch Mon – Fri
Dinner nightly
Chicago (Brown)

Ai's upscale Japanese cuisine meshes effortlessly with the chic shops and high-rise residences on the western outskirts of River North's design district. An action-packed open kitchen and sushi bar draws the eye in, while intricate wood and bamboo carvings and plush leather seating show attention to detail in the décor as well as the food. House cocktails make the lounge area just as popular as the capacious dining room. A lengthy menu encompasses traditional nigiri, sashimi, and maki along with contemporary bento boxes and fusion-inspired items. Pristine, delicately sliced red snapper and tempura-battered mozzarella and zucchini take a dip in an inventive dashi; while chicken *katsu* gets a zingy punch from mirin-based Japanese barbecue sauce.

Bar Umbriago

E3

Italian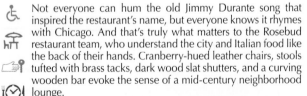

6 W. Hubbard St. (at State St.)

Phone: 312-494-1200
Web: www.barumbriago.com
Prices: $$

Lunch Mon – Fri
Dinner nightly
Grand (Red)

Not everyone can hum the old Jimmy Durante song that inspired the restaurant's name, but everyone knows it rhymes with Chicago. And that's truly what matters to the Rosebud restaurant team, who understand the city and Italian food like the back of their hands. Cranberry-hued leather chairs, stools tufted with brass tacks, dark wood slat shutters, and a curving wooden bar evoke the sense of a mid-century neighborhood lounge.

Italian-inspired dishes and wines bring a modern, *enoteca*-style touch to the throwback décor. *Bufala caprese* salad combines top ingredients for seasonal simplicity; and pastrami on toasted rye with homemade potato- and beet-chips brings a fresh face to a deli favorite. Finish with a rich Nutella *bomba* or scoop of gelato.

Benny's Chop House

E3

Steakhouse 𝕏𝕏𝕏

444 N. Wabash Ave. (bet. Hubbard & Illinois Sts.)

Phone: 312-626-2444   Lunch & dinner daily
Web: www.bennyschophouse.com
Prices: $$$ Grand (Red)

From its quiet location tucked into the shadow of the Trump Tower, this contemporary American steakhouse manages to shine. The art deco-inspired décor and casual yet very competent staff may be your first clues that Benny's stands above its many Chicago chophouse brethren, but the excellent food here is everyone's focus.

While many tables are topped with the likes of USDA Prime dry-aged steaks, other offerings are as enticing. Chopped salad is flawlessly rendered, and the only downside to oysters Rockefeller is that the preparation requires cooking such tasty shellfish. Playful, fun, and decadent treats abound in the likes of blue cheese tater tots. Portions are often generous here: the baked Alaska "for two" would more suitably feed an army.

Bin 36

E4

American 𝕏𝕏

339 N. Dearborn St. (bet. Kinzie St. & the Chicago River)

Phone: 312-755-9463   Lunch & dinner daily
Web: www.bin36.com
Prices: $$$ Lake

It's a wine store! It's a cheese shop! It's a restaurant! No, it's all three and much more inside this perennially popular downtown spot. The entrance of the cavernous multi-level space doubles as a specialty market with affordably priced bottles and a casual sit-down café with a curving bar. Further back, notice a spacious atrium and communal tables offering additional dining and sipping options from morning coffee to evening tastings and in-depth "Bin School" wine courses.

Though wine and cheese are the main focus at Bin 36, patrons interested in a more substantial nosh than a tasting plate or wine flight can sit down and choose a few of the tasty, generous, and eclectic dishes—including excellent seafood—from the contemporary American menu.

Bridge House Tavern

American XX

D4

321 N. Clark St. (on the Chicago River)

Phone: 312-644-0283   Lunch & dinner daily
Web: www.bridgehousetavern.com
Prices: $$ Lake

Take the elevator by the Clark Street bridge down to this riverside dwelling. When the sun is warm, Chicagoans clamor for Bridge House Tavern's spectacular tree-lined patio, exquisitely defined by the hum of cars crossing the bridge above and its compelling skyline vista. Inside, a brew of suits and locals crowd the onyx bar, attractively dressed with flagstone walls.

The service verges on erratic and your order may be wrong, but what a view! Grab your prime outdoor seat before the happy-hour hordes descend. An endless supply of sautéed Green City Market vegetables provide just the right crunch, while macaroni and cheese with Nueske bacon is pure decadence. The smoked salmon BLT is good, but when served with that bacon milkshake it is a showstopper.

Carson's

Barbecue XX

C2

612 N. Wells St. (at Ontario St.)

Phone: 312-280-9200   Lunch & dinner daily
Web: www.ribs.com
Prices: $$ Chicago (Red)

Fear not, barbecue fans. Though this Chicago classic underwent a face-lift, behind the slightly forbidding windowless brick walls of the Wells Street flagship, the restaurant's Old World sensibility and, most importantly, its recipe for sweet, smoky signature ribs all remain intact.

Steps away from other gut-busting Chicago food institutions including Al's Beef, Gino's East, and Mitchell's Ice Cream, Carson's continues to hold its own as the go-to spot for delectable barbecue. Pit-smoked with hickory wood for hours, the legendary slabs of baby back ribs are worth every messy bite and tender enough to gnaw all the way down to the bone. Travelers and Chicago expats can rest easy knowing that these supremely slathered wares ship overnight across the nation.

Chicago Cut

Steakhouse ✗✗✗

D4

300 N. LaSalle St. (at Wacker Dr.)

Phone: 312-329-1800
Web: www.chicagocutsteakhouse.com
Prices: $$$

Lunch & dinner daily

🛒 Merchandise Mart

In a town that's fanatically loyal to its meat, Chicago Cut rivals some of the well-tested classics that have "steaked" their claim on the city's bellies for decades. Diners pack the place wall-to-wall from breakfast through dinner, admiring the river views in this glossy modern steakhouse and choosing a bottle from the extensive iPad wine list.

Though it's a menu fixture, the gently charred, wet-aged, bone-in filet mignon sells out quickly, so snag the cut if it's available. It wouldn't be a steakhouse without lots of spuds and creamy greens on the side; the house-made hollandaise sauce served with asparagus is a perfect foil for both meat and vegetables. Split the dessert: one order of nutty, spicy carrot cake is large enough to feed a four-top.

Coco Pazzo

Italian ✗✗

C3

300 W. Hubbard St. (at Franklin St.)

Phone: 312-836-0900
Web: www.cocopazzochicago.com
Prices: $$

Lunch Mon – Fri
Dinner nightly
🛒 Merchandise Mart

Windows framed with cheery blue and orange awnings are the first sign of welcome, but the real Italian greeting comes upon entering Coco Pazzo to see a prosciutto leg displayed prominently on a carving cradle. Add this to bowls of antipasti laid out on a serving stand, and a Bellini atop the dark wood bar or linen-topped table, and you know the type of conviviality that is in store here.

Tuscan cuisine, rustic by nature, gets a polished sheen in the open kitchen, where the line takes great care to turn out unfussy but flavorful preparations. Freshly sliced smoked beef carpaccio with goat cheese sauce and roasted hazelnuts balances taste and texture; and a dusting of grated *bottarga* on crispy sea bass and tender, garlicky lima beans adds a luxe touch.

Cyrano's Farm Kitchen

C3

546 N. Wells St. (bet. Grand Ave. & Ohio St.)

Phone: 312-467-0546
Web: N/A
Prices: $$

Dinner Mon – Sat

Grand (Red)

A recent revamp of the River North standby Cyrano's still transports diners to the South of France via cuisine and décor—now however, it's more country farm mouse than city bistro mouse. Quaintly rustic touches like walls covered in gray hay-hued plaster and ancient farm implements as well as a few rooster decorations for effect, set the charming stage. As befits the newly rustic concept, the menu emphasizes farm-to-table food by way of Provence, while still retaining bistro classics. *Salade Niçoise* is expertly composed and layered with crisp beans, poached egg, and brined red onions; whereas onion soup remains a French standard. End by dipping decadent foie gras-filled beignets into a trio of sweet dipping sauces-cherry compote anyone?

David Burke's Primehouse

F2

616 N. Rush St. (bet. Ohio & Ontario Sts.)

Phone: 312-660-6000
Web: www.davidburkesprimehouse.com
Prices: $$$

Lunch & dinner daily

Grand (Red)

This outpost of prolific restaurateur David Burke is located in the chic James hotel. David Burke's Primehouse is true to its name and focus: the crux of the menu features bone-in cuts of USDA Prime dry-aged in-house, in a Himalayan salt-tiled aging room. This is an easy and suitably handsome space in which to enjoy an impressive steak—matched with two privately labeled bottles, a sauce named after their late bull 207L and another spicy-sweet variation.

Appetites are whet with fluffy cheese-topped popovers and surf and turf dumplings. Skip the sides to leave room for rich cheesecake lollipops. The clever weekend menu offers brunch in a box—maybe the "Hangover" stocked with a mini burger, bacon-filled mac and cheese, and a petite Monte Christo sandwich.

Eggsperience

American ✗✗

E2

35 W. Ontario St. (at Dearborn St.)

Phone: 312-870-6773
Web: www.eggsperiencecafe.com
Prices:

Lunch daily
Dinner Thu – Sat
Grand (Red)

When only a diner will do, Eggsperience delights with an egg at the ready. This spacious, dressed-up diner offers a multitude of seating options, including the veritable (and lengthy) counter. Outside, you may find fast-moving lines; inside it is a bright, cheery spot, with natural light and many representations of the almighty egg.

Find it also on the plate, in omelets, skillets, and frittatas, just to name a few dishes. The cast-iron skillets are chock-full of ingredients, such as the "mmmmmushroom" made with earthy mushrooms, spinach, two kinds of cheeses, potatoes, and onions. With that order come sides of pancakes, which are mercifully light and fluffy. Caffeine addicts rejoice: a whole tasty pot of coffee is placed on your table.

Epic

Contemporary ✗✗

D3

112 W. Hubbard St. (bet. Clark & LaSalle Sts.)

Phone: 312-222-4940
Web: www.epicrestaurantchicago.com
Prices: $$$

Lunch Mon – Fri
Dinner Mon – Sat
Grand (Red)

If M.C. Escher were still alive, he'd give a thumbs-up to the crisscrossing staircases winding seductively through each floor of Epic's three-story black brownstone. Ceilings that surpass the definition of "soaring" enhance the space's lofty layout, aided by walls of windows lining the warehouse-sized lounge and upper-level dining room, capped by a sexy rooftop bar. Equally statuesque servers in minimal tanks seem unfazed by the Chicago cold.

Despite the clubby, funky feel, the kitchen turns out enjoyable contemporary American fare with broad appeal for diners ranging from suits and out-of-towners to Ed Hardy-clad scenesters. Favorites may include Parmesan gnocchi with lamb sausage and herbs, or grilled salmon with ginger spinach and cucumber yogurt.

Farmhouse

Gastropub ✗✗

C1

228 W. Chicago Ave. (bet. Franklin & Wells Sts.)

Phone: 312-280-4960   Lunch & dinner daily
Web: www.farmhousechicago.com
Prices: $$ Chicago (Brown)

The pitchfork door handle might verge on silly, but the connection to regional farms is serious at Farmhouse. As is evident from blackboards scrawled with names of local purveyors and seasonal brews, the Midwest rules the menu, sourcing Illinois beef, Indiana chicken, Michigan wine, and soda syrup from Logan Square. Salvaged and industrial materials like steel and chunky wood mix with down-home inflections like faux sunflowers and a blues-meets-country soundtrack.

Split the Wisconsin cheese curds with alder-smoked catsup, or a bucket of mussels steamed in wildflower honey lager; before digging into short rib Sloppy Joes with blue cheese and sweet onion marmalade, or a chicken pot pie *pastie*. End with a slice of blueberry-lemon pie for true farm flavor.

Fleming's

Steakhouse ✗✗

E3

25 E. Ohio St. (bet. State St. & Wabash Ave.)

Phone: 312-329-9463   Dinner nightly
Web: www.flemingssteakhouse.com
Prices: $$$ Grand (Red)

In many ways Chicago is still a meat and potatoes town, and the famous Fleming's chain is as good a place as any to find these faves. A classic steakhouse, Fleming's lounge is painted a rich burgundy and shows off redwood-stained furnishings. The crowd may be a confusing blend of corporates, pre-theater touristas, and gaggles celebrating a special occasion, but they all flock here for staples like an iceberg wedge served with blue cheese dressing and crowned with cherry tomatoes; or potatoes, sliced paper-thin and baked gratin-style, with layers of cheese and jalapeños. A simply seasoned USDA Prime filet is served tender and enriched with spicy peppercorn sauce. More than 100 wines by the glass make it easy to sip the right vintage with your meal.

Frontera Grill

D3

Mexican 🍴🍴

445 N. Clark St. (bet. Hubbard & Illinois Sts.)

Phone: 312-661-1434
Web: www.fronterakitchens.com
Prices: $$

Lunch & dinner Tue – Sat

🚇 Grand (Red)

Loud, fun, and excellent, Frontera Grill is the more casual Chicago home of Chef Rick Bayless—perhaps America's best-known Mexican food enthusiast. While his commercial empire has burgeoned to include TV shows, books, and more restaurants, quality ingredients prepared with signature style remain the focus here.

Tortilla soup is the stuff of legend, and not to be missed by any first-timer. The menu goes on to offer the likes of Mexico City-style deep-fried quesadillas stuffed with locally crafted cheese, or the refined and comforting *posole rojo*, served with traditional garnishes.

Whether here for lunch, brunch, or dinner, know that this lively Mexican spot will be packed. Consider staking a claim at the bar and keeping a keen eye on the nearby tables.

Fulton's on the River

D4

Seafood 🍴🍴

315 N. LaSalle St. (at the Chicago River)

Phone: 312-822-0100
Web: www.fultonsontheriver.com
Prices: $$$

Lunch Mon – Sat
Dinner nightly

🚇 Merchandise Mart

The realtor's axiom on location might be tired, but it applies accurately to Fulton's on the River. This sizeable but warm space sports a warren of comfortable rooms, though the primo spot on a sunny day is an umbrella-shaded table outside. Salads, burgers, and bites like beer-battered fish and crispy calamari dominate the value-priced lunch menu.

A wood-paneled décor and glossy black-and-white photos keep company with steakhouse mains; while accompaniments like oysters or jumbo lump crab cakes are served at dinner as the crowd shifts to corporate and affluent regulars. Outdoor tables are first-come, first-serve, making early arrivals a must. The same killer scene makes Fulton's a prime wedding reception spot, so call ahead for weekend availability.

Gene & Georgetti

C3

Steakhouse XX

500 N. Franklin St. (at Illinois St.)

Phone: 312-527-3718 Lunch & dinner Mon – Sat
Web: www.geneandgeorgetti.com
Prices: $$$$ 🚇 Merchandise Mart

With such wonderful consistency for decades (and surely, for decades to come), dining here is akin to stepping into a time machine. Outside, cab drivers deliver women with hairdos that are still "set" at the beauty parlor. Inside, find crowds of suit-clad regulars who still believe in the three-martini lunch. Upstairs is a quieter, more subdued place to dine near a wintry wood-burning fireplace. Nonetheless, everyone is welcome here, from Chi-town politicos to the average Joe.

The menu offers a hybrid of Italian-American classics and standard steakhouse fare. The steaks are huge (get ready for that doggie bag) and sides equally so. The veal Parmesan is decadent and delicious. Cocktails trump the wine list, sticking with the feeling of the era.

Gilt Bar 😊

C4

Gastropub XX

230 W. Kinzie St. (at Franklin St.)

Phone: 312-464-9544 Dinner nightly
Web: www.giltbarchicago.com
Prices: $$ 🚇 Merchandise Mart

This speakeasy-on-steroids covers all its bases—tufted leather banquettes for comfort and worn wooden chairs for a studied distressed style; an impressively gilded bar for casual noshers and serious cocktailers; and a semi-exposed kitchen serving up rustic cuisine with refined touches. High-spirited conversation from the packed-in, dressed-up revelers keeps sound levels at a dull roar.

As with the space, there's a bite for every appetite. Mouthwatering nibbles like bone marrow and red onion jam, or steak tartare laced with shallots and capers populate the "On Toast" section of the menu. Hungrier guests will tear through exquisitely fuss-free entrées such as pan-roasted Gunthorp farm chicken with a rich jus; or bouillabaisse with red pepper rouille.

Gino's East

Pizza

 C2

633 N. Wells St. (at Ontario St.)

Phone: 312-943-1124   Lunch & dinner daily
Web: www.ginoseast.com
Prices:

 Grand (Red)

When sated diners cover the walls of this massive, dark, and dizzyingly loud Chicago deep-dish pizza parlor with scratchy graffiti–a Gino's East tradition–they tell their stories, add to the legend, and speak to their longstanding loyalty for this divey yet venerable institution.

Be prepared for a wait, as families, tourists, couples, and regulars linger side-by-side for the famous deep-dish and thin-crust pizzas, all made to order. Both versions start with a round of sturdy golden dough before piling on tomato sauce, then layers of toppings, and finishing with copious handfuls of cheese. Though pepperoni and sausage are requisite offerings, a cheese and spinach pie isn't just a halfhearted concession to health but a true regional specialty.

Giordano's

Pizza

 F1

730 N. Rush St. (at Superior St.)

Phone: 312-951-0747   Lunch & dinner daily
Web: www.giordanos.com
Prices:

Chicago (Red)

Value, friendly service, and delicious deep-dish pizza make Giordano's a crowd sweetheart. With several locations dotting the city and suburbs, this restaurant has been gratifying locals with comforting Italian-American fare for years. Come during the week–service picks up especially at dinner–to avoid the cacophony.

Giordano's menu includes your typical salads, pastas, et al., but you'd do well to save room for the real star: the deep-dish. Bring backup because this pie could feed a small country. The spinach pie arrives on a buttery pastry crust, filled with spreads of sautéed (or steamed) spinach and tomato sauce, and topped with mozzarella and Parmesan cheese. For those cold, windy nights, opt for delivery—their website sketches a detailed menu.

graham elliot ❀ ❀

C2

217 W. Huron St. (bet. Franklin & Wells Sts.)

Phone: 312-624-9975 — Dinner Wed – Sun
Web: www.grahamelliot.com
Prices: $$$$ — 🚇 Chicago (Brown)

Graham Elliot

Something here has changed. Inside this warehouse-chic fine dining destination, there is no library-hush over the food. Young crowds gather at unadorned dark wood tables spaced amidst timber columns or at the u-shaped copper bar, and seem to relish each dish as much as the carefully stripped-down, unpretentious vibe. The music isn't too loud to drown out excited conversations, but clearly makes Chef Elliot's indie-alternative mark. Servers in jackets and jeans are knowledgeable, synchronized, and never stuffy; everything seems serious but echoes the mantra, "I'm real."

The three menus are cleverly broken down and range from five to fifteen courses. Much here demonstrates the kitchen's mastery, yet equally conveys the chef's trademark humor and eccentricity. Some dishes make diners smile before they have even touched the tines of a fork: piped dots of pink trout mousse and dill gel atop peppery tuile with cream cheese ice cream, caper relish, Tasmanian sea trout and roe is a genius play on the "everything bagel."

Each flavor seems to top the next in poached lobster knuckles with intense roe gelée, tender lobster sausage, and lobster butter emulsion, garnished with lemon and verbena.

GT Fish & Oyster ⊛

Seafood ✗✗

C3

531 N. Wells St. (at Grand Ave.)

Phone: 312-929-3501
Web: www.gtoyster.com
Prices: $$

Lunch Mon – Fri
Dinner nightly
🚇 Grand (Red)

Chef Giuseppe Tentori of Lincoln Park's Boka goes fish shack-chic with this lively, sceney haunt that's an after-work favorite among the young professionals around River North. Planked wood floors and white wainscoting give just the right soupçon of nautical flair to an otherwise contemporary space.

The eponymous oyster bar groans under the weight of icy bivalves stacked high, so take a dozen or two off its pile while deciding on plates to share with your cohorts. Order à la carte, but don't worry about balancing your meal with anything green on the seafood-heavy menu. The lobster mac and cheese is a requisite choice for many a group; whereas subtle seasonings on tuna *poke* with pickled mango or crisp brandade croquettes keep flavors restrained.

Harry Caray's

Steakhouse ✗✗

E4

33 W. Kinzie St. (at Dearborn St.)

Phone: 312-828-0966
Web: www.harrycarays.com
Prices: $$$

Lunch & dinner daily

🚇 Grand (Red)

The gone-but-never-forgotten Chicago sportscaster Harry Caray was known for his trademark "Holy Cow!" Guests might feel the need to utter it as they see the famous broadcaster's bronze bust complete with giant glasses. As Harry Caray is iconic to the Windy City, so, too, are steakhouses, so it makes sense that the restaurant that sports his name is a classic steakhouse specializing in USDA Prime corn-fed beef.

Make sure you show up hungry here: the 18oz dry-aged, bone-in ribeye or 23oz Porterhouse are on the hefty side of what is an ample selection on this massive, meat-centric menu. Like most steakhouses, all the sides–classics including garlic mashed potatoes, creamed spinach, and sautéed mushrooms–are served à la carte.

Hubbard Inn

D3

International

110 W. Hubbard St. (bet. Clark & LaSalle Sts.)

Phone: 312-222-1331   Lunch Mon – Fri
Web: www.hubbardinn.com   Dinner Mon – Sat
Prices: $$ Grand (Red)

Handsome and invitingly decorated within an inch of its life, this turn-of-the-century European-style tavern spares no detail. A flotilla of warm brass-harnessed globe lamps hangs from the rafters, suspended over thick wooden plank tables. Upstairs, the vibe is more library lounge-chic, with couches and open seating set among book-lined walls.

Cocktails are the draw for mixology mavens, with an extensive list of classics and new favorites carefully etched on a wall-sized chalkboard behind the impressive marble bar. Pick your poison and embark on a relaxing lunch of globe-spanning plates like steak tartare, grilled duck bratwurst, or flatbread with merguez and pear chutney before the dinner crowd ambles in to fill each lounge chair and bar stool.

Hub51

E4

International

51 W. Hubbard St. (at Dearborn St.)

Phone: 312-828-0051   Lunch & dinner daily
Web: www.hub51chicago.com
Prices: $$ Grand (Red)

The twenty-something sons of legendary Chicago restaurateur Rich Melman are behind this bar-slash-eatery, which appeals to a hip, downtown crowd. A well-stocked bar pouring a multitude of draft beers and dark wood tables make up the spacious dining room—having a nightclub (SUB 51) right downstairs doesn't hurt.

The menu reaches out to the under-40 set with a hybrid offering of Tex-Mex, sushi, sandwiches, salads, and other things folks order when they get off of work. Fish tacos are well-conceived; the popular *shakishaki* tuna is crunchy and tangy; and the carrot cake super decadent with extra scoops of whipped cream and cream cheese icing. Drunker appetites can choose a green chile cheeseburger or the Dude, an aged 18oz ribeye with the works.

Japonais

A1

Fusion ✗✗✗

600 W. Chicago Ave. (bet. Larrabee St. & the Chicago River)

Phone: 312-822-9600
Web: www.japonaischicago.com
Prices: $$$

Lunch Mon – Fri
Dinner nightly
🚇 Chicago (Blue)

For nearly a decade, Japonais has remained sleek and sexy while attracting the see-and-be-seen contingent in droves. Sultry scenesters relax on oversized ottomans or take in romantic river views in the windowed lounge, while efficient servers nimbly take care of large parties and navigate the crowds.

The Asian fusion menu continues to impress from start to finish: a refreshing seaweed salad spiked with citrus and pickled cucumber; and The Rock, a signature preparation of tender New York strip steak cooked tableside on a sizzling-hot rock, are standouts. Finish on a high note with desserts that put exotic touches on all-American staples, like the kabocha squash cheesecake with five spices, frothy pineapple mousse, and a dense almond cookie crust.

Joe's

F3

American ✗✗✗

60 E. Grand Ave. (at Rush St.)

Phone: 312-379-5637
Web: www.joes.net
Prices: $$$$

Lunch & dinner daily

🚇 Grand (Red)

An outpost of the Miami landmark, this Joe's certainly feels like a Chicago original. A large bar area peppered with tables lingers up front and is packed with drinkers and diners. While it rocks a clubby vibe, Joe's is also ideal for a light bite. File it under the "when in Rome" rule and start with stone crabs sided with mustard sauce before moving onto tempting sides of fried green tomatoes which offer a taste of the South, while grilled tomatoes topped with spinach and cheese are classic Joe's.

This popular institution with its friendly service and adept kitchen is also beloved for its seafood spectrum (the fisherman's platter) and sinful treats like the Havana dream pie, a Joe's signature, and Key lime pie which tender a tasty slice of Americana.

Keefer's

Steakhouse

E4

20 W. Kinzie St. (bet. Dearborn & State Sts.)

Phone: 312-467-9525
Web: www.keefersrestaurant.com
Prices: $$$$

Lunch Mon – Fri
Dinner Mon – Sat
Grand (Red)

From the warm welcome and efficient service to the contemporary menu, everything Keefer's does, it does well. While Chicago has no shortage of steakhouses, this one distinguishes itself with a friendly bar area showing bistro-style booths and menu, and a vibe that is updated and upscale in the main dining room—this is a modern classic whose menu follows suit.

Find all the anticipated cuts of meat, sauces, and sides to feast on in an à la carte style. But also try the chef's signature items for something a little different: sides like the potato croquettes (imagine deep-fried mashed potatoes with all the toppings inside); braised endive in sauce Mornay; and broccoli salad combining florets, fennel, apple, and cheese with a lemon vinaigrette.

La Madia

Italian

D3

59 W. Grand Ave. (bet. Clark & Dearborn Sts.)

Phone: 312-329-0400
Web: www.dinelamadia.com
Prices: $$

Lunch & dinner daily
Grand (Red)

This contemporary take on the pizzeria, where subway tiles mix with marble at the pizza station, bustles with activity while remaining a comfortable spot for couples or crowds. Booths throughout the high-ceilinged space, barstools at the open kitchen, and sleek bar give ample room for *mangiare*. Peruse the extensive wine list, with options by the bottle or by the glass in four- and seven-ounce pours, and exquisite stemware to match.

The well-edited menu features modern riffs on Italian fare such as Sardinian flatbread filled with herbed chicken, almonds, and currants; or thin-crust pizzas with quality toppings like sweet Italian sausage, fresh mozzarella, and caramelized onions. Split the dense chocolate *tortino* with your tablemates for dessert.

Mastro's

E3

Steakhouse

520 N. Dearborn St. (at Grand Ave.)

Phone: 312-521-5100
Web: www.mastrosrestaurants.com
Prices: $$$$

Dinner nightly

 Grand (Red)

Big spenders and power brokers bring swagger to the latest steakhouse chainlet hoping to make its mark on Chicago's meat scene. Clubby, plush décor, a crooning pianist, and generously poured martinis telegraph old-school swank, though servers radiate genuine Midwestern friendliness, and the crowd eats it all up. Reservations are essential, even for this spacious, multi-floored setting with nooks for private dining.

Large and succulent portions of wet-aged Prime steak arrive simply broiled on screaming hot plates, with sauces and accompaniments upon request. Show restraint with the list of two dozen traditional sides like garlic mashed potatoes and creamed spinach in favor of a new classic: the rich, smooth, salty, sweet, and revelatory butter cake.

Mercadito

D4

Mexican

108 W. Kinzie St. (bet. Clark & LaSalle Sts.)

Phone: 312-329-9555
Web: www.mercaditorestaurants.com
Prices: $$

Lunch & dinner daily

Merchandise Mart

After conquering New York with their fresh, spicy, and upscale tacos and ceviches, brothers Patricio, Alfredo, and Felipe Sandoval brought their winning formula to the Windy City in 2009. Mercadito's weathered metal façade hides a bold décor: custom graffiti art, Mayan murals, and pebbled glass plates are casually colorful and hip, evoking a beach club that invites you to stay just a little bit longer.

Sample or share a few ceviches like the smoky-sweet dorado with Asian pear and hints of tamarind; or spicy *mixto* with octopus, shrimp, and mahi mahi. Then dig into a stack of satisfying *tacos al pastor* studded with glistening ancho-rubbed pork and grilled pineapple, along with one or three tangy margaritas with just the right dip of salt on the rim.

Nacional 27

C2

325 W. Huron St. (at Orleans St.)

Phone: 312-664-2727
Web: www.n27chicago.com
Prices: $$

Dinner Mon – Sat

Chicago (Brown)

Celebrating the 27 recognized Latin American countries through name and cuisine, Nacional 27 serves up sultry pleasures in a wonderfully diverting environment. From the dusky enticements of the central bar, energetic music, and weekly events like complimentary salsa dancing lessons, it's easy to get distracted before you sample the food.

The extensive menu of passionately flavored small plates, ceviches, paellas, and the signature N27 roast suckling pig *Cubano*, show off traditional Latin elements in unexpected combinations. Dishes like the *chimichurri*-crusted filet atop showstopping potato-chorizo hash with a malbec reduction; and the barbecued lamb taco with guava, black beans, sweet agave, and creamy avocado salsa hit all the right notes.

Osteria Via Stato

Italian

E2

620 N. State St. (at Ontario St.)

Phone: 312-642-8450
Web: www.osteriaviastato.com
Prices: $$

Dinner nightly

Grand (Red)

Though it is adjacent to the Embassy Suites, this pitch-perfect cozy *taverna* complete with stone walls and barrel-vaulted archways is a local standby for its across-the-board value in a neighborhood of pricey plates. The all-Italian wine list sparkles with well-priced gems, but those who can't decide can simply ask for the "just bring me wine" feature—a tasting flight of three different wines.

Order à la carte or bring a group for the *molto* popular "Italian dinner party" that lets diners choose their own entrée and share antipasti, pastas, and sides family-style. With hearty portions of mini meatballs in marinara sauce; braised lamb shank with cipollini onions and rosemary; or ravioli stuffed with tender short rib, no one leaves hungry.

NAHA

D3

500 N. Clark St. (at Illinois St.)

Phone: 312-321-6242
Web: www.naha-chicago.com
Prices: $$$

Lunch Mon – Fri
Dinner Mon – Sat
 Grand (Red)

Lara Kastner

Gazing through a wall of windows toward the corner of Clark and Illinois, it's easy to breathe a sigh of ease watching the urban tableau play out beyond the glass while comfortably ensconced in one of NAHA's banquettes. Surrounded by pacific shades of cream, gray, and taupe, a meal here is an instant soother—a simple luxury that never feels pretentious or stuffy.

If your idea of relaxation starts with pre-dinner drinks, the concrete-topped bar and austere lounge are an open invitation to begin. Natural and industrial elements mix freely and harmoniously inside this stylish fishbowl whose warm woods segue seamlessly into planters filled with grassy reeds.

The stark-meets-sophisticated poise of the space with equal parts charm and gusto extends to the plates spun out of Chef Carrie Nahabedian's kitchen: dribbles of Parmesan, sweet potato, and braised oxtail are star players in a lunchtime risotto, while no one will lift an eyebrow should you begin dinner with one of nearly a dozen starters—creamy scallops roasted with vanilla and citrus? Entrées bring pure joy with the likes of juicy duck breast lacquered in a Port-honey glaze, fortified with parsnips, broccoli rabe, and licorice root.

Paris Club

French   XX

59 W. Hubbard St. (bet. Clark & Dearborn Sts.)

Phone: 312-595-0800   Dinner nightly
Web: www.parisclubchicago.com
Prices: $$ Grand (Red)

Jammed with the top five percent of the city's hippest and most attractive residents, Paris Club might knock you flat with the sound waves ricocheting from the ceiling's iron beams to the subway-tiled walls to the communal wooden tables. A bar spanning the vast front room helps corral the pretty young things, but this lounge-cum-eatery nonetheless runs smoothly with the pampering service expected from the newest Lettuce Entertain You venture.

French gastropub fare that's a tasty step above typical lounge food offers a respite from the burger-centric menus at similar Chicago hot spots. Small plates like jars of pork rillettes, mac and cheese gratinée, or lamb meatballs with *harissa*-spiked tomato sauce are reliable options from the extensive menu.

Phil Stefani's 437 Rush

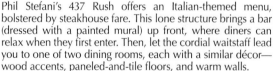

Italian   XX

437 N. Rush St. (bet. Hubbard & Illinois Sts.)

Phone: 312-222-0101   Lunch Mon – Fri
Web: www.stefanirestaurants.com   Dinner Mon – Sat
Prices: $$$ Grand (Red)

Phil Stefani's 437 Rush offers an Italian-themed menu, bolstered by steakhouse fare. This lone structure brings a bar (dressed with a painted mural) up front, where diners can relax when they first enter. Then, let the cordial waitstaff lead you to one of two dining rooms, each with a similar décor—wood accents, paneled-and-tile floors, and warm walls.

White-clothed tables carry a foray of food, presented in fine white china. Italian-born Federico Comacchio brings his native's sensibility to a tandem of treats including pappardelle with house-made sausage ragout and goat milk ricotta; or risotto with organic buttercup pumpkin, Swiss chard, and robiola. Less theatrical, but as tasty, are the Caesar salad, steaks, seafood, and sweets.

Pizzeria Uno

29 E. Ohio St. (at Wabash Ave.)

Phone: 312-321-1000   Lunch & dinner daily
Web: www.unos.com
Prices: 🚇 Grand (Red)

 Since 1943, this establishment has been laying claim to the (somewhat disputed) title of creating the original Chicago-style pizza. Its tiny booths and wood tables wear their years of graffiti etchings like a badge of honor. Nonetheless, an intricate pressed-tin ceiling reflects the cheerful atmosphere as everyone counts down the 40 or so minutes it takes for these deep-dish delights to bake.

Of course, the main attraction here is, was, and always will be the flaky, buttery crust generously layered with mozzarella, other toppings, and tangy tomato sauce that comprise this belly-busting pizza. The menu also includes a selection of good basic bar food like Buffalo wings and a simple salad, but most just save the room for an extra slice.

Pops for Champagne

601 N. State St. (at Ohio St.)

Phone: 312-266-7677   Dinner nightly
Web: www.popsforchampagne.com
Prices: $$ 🚇 Grand (Red)

 Who needs a celebration–or any excuse–to enjoy a glass of bubbly? With its prime State Street location, Pops for Champagne makes the idea irresistible. Tourists, shoppers from nearby Bloomie's and Nordstrom, and happy hour-ready clusters slouch into low sofas or crowd around crackled green glass tables with built-in champagne buckets to sip a flute or two.

Pops offers full and half pours of all things fizzy from Champagne and Cava to obscure sparkling wines and bubbling cocktails. A succinct menu of nibbles like oysters, charcuterie and desserts help offset the heady effervescence. Crispy black tiger shrimp with a sweet clementine glaze and "foie gras dust" are appropriately rich; whereas beef tartare is perked up by truffled edamame relish and chili oil.

217

Prosecco

Italian

C2

710 N. Wells St. (bet. Huron & Superior Sts.)

Phone: 312-951-9500
Web: www.prosecco.us.com
Prices: $$

Lunch Mon – Fri
Dinner Mon – Sat
Chicago (Brown)

Make no mistake; Prosecco is no mediocre joint. Champagne hues and vintage Venice-inspired style create an atmosphere of casual elegance here, where bountiful portions of sumptuous Italian fill adoring locals. Of course, the namesake beverage is offered in fifty different varieties. But first, let the affable staff steer you through a bowl of *orecchiette tartufate* showcasing wild mushrooms, sun-dried tomatoes, and Grana Padano in a black truffle cream. For a bit of zest, the pistachio-crusted prawns with red pepper purée gets things right.

Whether at their classically chic dining room or under the glossy awning of the sidewalk patio, one bite of the *costoletta di agnello*, lamb with a red grape and balsamic reduction will have you glowing.

Quartino

Italian

E2

626 N. State St. (at Ontario St.)

Phone: 312-698-5000
Web: www.quartinochicago.com
Prices: $$

Lunch & dinner daily
Grand (Red)

Centrally located on State Street is this boisterous gathering place, where Quartino pulled off the coup of making a two-floor space, with bar room and outdoor seating, seem relaxed and comfortable. The kitchen hums, but doesn't miss a beat catering to the clamor to keep the *cicchetti* coming and wine flowing.

Salumi and cheese flights, along with wine pourings ranging from the quarter-carafe to the bottle, make sharing a priority among groups out for a good time. Smart servers stack white appetizer plates on each table for ease of distribution. Crisp and light polenta fries won't spoil the appetite for heartier fare like rigatoni with poached chicken and broccoli cloaked in béchamel; or pizza soprano with sliced veal meatballs and *giardiniera*.

RL

American ✗✗

F1

115 E. Chicago Ave. (bet. Michigan Ave. & Rush St.)

Phone: 312-475-1100   Lunch & dinner daily
Web: www.rlrestaurant.com
Prices: $$$ Chicago (Red)

Book a table at RL and you'll instantly feel like a member of the pedigreed elite. The place resembles a stage set for the American dream, so it should be of no surprise that the style icon is behind it. The crowd is both attractive and attracted to this posh scene, housed inside the Ralph Lauren store. Here, the décor is the climax with mahogany paneled walls, leather banquettes, and glinting crystal. Thanks to the sociable staff you'll never feel like an outcast, but don't forget about those reservations.

A hot spot for Bloody Mary's and brunch, the burger on a challah bun is loved by the bold and beautiful. Echoing the brand's American sensibility is a chicken hash topped with poached egg; or creamy lobster bisque to go with the lobster club.

Roka Akor

Japanese ✗✗

D3

456 N. Clark St. (at Illinois St.)

Phone: 312-477-7652   Lunch Mon – Fri
Web: www.rokaakor.com   Dinner nightly
Prices: $$$ Grand (Red)

Chicagoans love their grilled meat, especially when it's Wagyu beef cooked over a charcoal-fueled *robata* grill. At palindromic Roka Akor ("roka" means fire), the grill may be the centerpiece, but the entire space is a sexy, sleek, and energetic hybrid lounge. Oversized wood accents are simple and artfully positioned—as if Frank Gehry had free reign of life-sized Lincoln Logs.

Expect very fresh and neatly cut sashimi plates, or large cubes of tender ribeye beef in *wafu* dressing. Other dishes include butterfish *tataki* with white asparagus and yuzu or shishito peppers with bonito. The omakase may range from "signature" to "decadent" which tend to speak for themselves. Fashionable foodies appreciate the wasabi grated tableside and house-brewed soy sauce.

Roy's

E2

720 N. State St. (at Superior St.)

Phone: 312-787-7599 — Dinner nightly
Web: www.roysrestaurant.com
Prices: $$ — Chicago (Red)

Roy's may celebrate its Hawaiian roots in its food and background music, but this sophisticated spot with floor-to-ceiling windows and elegant seating does not play to any clichés.

The extremely popular outpost of the nationwide chain has many signature dishes (like macadamia nut-crusted mahi mahi or hibachi grilled salmon), but it also includes selections created specifically by the on-site chef. The Hawaiian fusion cuisine that Roy's is known for focuses heavily on simply prepared, quality seafood such as Hawaiian-style *misoyaki* butterfish with wasabi-ginger-cilantro cream; and crab dynamite-crusted *hebi* with coconut rice and kimchi-lime butter sauce.

Hit the packed bar for the budget-friendly $5 Aloha happy hour (Sunday-Thursday).

RPM

Italian

E3

52 W. Illinois St. (at Dearborn St.)

Phone: 312-222-1888 — Dinner nightly
Web: www.rpmitalian.com
Prices: $$ — Grand (Red)

When powerhouse restaurant group Lettuce Entertain You partners with reality-TV couple Bill Rancic and his *E! News*-hosting wife, Giuliana, you get a high-wattage happening rather than family-style Italian. Carrara marble and black walls add modern glamour to the bar area, where a loud, see-and-be-seen crowd rubbernecks amid the first come, first served booths and tables. The stark white dining room suits anyone with a Milanese sense of fashion.

Snacks like antipasti, *salumi*, and (slightly) truffled garlic bread take precedence on the menu. Larger dishes include family recipes like Mama DePandi's *bucatini pomodoro* alongside urban rustic plates like wood-grilled and braised octopus tossed with celery and garbanzo beans, as well as gluten free options.

Sable

E3

American   ✗✗

505 N. State St. (at Illinois St.)

Phone: 312-755-9704   Lunch & dinner daily
Web: www.sablechicago.com
Prices: $$ 🚇 Grand (Red)

Like its lavish namesake, this cosmopolitan spot wraps itself in shades of pewter, bronze, and chocolate as it stretches the length of Palomar Hotel's first floor. Sable labels itself a gastro-lounge with cocktails that get top billing in the ample bar, but patrons can also unwind in the garden patio that runs alongside the dining room.

Eclectic elements like hints of smoke and soy in homemade beef jerky elevate a carte of contemporary American food. Pickled mustard seeds dot the apricot chutney that dresses fennel sausage; while Bourbon-caramel sauce offers a heady finish to a banana cream tart. Almost every item is listed with two prices: one for a smaller portion and one for a full-size dish, letting guests decide if they'd rather share or hoard.

Scoozi

B2

Italian   ✗✗

410 W. Huron St. (bet. Hudson Ave & Sedgwick St.)

Phone: 312-943-5900   Dinner nightly
Web: www.leye.com
Prices: $$ 🚇 Chicago (Brown)

Dining at Scoozi is like popping in on a neighbor who happens to be a fabulous cook. It is the kind of place filled with families (both literal and metaphorical) settling into oversized leather booths, adding to the fun yet relaxed vibe—its enormous size makes this feat all the more impressive. Reasonable prices have everyone planning to return soon.

On the menu, expect lovely Italian-American classics, perfectly cooked and satisfying, that boast the marks of a very professional kitchen. Linguini *frutti di mare* is spiked with just the right amount of heat, and a tender Italian pot roast with pearl onions, carrots, and fresh rosemary is enrobed in a wonderfully full-bodied sauce. Desserts like deep-fried apple "ravioli" are a sweet twist on tradition.

Shanghai Terrace

F1

Chinese ✗✗

108 E. Superior St. (bet. Michigan Ave. & Rush St.)

Phone:	312-573-6695
Web:	www.peninsula.com
Prices:	$$$

Lunch & dinner daily

Chicago (Red)

While its design could be described as chinoiserie, Shanghai Terrace fashions an ethereal Asian look. Its class and distinctive style carries from the elegant dining room to the sunny terrace, open during warmer months. Set inside the aristocratic Peninsula Hotel, this sanctum draws an affluent crowd who come as much for the setting (rife with Chinese antiques, furnishings, and a staff robed in Mandarin jackets), as they do for the highly regarded food.

Dim sum craving sophisticates can choose from a nice medley of dishes friendly to Western palates. Entrées include the likes of *yang zhao* fried jasmine rice with rock shrimp and duck; Hong Kong beef tenderloin, or chrysanthemum-infused pork spareribs. Reasonably priced brunch is a popular option.

Shaw's Crab House

E4

Seafood ✗✗

21 E. Hubbard St. (bet. State St. & Wabash Ave.)

Phone:	312-527-2722
Web:	www.shawscrabhouse.com
Prices:	$$$

Lunch & dinner daily

Grand (Red)

There aren't that many restaurants that have tuxedoed waiters welcoming guests in jeans, as well as a kid-friendly menu. But that's the story at Shaw's, a mainstay for both locals and visitors. The ambience is old-school with black patent leather booths and big band music.

Crab is always on the menu, though it varies by season: Dungeness, king, stone, soft shell, and blue. The crab cakes are as simple a presentation as imaginable, yet tasty. The single round patty is all large lump Maryland crab with very little filler, served golden brown and kissed with spiced mayonnaise. For a non-crab option, try the horseradish-crusted grouper, prepared simply, but just right. Tuesdays, Thursdays, and Sundays the joint is jumping with live music at the oyster bar.

Sixteen ✿

Contemporary XXXX

E4

401 N. Wabash Ave. (bet. Hubbard St. & the Chicago River)

Phone: 312-588-8030
Web: www.trumpchicagohotel.com
Prices: **$$$$**

Lunch & dinner daily

🚇 State/Lake

Steve Hall/Hedrich Blessing Photographers

As the signature restaurant of the Trump International Hotel & Tower, Sixteen spares no expense in creating a dramatic impression. Propitiously, all elements unite sumptuously and effortlessly. Gracious hosts glide guests past the 900-bottle glass-enclosed wine gallery to the Tower Room, where breathtaking views of the Chicago River, Tribune Tower, and Wrigley building clock compete for attention with a curvy African rosewood wall and 14-foot Swarovski crystal chandelier.

Showy presentations talk the talk, but the flavors of each dish walk in an explosive and ingenious parade of fine ingredients. Potatoes cooked in seaweed lend minerality to Columbia River sturgeon with osetra caviar and two-minute oysters; while tender Dover sole floats in a yuzu-spiked carrot-ginger *nage* with sea beans and edible flowers.

Even Diver scallops with uni and coffee-scented *pommes* purée; or bite-size palate cleansers like strawberry sorbet with almond-lemon curd and tweezer-set flake of gold leaf are memorably balanced. Dessert nearly steals the show with chocolate confections like *gianduja cremeux* atop crunchy *feuilletines* of milk chocolate, praline, and peanut butter, or cactus-pear jelly mignardises.

Slurping Turtle 😋

D3

Japanese ✗✗

116 W. Hubbard St. (bet. Clark & LaSalle Sts.)

Phone: 312-464-0466
Web: www.slurpingturtle.com
Prices: $$

Lunch Mon – Sat
Dinner nightly
🚇 Merchandise Mart

Chef Takashi Yagihashi takes a break from his eponymous Bucktown flagship at this casual spinoff dedicated to belly-warming noodles and other simple Japanese dishes. The restaurant's design seems bento box-inspired with booths, nooks, and communal tables—all of which are snatched up quickly at both lunch and dinner. Be quick like the hare to get a seat at the Turtle.

Graze on meaty skewers off the *bincho* charcoal grill or steamed buns with lacquered pork belly before diving into a deep ceramic bowl of rich, brothy noodles. Don't be shy, for slurping is a compliment to the chef. The über crispy duck fat-fried chicken is outrageously good. Finish up with a Yamazaki whiskey, bottle of Japanese craft beer, like Hitachino Nest, or a caramel-soy macaron.

Smith & Wollensky

E4

Steakhouse ✗✗

318 N. State St. (at the Chicago River)

Phone: 312-670-9900
Web: www.smithandwollensky.com
Prices: $$$

Lunch & dinner daily

🚇 State/Lake

While mighty steakhouses may be a favorite among Chicagoans, this babe (of the famed national chain) sits gorgeously on the Chicago River bank, and thus, lures all. Inside forever loved Smith & Wollensky, find handsome décor details like dark wood furniture, polished brass, and other accoutrements. The crowds are large (a common sight here), but the staff navigates them with little trouble.

The kitchen churns out steakhouse classics like dry-aged cuts with heaping sides of mashed potatoes and onion rings; and shrimp cocktail—three prawns lying beside three (mustard, tomato, and avocado) sauces. But you're here for the steaks, and they are well charred and perfectly cooked. Don't skip their signature sauce—it adds a great kick to the meat.

Sunda

D3

Fusion ✗✗

110 W. Illinois St. (bet. Clark & LaSalle Sts.)

Phone: 312-644-0500
Web: www.sundachicago.com
Prices: $$

Lunch Sun – Fri
Dinner nightly
🚇 Grand (Red)

The name is derived from the Sunda shelf–submerged in Southeast Asia–whose thriving trade routes made it an exotic stew of cultures and cuisines. At this Asian-fusion hot spot, fresh Japanese fish blends with bordering Pacific Island flavors amidst marble floors and warm, rust-colored couches. It's a restaurant as much as it is a scene, and there are plenty of cocktails, sake, and clubby tunes to keep the pretty people groovin'.

Hanging box lanterns dim at sundown, perhaps announcing the arrival of such colorful, creative, and tasty dishes as a Brussels sprout salad tossed with shallots, red chilies, ground shrimp, and *nuoc cham*. Pan-fried oxtail potstickers with a wasabi cream and lemongrass lollipops of grilled beef complete the experience.

Tavernita

D2

Spanish ✗✗

151 W. Erie St. (at LaSalle St.)

Phone: 312-274-1111
Web: www.tavernita.com
Prices: $$

Lunch Sun – Fri
Dinner nightly
🚇 Chicago (Brown)

Don't bother complimenting any of the head-turners basking in the warm amber glow of Tavernita. They'll never be able to hear you over the high-decibel din in this sexy space. But fear not; they know they look damn good anyway. Everybody's here to indulge in food and drink, not deep conversations.

Dozens of wooden taps behind the bar pour homemade sodas, sangria, wine, beer, and ready-made cocktails to ensure the party keeps going and flowing. Take a seat if you can grab one and pass around modern tapas like corn pudding studded with rock shrimp and chile poblano; or baguettes artfully smeared with eggplant, pepper, and hazelnut romesco.

Late-night noshers will adore Barcito, the glass-enclosed *pinxtos* bar-within-a bar inside the restaurant.

Topolobampo

445 N. Clark St. (bet. Hubbard & Illinois Sts.)

Phone: 312-661-1434
Web: www.rickbayless.com
Prices: $$$

Lunch Tue – Fri
Dinner Tue – Sat
🏛 Grand (Red)

Jeff Maimon

Unsurpassed refinement and a judicious approach to the cuisine of Mexico has thrust Rick Bayless' celebrated flagship into the spotlight, where it has remained since 1989.

Sharing its location with the casual and bustling sister spot Frontera Grill, "Topo" feels dramatic, warm, and vibrant, as it melds traditional elements like terra-cotta floors with modern copper and cobalt accents. The sounds of horns from the playlist and margaritas shaken tableside further stimulate the senses.

Dishes please the eyes and palate with wonderful textures and flavors, as in the *envuelto de trucha ahumada*—a Mexican maki of sorts rolling smoked local trout infused with pasilla chilies, draped with ripe avocado, pickled garlic, trout roe, and chef's own garden greens. This might be followed by *pescado en chileatole* combining day-boat striped bass sluiced tableside by a rich elixir of fresh corn masa, tomatillos, red poblano, fragrant herbs, and arranged with salt-roasted butterball potatoes and suckling pig bacon. The kitchen's uniquely creative touches even ameliorate the beloved flan, here infused with cinnamon and black pepper and embellished with doses of tequila meringue and boozy caramel sauce.

Union Sushi + Barbeque Bar

Japanese

C2

230 W. Erie St. (at Franklin St.)

Phone: 312-662-4888
Web: www.eatatunion.com
Prices: $$

Lunch Mon – Fri
Dinner nightly
Chicago (Brown)

It's loud, graffiti-tagged, and mad fun in this über-contemporary, hopping Japanese joint. The bi-level space rocks a colorful, urban design, drawing in a young, hip crowd hungry for the likes of *robata* specialties, noodle dishes, and traditional and creative takes on sushi.

Sample skewers of grilled *kushiyaki* (though alligator can be an acquired taste) then dig your chopsticks into a prosciutto-wrapped scallop topped with wasabi-avocado purée, fried ginger, and sweet plum sauce; or the excellent Bay Street California roll, with crunchy cucumber, spicy chili-mayo, golden brown crab cake, wrapped in nori and rice topped with fresh *masago*. Sate the sweet tooth with Killer Yuzu Pie—a tangy, rich, creamy sensation crowned with whipped cream.

Untitled 😋

Contemporary ✗✗

D4

111 W. Kinzie St. (bet. Clark & LaSalle Sts.)

Phone: 312-880-1511
Web: www.untitledchicago.com
Prices: $$

Dinner Tue – Sun
Merchandise Mart

Yep, that is a doorman keeping watch over a pair of heavy wooden doors between a CVS and parking garage...and that's also the entrance to the warren of rooms comprising this surreptitious speakeasy. Servers decked in suspenders and fedoras navigate the cacophonous and cavernous club's four full bars, parlor, library, and private cabanas, making sure no guest ever runs dry.

The menu sports the de rigueur cheese and charcuterie choices along with inventive small plates that pair harmoniously with the vast whiskey and made-to-order cocktail list. Crispy wontons wrap up braised goat with a tangy blackberry sauce; boneless short ribs sit beside seared scallops atop herbed bread pudding; and a Key lime custard tartlet refreshes after such savory indulgences.

227

Vermilion

E3

Indian ✗✗

10 W. Hubbard St. (bet. Dearborn & State Sts.)

Phone: 312-527-4060
Web: www.thevermilionrestaurant.com
Prices: $$

Lunch Mon – Fri
Dinner nightly
🚇 Grand (Red)

From the stunning oversized photographs shot by India's leading fashion photographer Farrokh Chothia, to the bold, modern styling crafted by architectural firm Searl, Lamaster and Howe, this sleek, sultry, and sexy spot is clearly not your average Indian restaurant.

The surprises continue to the palate, where dishes marrying the marvelous flavors of India and Latin America dazzle and delight. Peruse the menu, and your eye will stop on some seemingly familiar dishes, but expect the unexpected at this bold and inventive scene. Dishes like a duck *vindaloo arepa* brushed with pomegranate molasses, curry leaf, and mango, or white chocolate and cauliflower soup are outstanding; while the heady spices of the lamb shank *gassi* are simply intoxicating.

Zealous

B1

Contemporary ✗✗✗

419 W. Superior St. (bet. Hudson Ave. & Sedgwick St.)

Phone: 312-475-9112
Web: www.zealousrestaurant.com
Prices: $$$

Dinner Tue – Sat
🚇 Chicago (Brown)

Understated in décor but ambitious with its food, Zealous has always marched to its own offbeat tunes. A longtime resident of a loft-like space on a less-traveled block of River North, the room–designed by Chef/owner Michael Taus–feels vaguely Zen, with Asian touches like bamboo, Japanese screens, and quiet murmurs of conversation rippling over the New Age music and bouncing off the 15-foot glass-enclosed wine cellar.

In the kitchen, Taus plays with an eclectic mix of ingredients pulled from cuisines around the globe–Scottish gravlax with *garam masala*-fried Brussels sprouts, for example–piled into intricate towers and platings. Pick à la carte or submit to the chef's whims with tasting menus like the seven-course omakase-style Spontaneous tour.

CHICAGO
CHICAGO
CHICAGO PUBLIC RADIO & DIREC TV
PRESENTS THIS AMERICAN LIFE
CHICAGO PUBLIC RA
& DIRECTV PRESE
THIS AMERICAN L
NOW PLAYING
SHEAR MADNESS

Streeterville

If you simply had to pick a neighborhood that truly recapitulates Chicago, it would be Streeterville. Home to the Magnificent Mile, the iconic John Hancock Building, and the fun-loving Navy Pier, skyscraping and stirring Streeterville takes the cake.

Absorb the sights and smells of the stunning surroundings, especially upon arrival at Water Tower Place's **foodlife**—a simple food court elevated to an art form, located on the mezzanine floor of the shopping mall. Before going further, know that this isn't your average mall or airport food court. Instead, this United Nations of food courts satiates with 14 different kitchens whipping up everything from Chinese potstickers and deep-dish pizza to fried chicken. **Wow Bao** (also located within the

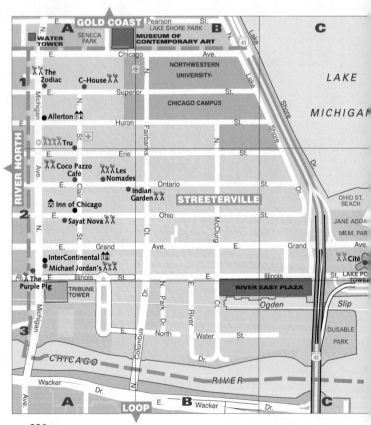

landmark building), doles out some of the best handheld treats in town (like steamed veggie-and-meat-filled buns), and is so popular, they had to open a second spot in the Loop. The coolest part? Buy a card that gives you access to the many stands.

Food Court Fun

Prefer panini and pastry? Stop by the legendary **Hancock Building**, otherwise known as food lovers' paradise. The Italian deli **L'Appetito** is perfect for comforting breakfasts, Italian-and American-style sandwiches, baked goods, and other classic delights. Lucky locals and office types can shop for groceries with sky-high prices to match the staggering view at **Potash Brothers**, a supermarket stunningly set on the 44th floor of the Hancock Building.

Museums and Markets

The Museum of Contemporary Art houses one of the world's leading collections of contemporary art, but it's also the peppers and potatoes that lures gaggles far and wide, to the farmer's market held here on Tuesdays from June through October. Those with fat wallets should hit up posh gourmet supermarket **Fox & Obel** for gorgeous groceries year-round. With a mission to showcase the love and creativity surrounding quality food, this European-style enterprise also houses a delightful café (or market bistro) whose menu struts a spectrum of spectacular treats for all-day dining. Such fine brunch, lunch, and dinner menus combined with boutique wines makes this place a huge highlight (especially among gourmands) in vibrant Streeterville. Carry on this darling adventure at **Teuscher**, **Godiva**, and **Lindt**—they all have boutiques here; but it is Chicago's own **Vosges Haut-Chocolat** that has made a name for itself by rocking taste buds with exotic ingredients—curry and chocolate anyone?

Tasty Treats

Where do all the savvy foodies and fashionistas in Chicago convene? Most likely at artisan food paradise, also known as **Dose Market**. This year-round bazaar features the finest in food and chefs (together with some

D
Streeterville

N

1

E. Ohio St.

JARDINE
WATER PURIFICATION
PLANT

OLIVE PARK

Ohio St.

St.

Ohio

E. Ohio St.

2

Park

E. Grand Ave.

NAVY PIER

Dr.

N. Streeter Dr.

Riva

LAKE
MICHIGAN

3

NAVY PIER PARK

● Hotels
● Restaurants

D

of their secret ingredients) all under one roof. From acclaimed "dosers" (think Pasta Puttana and Saigon Sisters) to passionate "dosettes", Dose Market offers "a beautiful setting full of happy people." After such epicurean prowling, move on to more substantial chow like an all-natural Chicago-style dog (with mustard, onion, relish, sport peppers, tomato, pickle, and celery salt) from **America's Dog**. This dog heaven showcases a gargantuan repertoire of city-style dogs from Houston, New York, and Philadelphia, to Detroit, Kansas City, and San Francisco. In the mood for some crunch? Venture towards world-famous **Jiminy Chips** for some of the most addictive kettle-cooked, made-to-order potato chips. Also on the menu and prepared with top-notch techniques are crispy sweet potato chips, pita chips, and tortilla chips. The choices are plenty, so make your pick and settle down for a fried feast.

Streeterville Faithfuls

The **Billy Goat Tavern** is a Streeterville institution. Now known more for its famous "cheezeborger, cheezeborger" Saturday Night Live skit, this is a "buy the tee-shirt" type of place with a spot in Navy Pier, and the original just off Michigan Avenue. The tavern's menu, which includes breakfast specials, an array of steaks, and sandwiches galore, is sure to please all who may enter its hallowed portals. Jonesing for a juicy burger? Hit up **M Burger** (another outpost thrives in River North), along with the hordes of business lunchers, tourists, and shoppers. It should be renamed

"mmm" burger for its tasty, meaty gifts. Bacon, cheese, and secret sauce comprise the signature M burger, but if overcome with guilt, you can always order the all-veggie Nurse Betty. If you're the type who adores breakfast for dinner, linger at Michigan Avenue's **West Egg Cafe**. This comfortable coffee corridor may serve lunch and dinner as well, but crowds really flock here for their deliciously fluffy omelettes, pancakes, wafflcityes, and other "eggcellent" dishes including "The Swiss Account" featuring eggs, ham, mushrooms, and Swiss cheese baked to perfection, and crowned with olives, tomatoes, and sour cream.

Sip and Savor

And for those whose tastes run more toward champagne and cocktails than cheeseburgers and crinkle-cut fries, there's always the **Signature Lounge**, located on the 96th floor of the John Hancock Center. An idyllic spot for nightcaps, the Signature Lounge also presents staggering brunch, lunch, dinner, and dessert menus that employ some of the freshest and most fine ingredients in town. While their creative concoctions are a touch pricey, one glimpse of the sparkling cityscape will have you lilting in delight. And finally, the Northwestern Hospital complex is another esteemed establishment that dominates the Streeterville scene. Besides its top medical and surgical services, also catering to the spectrum of staff and visitors is a parade of dining gems (cafés, lounges, and ethnic canteens) that loom large over the neighborhood and lake.

C-House

Contemporary

166 E. Superior St. (at St. Clair St.)

Phone: 312-523-0923   Lunch & dinner daily
Web: www.c-houserestaurant.com
Prices: $$ Chicago (Red)

Housed in the MileNorth hotel, C-House has a definitive buzz about it. However, don't come expecting to see the celeb chef in action at this casually stylish yet contemporary space designed by Brazilian architect, Arthur Casas.

Meals here may begin with a fresh house-pickled herring coupled with pickled onions and rye bread. The kitchen supports a host of local farms and fisheries and the same is revealed in such concise entrée selections as venison loin with spruce-roasted carrots, pancetta, and apple; and grilled Running Waters trout with black radish, fennel, and Meyer lemon. The dessert menu offers a whimsical "Candy Bar" selection of chocolate for those with a sweet tooth.

Cité

Contemporary

505 N. Lake Shore Dr. (entrance on Grand Ave.)

Phone: 312-644-4050   Dinner nightly
Web: www.citechicago.com
Prices: $$$

Any restaurant with 360-degree views of a magnificent city skyline and the expanse of Lake Michigan has to know that what's outside is likely to detract from what's inside. That's true at this 70th floor establishment atop Lake Point Tower, where the views of Navy Pier and the lake are particularly breathtaking.

In recent years, neither the décor nor the continental menu has been able to compete with the panoramic views, but that doesn't mean the kitchen isn't trying to keep the competition interesting. Perhaps start with braised morels beside sweet English peas and a creamy egg yolk before moving on to a hearty bone marrow-crusted beef tenderloin. For dessert, bananas Foster flambéed tableside will challenge the Navy Pier for your attention.

Coco Pazzo Café

A2

Italian ✗✗

636 N. St. Clair St. (at Ontario St.)

Phone: 312-664-2777   Lunch & dinner daily
Web: www.cocopazzocafe.com
Prices: $$ 🚇 Grand (Red)

Doctors from nearby Northwestern Hospital, tourists, and local denizens all adore the cheery atmosphere and Tuscan-style décor of Coco Pazzo Café. This nice little haunt is one of the better options in the nabe by dint of its good service and tasty food. The inviting colors of Italy create a calming ambience in their small though snug dining room.

This kitchen delivers a Tuscan- and Chicago-flecked menu with easy, appealing salads, antipasti, pastas, and mains. Lunch is light with sandwiches on grilled ciabatta, while dinner is more substantial offering crowd-pleasing plates of rigatoni *"buttera"* with sausage, peas, and a whirl of cream. A side of seasoned fries will have you pining for the "Tuscan sun" in just a matter of minutes.

Indian Garden

A2

Indian ✗✗

247 E. Ontario St. (bet. Fairbanks Ct. & St. Clair St.)

Phone: 312-280-4910   Lunch & dinner daily
Web: www.indiangardenchicago.com
Prices: $$ 🚇 Grand (Red)

Frequent diners know it as "The IG," but first-timers will appreciate the copious lunch buffet as much as the doctors, med students, and locals. These faithful droves routinely make the trip up a few flights of stairs to get their *pakora* and tandoori fix on, among kitschy but ornate touches like richly colored fabrics and wafting incense.

Though the à la carte menu offers Northern Indian dishes brought to the table in shiny copper vessels, the lunch buffet covers all bases with vegetarian, chicken, and lamb items. Staples like *saag*, *dal*, naan, and basmati rice are freshly made; *bhuna gosht* mixes succulent lamb with tomatoes, onions, and spices; while *lassi* or masala tea provide refreshment along with a decent selection of wine, beer, and cocktails.

Les Nomades

A2

French ✕✕✕

222 E. Ontario St. (bet. Fairbanks Ct. & St. Clair St.)

Phone: 312-649-9010   Dinner Tue – Sat
Web: www.lesnomades.net
Prices: $$$$ 🚇 Grand (Red)

The hush of old-world formality and restrained elegance fills this sliver of a two-story brownstone that houses Les Nomades. Whether greeted personally by Owner Mary Beth Liccioni or any of her besuited staff, courtesy and civility reigns among the dining room's voluminous floral arrangements, properly chilled martini glasses, and seated gentlemen in jackets.

With the return of Executive Chef Roland Liccioni, contemporary touches enliven classic French cuisine available through four- and five-course prix-fixe menus. Lemongrass-infused tomato purée and black olive tapenade complement a firm piece of Arctic char. Whereas escargots in a yellow tomato coulis, or kabocha squash soup with caramelized fennel and truffle foam supplement sweet and savory flavors.

Michael Jordan's

A2

Steakhouse ✕✕✕

505 N. Michigan Ave. (bet. Grand Ave. & Illinois St.)

Phone: 312-321-8823   Lunch & dinner daily
Web: www.mjshchicago.com
Prices: $$$ 🚇 Grand (Red)

In the swank InterContinental Hotel on Michigan Avenue (a prime location befitting the greatest), the namesake steakhouse of His Airness holds court. Subtle shout-outs to the game like oversized sepia prints that on closer inspection depict nylon basketball netting, appear among leather chairs and burgundy booths.

MJ is a Southern gent at heart, and the menu makes reference to his North Carolina upbringing by way of dishes like shrimp and grits; or fried chicken and waffles. Should you want to threepeat with your meal, slam-dunk menu items include dry-aged steaks with trophy-worthy char and minerality set beside mushrooms; toasted garlic ciabatta laden with Wisconsin Roth Käse buttermilk blue cheese fondue; and a 23-layer (get it?) chocolate cake.

The Purple Pig

A2

Mediterranean

500 N. Michigan Ave. (at Illinois St.)

Phone: 312-464-1744
Web: www.thepurplepigchicago.com
Prices: $$

Lunch & dinner daily

Grand (Red)

Grace under pressure defines the atmosphere at this fantastically busy spot overlooking the Chicago River. Despite the constant hum of action, comfort radiates from every corner of the wide room, where friendly conversations from skillful bartenders and strangers at the next seat all become pleasant dining companions whether seated at the counter or one of the many communal tables.

Once you've pulled up a stool and taken a first sip of wine from the wall-mounted selection, thoughts of devouring the entire menu set in. Try the aromatic charred octopus with green beans, fingerling potatoes, and salsa verde; or dunk some woodsy and earthy *jamón serrano*, oyster and black trumpet mushrooms, and grilled bread into the yolk of an oozing duck egg.

Riva

D2

Seafood

700 E. Grand Ave. (on Navy Pier)

Phone: 312-644-7482
Web: www.rivanavypier.com
Prices: $$

Lunch & dinner daily

Wind your way down Navy Pier's perennially crowded boardwalk and catch your breath just past the Ferris wheel. Yachts and tall ships are picture-perfect backdrops at this seafood-driven haven, which stays family-friendly without verging on touristy. Parents might want to cool their heels at the expansive bar area both in the upstairs dining room and downstairs café.

Cherished dishes have included horseradish-rich crab cocktail with jumbo lump chunks; a chopped seafood salad mingled with greens and tossed in a Dijon vinaigrette; or a crisp-skinned, pan-roasted salmon fillet drizzled with sweet barbecue sauce. Non-pescatarians will be happy to see prime steaks and other land-based entrées on offer, and everyone will steal a bite of the tasty tiramisu.

Sayat Nova

Middle Eastern ✗✗

A2

157 E. Ohio St. (bet. Michigan Ave. & St. Clair St.)

Phone: 312-644-9159
Web: www.sayatnovachicago.com
Prices: $$

Lunch Mon – Sat
Dinner nightly
🚇 Grand (Red)

Streeterville's business crowd knows a good deal; that's why they flock to Sayat Nova. Here generous portions and reasonable prices are always on the menu. Also adding the to allure inside are tables tucked intimately along the wall, while intricately designed metal luminaries lend a pleasant exoticism to the space.

The menu is made up of tasty, boldly flavored Armenian and Middle Eastern treats. Perhaps begin with creamy *hommos*, heaped with tahini, garlic, and olive oil and finished with a spike of paprika and chopped parsley. Follow it up with a satisfying entrée: choose from a variety of kebabs, or go for a lesser-known dish such as ground lamb *kibbee* (like a well-seasoned and spiced meatloaf) served with *jajik*, a refreshing yogurt sauce.

The Zodiac

A1

American ✗✗

737 N. Michigan Ave. (at Superior St.)

Phone: 312-694-4050
Web: www.neimanmarcus.com
Prices: $$

Lunch Mon – Sat

🚇 Chicago (Red)

Even if you subscribe to the philosophy that nothing tastes as good as skinny feels–as many of the slender diners chatting and sipping flutes of Aperol-spiked arancia spritzes no doubt do–The Zodiac offers much to entice and satisfy beyond just salads. The hushed retreat on the fourth floor of Neiman Marcus is coolly elegant but genuinely welcoming.

A complimentary popover, served to all guests with a tiny amuse of consommé, should be set on a pedestal for its lasting pleasure: dense, chewy, and buttery, it's tempting to ask for a second one. While sandwiches like the turkey melt with applewood-smoked bacon and roasted Roma tomatoes, or freshly made soups like a filling cup of brothy lentils with a dollop of sour cream, are far more than deli faves.

Tru ✿

A1

676 N. St. Clair St. (bet. Erie & Huron Sts.)

Phone: 312-202-0001

Dinner Mon – Sat

Web: www.trurestaurant.com

Prices: $$$$

🚇 Chicago (Red)

Mark Ballogg

Serious but not stuffy and imposing but not showy, Tru is a mind-reader of a restaurant, effortlessly giving you what you want before you can even consider asking. The high-ceilinged dining room has a cool, muted gallery feel with pops of winking, playful color and contemporary art dispersed throughout. Plush drapes and tufted blue banquettes (with matching purse stools for the ladies, no less) leave a striking impression against glossy white walls.

Finesse and charm work in concert throughout the three- six- and nine-course prix-fixe menus. Delightfully executed plates show lighthearted touches like pearls of smoked, poached, and puréed white sturgeon presented in a caviar tin; and an entire hollowed-out kohlrabi filled with chilled curry-flecked soup. Simpler dishes are no less elegant in taste, like Jidori chicken roulade stuffed with a foie gras farce.

Desserts and mignardises mix sweet and savory to stunning effect in grown-up pleasures like semifreddo gumdrops of honey and *fromage blanc*; or mini yet mighty tasty cranberry macarons. The wine list, with exotics from India and Greece along with a notable stable of premium bottles from Europe and the U.S., is another treat to peruse.

West Loop
Greektown · Market District

THE NEW WEST LOOP

What a difference a century (or two) makes—the West Loop was once home to smoke-spewing factories and warehouses, but walk through this natty neighborhood now, and you'll find young professionals instead of struggling immigrants. Transformed into luxurious lofts, cool nightclubs, art galleries, and cutting-edge restaurants, the warehouses and factories are a far cry from their former existence. Immigrants staked their claim to this neighborhood years ago, and traces of ethnic flavor are still found here. It's not as big as it once was, but nearby Taylor Street still buzzes and lures with its old-world, slightly kitschy feel. It is delis, groceries, and, restaurants galore.

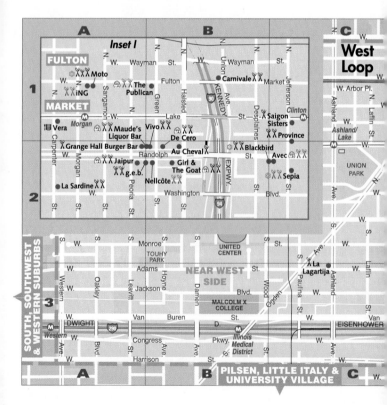

A Taste of Greece

Maintain this Mediterranean vibe by heading over to Greektown, where everybody's Greek, even if just for the day. Shout "oopa" at the Taste of Greece festival, held each August, or stop by the **Parthenon** for gyros and some serious showmanship—they even serve flaming *saganaki* cheese. If Greek and Italian foods don't fit the bill, there's definitely something to whet your appetite along Randolph Street, often referred to as "Restaurant Row." From sushi to subs, this street has it all. For those who enjoy binging at breakfast, head on over to **Dodo at Dino's**. This local favorite satiates all and sundry with its daily brunch proffering of seasonal frittatas, French toast, and yes, heart-warming Japanese pancakes! Speaking of gratification, **Next** is an innovative and ever-changing restaurant from Chef Grant Achatz of Alinea (in Lincoln Park) fame. Next channels a different place in time each quarter (year). Its themes may vary from Escoffier-inspired dishes from Paris 1906 and childhood memories turned on their head, to chronicling the evolution of El Bulli over

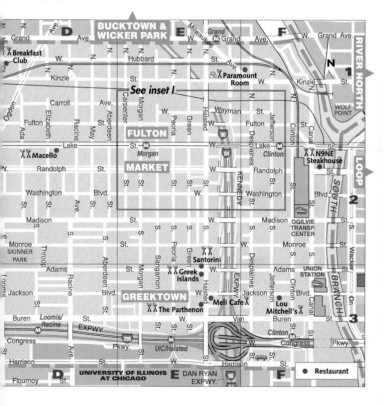

the years. What also sets this hot spot apart is its unique on-line reservation system, where a countless number of fans refresh their computer screens everyday in hopes of snagging a non-refundable ticket and coveted seat. Achatz's cocktails over ice at **The Aviary** next door also appreciate the buzz. Here, spherification and other playful techniques mix with booze to create such theatrical concoctions, where the ice is often a work of art in its own right.

For a magnificent night about town, you can even round up 1,000 of your closest peeps to dine at one of the many Moroccan-Mediterranean restaurants flaunting delights from hummus and baba ghanoush, to more faithful spreads like shrimp *charmoula* and *dolmeh*. Further west on Randolph, find **The Tasting Room**, a two-level stop for excellent wines accompanied by a good selection of à la carte dishes, artisan cheeses, small plates, and rich desserts.

Crafting Culinary Skills

Rather whip it up than wolf it down? Beef up your kitchen skills at the Calphalon Culinary Center, where groups can arrange for private hands-on instruction. Mastered the bœuf Bourguignon? Get in line at **Olympic Meat Packers**. This leading, old-school meatpacking jewel is one of the last holdouts in the area. It's certainly not for the squeamish, but the butchers slice and dice the perfect meat to order. Troll the stalls at the **Chicago French Market** for organic cheeses, roasted nuts, gourmet pickles, flowers, and other specialty items for your next dinner party. If you don't have a ramekin or Dutch oven, Northwestern Cutlery Supply stocks everything a chef could need—even the requisite white coat. Treasure hunters mark the spot at the Chicago Antique Market. This massive indoor/outdoor market is held the last Saturday of each month from May through October, and stocks everything from jewelry to furniture.

Beer and the Ballgame

Hoops fans whoop it up at Bulls games at the United Center, also home to the Stanley Cup winners—the Blackhawks. Depending on the score, the most exciting part of the night might be post game, especially if over a beer at **Beer Bistro**. You'll need to bring your most decisive friends as this place has 124 varieties of bottled beer (and 21 on tap). To nibble on the side, bona fide pub grub like spinach-and-artichoke dip, fried calamari, and beer-battered chicken fingers are sure to sate. Another spot for those who like a little brawl with their beer is **Twisted Spoke**. This proverbial biker bar (serving shrimp Po'Boys and smut & eggs after midnight on Saturdays) is complete with tattoos and 'tudes to match. The music is loud, crowds are big, and drinks are plentiful, but it's all in good testosterone-and-alcohol-fueled fun. Switching gears, lovely ladies sip champagne at Chicago's hip and hot **Plush** restaurant and lounge. If you've indulged in one too many sips of bubbly, grab a blanket (and fresh air), and head to Union Park for a much-needed alfresco nap.

Au Cheval

American

B2

800 W. Randolph St. (at Halsted St.)

Phone: 312-929-4580
Web: N/A
Prices: $$

Dinner nightly

 Morgan

A new entry on West Randolph's ever-growing restaurant row, Au Cheval caters to the kind of go-with-the-flow crowd that doesn't mind waiting (and often eating) at the zinc-topped bar. They happily chatter above the hip tunes coming from the authentic reel-to-reel by the door, making a fun-loving ruckus.

Fitting the "diner for grownups" theme, the menu is packed with satisfying dishes that pair well with draft (or root) beer options. In-house butchers offer sausages like bratwurst (served with roasted garlic gravy); cure peppered bacon (sliced thick enough to be mini steaks); and accordion sliced 32-ounce pork Porterhouse stuffed with foie gras and roasted apples. Salmon rillettes with soft-cooked eggs and house-made pickles work for lighter appetites.

Avec

American

C2

615 W. Randolph St. (bet. Desplaines & Jefferson Sts.)

Phone: 312-377-2002
Web: www.avecrestaurant.com
Prices: $$

Dinner nightly

 Clinton (Green/Pink)

Extremely loud and incredibly close isn't just a critically acclaimed novel—it's the unofficial motto of Avec, where the wooden-planked room jams 'em in every night. A strict no-reservations policy means prime-time waits can be brutal, but well-selected wine and beer lists can help pass the time. You might even meet a new best friend seated hip-to-hip at the bar or one of the long communal tables.

Menu items seem simply prepared, but explode with whimsical touches and big flavors. Plates arrive as the kitchen finishes them, so be ready to share such fresh, delicious goodies as sunchoke crostini with briny salmon roe, wafer-thin radishes, and brown butter; or a crock with tangles of tender baby squid laced in a rich tomato sauce studded with *guanciale*.

Blackbird ✣

B2

Contemporary ✗✗

619 W. Randolph St. (bet. Des Plaines & Jefferson Sts.)

Phone: 312-715-0708	Lunch Mon – Fri
Web: www.blackbirdrestaurant.com	Dinner nightly
Prices: $$$	🚇 Clinton (Green/Pink)

Doug Fogelson

The fine dining pioneers of Randolph Street, Paul Kahan and team, keep this somewhat industrial stretch of the neighborhood lively, pushing forward with this perennial favorite. Blackbird's polished white façade shimmers across the alley from its more rustic sibling restaurant, Avec.

The understated design makes it easy to mistake the setting for a contemporary Japanese restaurant in Tokyo or New York. Through the plate-glass window that spans the entire façade, a long, glossy white bar leads the eye into the narrow room then down walls lined with dove-gray banquettes that face retro-modern, pedestal-mounted wooden chairs. Even the most virtuous can't help eavesdropping across the tight-knit tables.

The globally inspired and seasonally focused menu builds flavor through every detail, large and small, on each creative dish. Expect grilled asparagus and briny sea beans with fresh dill and chervil to accent a pleasantly rare grilled Pekin-style duck breast; or stewed rhubarb and pine nut granola balancing a mousse that converts even those with misgivings on white chocolate. Lunch offerings are casual with sandwiches, *croques madames*, a short rib burger, as well as substantial entrées.

Breakfast Club

D1

American

1381 W. Hubbard St. (at Noble St.)

Phone: 312-666-2372

Lunch daily

Web: www.chicagobreakfastclub.com

Prices:

 Ashland (Green/Pink)

Brains, athletes, basket cases, princesses, and juvie thugs are all welcome at this Breakfast Club on the West Side. You can't miss the clapboard house with striped pink-and-brown awnings, though you might have to circle the block a few times for parking. Inside, it's quirky and quaint with light fixtures made of milk bottles and a marble counter for cocktails if the hair of the dog is what you need.

The menu covers all the breakfast, lunch, and even early dinner bases. House specialties include eggs Benedict, breakfast burritos packed with bacon and avocado, or stuffed French toast. Hungrier fiends may go for comfort food like a burger or grilled cheese sandwich. Open till 5:00 P.M., there's no reason not to make a visit to this club an all-day affair.

Carnivale

B1

Latin American

702 W. Fulton Market (at Union Ave.)

Phone: 312-850-5005

Lunch Mon – Fri

Web: www.carnivalechicago.com

Dinner nightly

Prices: $$

 Clinton (Green/Pink)

As much a spectacle as it is a restaurant, Carnivale aims for a festive feel on all levels. In a lofty dining room that could double as a hangar for parade floats, the décor explodes in a Technicolor kaleidoscope that may over-stimulate even the color-blind. Coupled with the pulsing Latin music, it's a riot for the senses that gets even wilder with a choice from the vast rum, tequila, and cocktail list.

The smaller lunch menu serves as the warm-up act with salads, sandwiches, and daily specials, but the real show begins at dinner. Dishes from Latin America, Spain, and the Caribbean mix and mingle in an all-embracing menu unveiling a Yucatan chicken soup with roasted chiles. Artisanal hams, cheeses, and *arrachera* with *chimichurri* also steal the spotlight.

De Cero

Mexican ✗✗

814 W. Randolph St. (at Halsted St.)

Phone: 312-455-8114
Web: www.decerotaqueria.com
Prices: $$

Lunch Tue – Fri
Dinner Tue – Sat
📮 Morgan

Fun, lively, and edgy, De Cero is modern Mexican with much to offer—starting with an excellent and limey-crisp margarita from the u-shaped bar. The loud music may impart a slightly raucous vibe, but its low-key locale, amiable staff, and cliché-free style keep things in check. The décor is urban yet rustic, with two main rooms dominated by loft-like ceilings and hefty furniture. Views into the open kitchen and the sight of a designated tortilla-maker ensure that the focus is on the food. While the hours of operation spin with the season, its simple, refined cooking is a constant. Relish fragrant, fresh tacos filled with battered shrimp and avocado *crema*; *rajas* with potatoes and *cotija* cheese; or chipotle chicken with bacon-mashed pinto beans.

g.e.b.

American ✗✗

841 W. Randolph St. (bet. Green & Peoria Sts.)

Phone: 312-888-2258
Web: www.gebistro.com
Prices: $$

Dinner nightly

📮 Morgan

Stacked Marshall amps comprise the host stand; menus are on notebook paper taped to old records; and the marble bar is devoid of stools. At the rock concert that is a Graham Elliot production, you gotta stand while you grab a canned beer served in its own foam coozy. Mixed with the rock n' roll imagery is a bit of hero worship: votive-style candles through the room are embellished not with saints, but with icons from the music and cooking worlds like Julia Child and Gordon Ramsay.

Don't be fooled by the loud and playful vibe as the food blends simplicity and finesse with ingredient trios listed as main elements for each dish. Golden trout + sorrel spaetzle + forest mushrooms sounds minimal, but each component perfects the other in flavor and execution.

Girl & The Goat

Contemporary ✗✗

B2

809 W. Randolph St. (bet. Green & Halsted Sts.)

Phone: 312-492-6262   Dinner nightly
Web: www.girlandthegoat.com
Prices: $$ 🚇 Morgan

If you're not one of the fortunate reservation holders, it helps to be nimble as a mountain goat to score a seat at *Top Chef* champ Stephanie Izard's hot spot. This cavernous space fitted with timber and steel is forever filled with tenaciously hungry diners—from its comfy lounge to the communal benches.

Izard and team take their ingredients seriously by doing all butchering in-house and employing an artisan bread baker. Though the menu's simply sectioned into Vegetables, Fish, and Meat, the kitchen packs complex, bold flavors into each dish. Green beans tossed with a fish sauce vinaigrette and crushed cashews keep their al dente snap, but gain a caramelized char. Meanwhile, head-on smoked blue prawns mix it up with mushroom *gribiche* and creamy polenta.

Grange Hall Burger Bar

American ✗

A2

844 W. Randolph St. (bet. Green & Peoria Sts.)

Phone: 312-491-0844   Lunch & dinner Tue – Sat
Web: www.grangehallburgerbar.com
Prices: 🍴🍴   🚇 Morgan

American Gothic accents (think Grant Wood) invade the big city at Grange Hall, where a down-on-the-farm vibe is telegraphed loud and clear through swinging barn doors, quilted panels hanging above the lunch counter, and mismatched knit napkins set atop tables with wooden chairs and stools. The glassed-in pie kitchen in the back hints dessert won't be an afterthought.

Choose your own adventure when building a burger, starting with a six- or nine-ounce grass-fed beef patty and adding toppings like Midwestern cheeses, smoked bacon, jalapeños, or homemade pickles. If a wedge of strawberry rhubarb pie or Bourbon-spiked milkshake is calling your name (especially when freshly churned ice cream is involved), go easy on those hand-cut farmhouse chili fries.

Greek Islands

E3

200 S. Halsted St. (at Adams St.)

Phone: 312-782-9855
Web: www.greekislands.net
Prices: ⊖⊖

Lunch & dinner daily

UIC-Halsted

More crowded than the streets of Athens and just as busy—that's Greek Islands for you. This Chicago retreat sports multiple dining areas as well as a bar filled to capacity. Diners sup among a Disney-fied décor of faux terraces and balconies, overhangs topped by terra-cotta tiles, and a trellised ceiling entwined with artificial greenery. The chances of a courteous-someone whose name ends in "os" attending to you is good, but it's the food that has kept the joint hopping for 40 years. Try classic Greek fare like baked *saganaki*, grilled octopus, gyros straight off the rotisserie, and warming *pastichio*. Fresh seafood doesn't disappoint: fish are grilled whole, filleted, and dressed simply with herbs, a few glugs of olive oil, and a squeeze of lemon.

iNG

A1

951 W. Fulton Market (bet. Morgan & Sangamon Sts.)

Phone: 855-834-6464
Web: www.ingrestaurant.com
Prices: $$$

Dinner Tue – Sat

Morgan

Set on the stretch along Fulton Market which has the highest food IQ in the country, this playful and eccentric concept from Homaro Cantu walks the line between delicious and crazy. Here, the always contemporary fare changes every six weeks but consistently unveils a world of tasty treats.

Even the background music stays in tune with the carte du jour. A heavy metal themed menu may offer Blue Oyster Cult starring crispy "blue" oysters with powdered mignonette. Some menu cycles pay homage to Martin Scorsese films, while others focus on "Miracle Berries"—a mystery fruit that tricks the palate into believing sour foods are sweet. Imagine a Back In Black donut soup floating with toasted pecans and chocolate lightning bolt and you will get the picture.

Jaipur 😊

Indian 🍴🍴

A2

847 W. Randolph St. (bet. Green & Peoria Sts.)

Phone: 312-526-3655   Lunch & dinner daily
Web: www.jaipurchicago.com
Prices: $$ Morgan

 Wait...a popular lunchtime Indian restaurant that doesn't do a buffet? And yet, these midday business diners digging into tandoor-charred and cheesy garlic naans don't seem to mind at all. They're coming for the equally affordable, full-service, daily specials served in a parade of hammered copper bowls that are filled to the brim. With soft music and dusky pomegranate walls, it's an elegant way to spend lunch hour. Tender morsels of chicken *kadahai* are boldly flavorful with galangal and curry, and the Jaipur platter is a golden-fried crunch fest of stuffed samosa and *pakoras* like banana peppers stuffed with spiced cheese. Dinner guests know to start with a martini before choosing from a vast selection of chicken, seafood, lamb, and vegetarian options.

La Lagartija

Mexican 🍴

C3

132 S. Ashland Ave. (bet. Adams & Monroe Sts.)

Phone: 312-733-7772   Lunch & dinner Mon – Sat
Web: www.lalagartijataqueria.com
Prices: 😊😊   Ashland (Green/Pink)

From sunrise to sundown, La Lagartija serves up heart-warming *blanquillos*, platters of *alambres*, crocks of *cazuelitas* with melted *chihuahua* cheese, and more in this contemporary-psychedelic space. Don't know what any of the food terms mean? Just check the tall walls, which illustrate the terminology in colorful fonts for an impromptu Spanish lesson your stomach will appreciate.

Pull up a brushed aluminium stool to one of the long counters and sink your teeth into a juicy *taco al pastor* made with pork spit-roasted with pineapple, then folded in one the taqueria's made-from-scratch tortillas. Cut through the spicy chili kick found in dishes and fresh salsas that accompany each platter with a refreshing pineapple or hibiscus *agua fresca*.

La Sardine

French ✗✗

111 N. Carpenter St. (bet. Randolph St. & Washington Blvd.)

Phone: 312-421-2800
Web: www.lasardine.com
Prices: $$

Lunch Mon – Fri
Dinner Mon – Sat
 Morgan

 A dependable French-style bistro, La Sardine has one of the most American of claims to fame: it is located literally in front of the entrance to Harpo Studios, Oprah Winfrey's media empire. For years, live television tapings fed audience-member diners into this eatery, although it is also popular with locals and staffers who appreciate its solid food and warm ambience.

Many bistro-goers expect French onion soup as a bellwether, and on this point La Sardine's rich, brothy, sweet, and cheesy stew brimming with onions cooked until tender but still recognizable, does not disappoint. Specials like the halibut are simple, well-priced, and made with the freshest ingredients. A nice wine list and excellent espresso finish off the meal with French flair.

Lou Mitchell's

American ✗

565 W. Jackson Blvd. (bet. Clinton & Jefferson Sts.)

Phone: 312-939-3111
Web: www.loumitchellsrestaurant.com
Prices: ⬤⬤

Lunch daily

 Clinton (Blue)

At the top of Chicago's list of beloved names is Lou Mitchell. This eponymous diner is by no means an elegant affair, but thanks to its fluffy omelets and iconic crowd, it has been on the Windy City's must-eat list since 1923. Don't panic at the length of the lines: they are long but move fast, and free doughnut holes (one of the restaurant's signature baked goods) make the wait go faster.

Back to those omelets: they may be made with mere eggs, like everyone else's, but somehow these are lighter and fluffier, almost like a soufflé, stuffed with feta, spinach, onions, or any other ingredients of your choice. They arrive in skillets with an Idaho-sized helping of potatoes. Save room, because everyone gets a swirl of soft-serve at the meal's end.

Macello

 D2   Italian

1235 W. Lake St. (bet. Elizabeth St. & Racine Ave.)

Phone: 312-850-9870   Dinner nightly
Web: www.macellochicago.com
Prices: $$ Ashland (Green/Pink)

Around the corner from the meatpacking district and within earshot of the roaring El train, find Macello (slaughterhouse in Italian). It's an apt name, since it was one in the 1920s; the front deli still evokes the old days with its polished white subway tiles and dangling meat hooks. Large painted orbs hanging from the vaulted ceiling and renderings of the joker from Sicilian card games add a bit of a carnival feel to the dining room.

Cuisine and wines hone in on Puglia, or the heel of the boot. A duo of wood-burning ovens turn out thin-crust pizzas, modestly adorned with toppings like creamy *burrata* and mortadella, or artichokes and olives. Orecchiette and *trofiette* are prepared in myriad ways, as are steak, chops, and seafood dishes.

Maude's Liquor Bar

B2   Gastropub

840 W. Randolph St. (bet. Green & Peoria Sts.)

Phone: 312-243-9712   Dinner Tue – Sat
Web: www.maudesliquorbar.com
Prices: $$ Morgan

Bring your vintage Miu Miu bag to the party at Maude's, where industrial and antique mix in a sea of candlelit tables, bistro-style mirrors, and aluminum chairs. It's trendy, sure, but who can fault the crowd for appreciating a bar that puts as much thought into its food as the cocktail program and whiskey flight? The first floor dining room can get just as loud as the bar upstairs, which packs 'em in on the late night.

Helpful servers suss out how many plates you'll need based on your hunger levels. A range of ingredients change daily, but don't miss the excellent grilled sausage; or subtle chicken liver mousse with a shallot marmalade. Need a breather? A crunchy shaved vegetable salad balances out the indulgent richness of a dark chocolate mousse.

251

Meli Cafe

%

E3

301 S. Halsted St. (bet. Jackson Blvd. & Van Buren St.)

Phone: 312-454-0748   Lunch daily
Web: www.melicafe.com
Prices: UIC-Halsted

Locals love this Meli Cafe (there's a sister located in River North), not just for the food but because it offers something other than the traditional Greek eats in the heart of Greektown. The proximity to UIC and the Loop packs folks into this yellow dining room decorated with rows of marmalades. Pick homemade apricot and grape or another favorite for your toast.

Meli is open through lunch, but breakfast is where it's at. The kitchen specializes in organic egg dishes such as omelettes, frittatas, and Benedicts. The sun-dried tomato and basil frittata, for example, is mighty wholesome and chock-full of ingredients. Waffles, French toast, and fancy sweet and savory pancakes and crêpes are alternatives for those who don't feel eggy.

Nellcôte

XX

B2

833 W. Randolph St. (at Green St.)

Phone: 312-432-0500   Lunch Sat – Sun
Web: www.nellcoterestaurant.com   Dinner nightly
Prices: $$ Morgan

Nellcôte is pervaded by a sexy, tactile presence: inspired by the French villa where the Rolling Stones recorded in the 1970s, it exudes a louche but luxe rocker vibe with a lacquered ivory counter, Italian marble staircase, and herringbone-patterned wood. Antique crystal chandeliers draw eyes up, as a showy bar runs down the room like a runway for those who want the spotlight.

Equally decadent is a creamy, chilled slice of foie gras torchon, poached in duck fat, rolled in crushed pistachios, and served with mini brioche and *marasca* cherries. Slightly more down-to-earth plates present fava bean- and spring onion-agnolotti mounded with shavings of *ricotta salata*; or halibut crowned with scrambled egg sabayon and black sturgeon caviar.

Moto ✿

Contemporary XXX

A1

945 W. Fulton Market (bet. Morgan & Sangamon Sts.)

Phone: 312-491-0058   Dinner Tue – Sat
Web: www.motorestaurant.com
Prices: $$$$

🚇 Morgan

Mike Silberman

Moto is rather easy to miss amid the meatpacking's loading docks (look for tiny letters on the window). Yet the mod setting offsets its urban surrounds in a monochromatic and minimalist space combining wood paneling, gray fabrics, and granite with booths that offer near-private isolation. Staffers donning dark suits and earpieces present guests with menus while informing them that it's being prepared—only one prix-fixe is offered.

There is a special occasion wow-factor here: it's where you take someone whom you'd like to convince that you're cool (and well-to-do). This is also a place of entertainment, as mad scientists flaunt their whimsy and skill through numerous courses that read like riddles, as in "Kentucky-fried noodle" or "forest foraging." The "black out" might consist of olive oil-poached mahi mahi topped with forbidden rice, black bean, and black garlic purées. The reconstructed corn features a popsicle of popcorn ice cream studded with freeze-dried kernels to resemble a cob's cross-section.

Desserts like the milk chocolate-coated truffle "ACME bomb" are outrageous fun, with a fuse that fizzles when ignited by the server. Its liquid graham cracker filling explodes in the mouth.

253

N9NE Steakhouse

F2

440 W. Randolph St. (at Canal St.)

Phone: 312-575-9900
Web: www.n9ne.com
Prices: $$$

Lunch Mon – Fri
Dinner Mon – Sat
 Clinton (Green/Pink)

"New" is typically the watchword that determines whether or not a night spot is trendy. But even after a decade N9NE Steakhouse still attracts the city's beautiful people for mingling, ogling, and, eating. The restaurant's name comes from the age the owners were when they first met. Those owners include Michael Morton, of Morton's steakhouse fame.

So, it stands to reason that N9NE can serve a good steak. The food is taken seriously, and the menu is simple, but not staid. Also fitting the nightlife vibe are the surf and turf specials, prepared like sliders, with beef tenderloin on one tiny sandwich and Maine lobster on the other. The shrimp cocktail is a little pricey but worth it simply for the kick of the horseradish-tomato cocktail sauce.

Paramount Room

F1

415 N. Milwaukee Ave. (bet. Hubbard & Kinzie Sts.)

Phone: 312-829-6300
Web: www.paramountroom.com
Prices: $$

Lunch Thu – Sun
Dinner nightly
 Grand (Blue)

In some ways, this popular gastropub merits multiple listings for its fittingly adult crowd—as each of its levels have a different vibe, depending on your mood. Housed in a former speakeasy, Paramount Room offers a friendly American Tavern inside this resurrected Prohibition-era basement lounge.

Check out the beer list which may include Belgian, craft-brewed, domestic, and imported varieties. The menu is all about nibbling–an activity that pairs perfectly with drinking–on such delicious dishes as skirt steak with roasted potatoes, sweet onion succotash, and peppercress; ale-steamed mussels infused with garlic and shallots; or a completely indulgent and decadent chocolate turtle-chocolate brownie with a dollop of whipped cream and whole pecans.

The Parthenon

Greek ✗✗

E3

314 S. Halsted St. (bet. Jackson Blvd. & Van Buren St.)

Phone: 312-726-2407 — Lunch & dinner daily
Web: www.theparthenon.com
Prices: 💰💰

🚇 UIC-Halsted

"Opaa!" From the signature shout, the crowds, and decor, to the size of the room and its well-connected clientele on down to the spits with gyros meat roasting in the front windows, this Greek mainstay is stereotypical Greektown. It is loud, bustling, and fun—the kind of place you'd go with a group of co-workers, not for a romantic tête-à-tête.

The menu is large and classic; all the traditional Greek favorites are here. Order the *dolmades*, tender grape leaves filled with a mixture of onion-scented ground beef and rice, and you'll have enough to share with friends or to munch on for lunch the next day. End the meal with the baklava, which has a lovely infusion of cinnamon in the filling, complemented by the well-browned flaky dough.

Province

American ✗✗

C1

161 N. Jefferson St. (bet. Lake & Randolph Sts.)

Phone: 312-669-9900 — Lunch Mon – Fri
Web: www.provincerestaurant.com — Dinner Mon – Sat
Prices: $$

🚇 Clinton (Green/Pink)

Natural and industrial elements complement one another at Province, where recycled cork tables and white tree branches "growing" from the ceiling mix with steel, glass, and walls splashed with magenta accents. The convenient Jefferson Street location makes it a hit with business types—an $18 lunch prix-fixe gets them in and out in a jiffy, and the bar sees its share of after-work revelers.

The carte is divided into categories like Bites, Raw, Small, Big, and Bigger and lets each diner dictate his or her level of hunger and propensity to share the American fare spiked with Central American flavors. Dishes have featured spice-rubbed ahi tuna tacos laced with a serrano chile-tartar sauce and julienned jicama; or pan-roasted salmon with parsnip gnocchi.

The Publican

B1

837 W. Fulton Market (at Green St.)

Phone:	312-733-9555	Lunch Sat – Sun
Web:	www.thepublicanrestaurant.com	Dinner nightly
Prices:	$$	Morgan

The sceney Publican conjures the age-old tradition of a public house (offering a communal setting for animated conversations over a plate of food and pint of beer) to the modern gastropub age. Judging from its packed-to-the-rafters crowd emboldening themselves with beers from tasty on-tap options, it seems as if the new cohorts have no problem keeping this custom alive.

Though warned by the staff, courses come out willy-nilly. Entrées may arrive before appetizers, desserts before veggies. But who really cares if dry-aged duck breast with romesco and lentils share belly time with fried Lake Erie walleye, or caramelized blueberry *crostata*? The results are always dazzling.

Use the valet if trucks from the nearby meatpacking plants make parking scarce.

Saigon Sisters

C1

567 W. Lake St. (bet. Clinton & Jefferson Sts.)

Phone:	312-496-0090	Lunch Mon – Fri
Web:	www.saigonsisters.com	Dinner Mon – Sat
Prices:	🪙🪙	Clinton (Green/Pink)

Saigon Sisters is two restaurants in one: during lunch hours, Fulton River District workers line up for lively grab-and-go casual counter service; which transforms at dinner into a cozy, low-lit, sit-down restaurant with ambitious, westernized Vietnamese fare.

Stopping by at lunch, it's easy to fill up on the killer *bánh bao*: steamed buns filled with a choice of caramelized chicken, Wagyu beef in coconut milk, or to-die-for hoisin-glazed pork belly, all dressed with pickled carrot, daikon, cilantro, and jalapeño. Or try one of many modern variations on the classic *bánh mì*. Dinner is a more upscale affair, tasting menus and prix fixe options–cleverly displayed on blackboards–offer great value, along with à la carte starters and entrées.

Santorini

 E3

Greek ✗✗

800 W. Adams St. (at Halsted St.)

Phone:	312-829-8820
Web:	www.santorinichicago.com
Prices:	

Lunch & dinner daily

🖥 UIC-Halsted

Named for the idyllic Greek island, Chicago's Santorini honors its home country by serving some of the best Greek food this city has to offer. Its charming taverna-style dining room, amiable service, and authentic ambience likewise deserve accolades for being among the most pleasant to be found in Greektown. Whitewashed walls, copper pots, and wood-beamed ceilings define the look, while upbeat Greek music sets a lively tone. Everyone feels like family here—note the groups arriving in droves.

All of the usual classics are on the well-rounded menu, but pay attention to rotating specials, like the hearty lamb *stamnas*, roasted until tender, and tucked with sautéed vegetables inside fluffy crêpes, then blanketed in melted Greek cheeses.

Vera

A1

Spanish 🍽

1023 W. Lake St. (at Carpenter St.)

Phone:	312-243-9770
Web:	www.verachicago.com
Prices:	$$

Dinner Tue – Sun

🖥 Morgan

Cheese, ham, and wine are always enjoyable happy hour companions, especially when their names are Manchego, Iberico, and Oloroso. Ask the urban barflies–contentedly nibbling under Vera's bare filament Edison bulbs and over the ruckus of sherry-fueled chatter–and they'll agree wholeheartedly.

The range of *escabeche* and crudo change nightly, but sexified stalwarts like paella with rabbit, or grilled octopus with potatoes keep the menu purring. Adventurous types might go for rich *morcilla* rounds topped with a runny fried eggs and spicy mizuna; while now-standard roasted Brussels sprouts perk up with crumbles of crispy Iberico ham. A traditional crème Catalan may be an established hit, but why not sip another sherry or share a selection of cheeses?

Sepia ⍟

American 🍴🍴

123 N. Jefferson (bet. Randolph St. & Washington Blvd.)

Phone: 312-441-1920
Web: www.sepiachicago.com
Prices: $$$

Lunch Mon – Fri
Dinner nightly
🚇 Clinton (Green/Pink)

Doug Snower

Imagine the flash, pop, and puff of an old-fashioned camera bulb as you give a hearty tug on Sepia's wooden door. As the (mental) smoke clears upon entering this haven, the 19th century patina remains. The building's industrial roots as a one-time print shop remain evident, from the old freight elevator doors on the walls, to raw materials like weathered brick and linoleum floors throughout.

Sepia's room may be intentionally rough around the edges, but service is polished and energetic, smoothly keeping pace with business lunchers, first-daters, and regulars filling the seats. Jazz wafts through the room over the thud and clink of sturdy barware and flatware, buoying the vintage vibe.

The kitchen presents American bistro food done with finesse: a crisp and seasoned walleye fillet atop buttery chanterelles gets a crunchy, salty kick from a dusting of crumbled chicken skin; whereas juicy braised lamb ravioli brightens up with fresh horseradish and tart crème fraîche. Dessert divulges an adult candy bar that even Willy Wonka can't top—peanut butter *feuilletine* and malted milk chocolate mousse covered in bittersweet chocolate ganache. Shards of pretzel bark are icing on the cake, as it were.

Vivo

Italian XX

B2

838 W. Randolph St. (bet. Green & Peoria Sts.)

Phone: 312-733-3379
Web: www.vivo-chicago.com
Prices: $$

Lunch Mon – Fri
Dinner nightly
Morgan

Life is lovely at Vivo, on Randolph Street's restaurant row. This Italian idol's congenial vibe is palpable both outside on the patio, and inside the lofty dining room outfitted with exposed ductwork and brick walls. Those on the ball aim for the most desired table in the house—perched in the converted elevator shaft with bird's-eye views. Expect well-prepared, rustic food here, brought to you by casual yet attentive waiters.

A fully stocked wine wall keeps good company with *linguine nere alla polpa di granchio*, black linguine with crab meat in a spicy tomato sauce; *costolette di maiale*, cranberry-glazed and wood-grilled pork chop atop horseradish mashed potatoes; and pistachio-crusted tilapia bathed in romesco. It's nothing new, but tasty all the same.

Look for our symbol 🍇,
spotlighting restaurants
with a notable wine list.

259

North &
Northwestern
Suburbs

North & Northwestern Suburbs

Evanston is the suburb that even city-dwellers love. As is the case in any metropolis, sometimes the suburbs fall victim to urban one-upmanship, but Chicago's first stop over the northern border lures a cluster of city folk with its lakefront charms and foodie finds. Additionally, Evanston is home to famed Northwestern University and the Woman's Christian Temperance Union, resulting in an incongruous mash-up of college-town hangouts and odd liquor laws.

Hotbed for Goodies

Evanston's Central Street is a swath of boutiques and cafés. Serious gourmands stock up at the renowned **Spice House**, reputed for their incredible spectrum of high-quality and unique spices, seasonings, rubs, and mixes. All these flavors will certainly inspire and nurture your inner Grant Achatz. It's also a solid choice for housewarming gifts. Nearby on Central Street is **Rose's Wheatfree Bakery and Café**. A rare and relevant establishment, they've garnered a giant following, all of whom come routinely for a treasure trove of gluten-free goodies including breads, cookies, cakes, cupcakes, and muffins to take home. Also sought after is the café menu of pizzas, salads, and sandwiches. Moreover, they carry the precious Tennessee-style Grampa Boo's Basting and Barbecue Sauce for some thrilling at-home grilling. Evanston and the tony North Shore are also

known for **Belgian Chocolatier Piron**—this decadent den features a variety of handmade chocolates and gift items, and also brings some of the finest and richest Belgian chocolates to Evanston.

Dog Day Delights

On the other side of the spectrum and shunning all things gluten-free and highbrow is **Wiener and Still Champion**, a hot dog stop where National Corn Dog Day is celebrated with the works (*sans* ketchup). When ordering, remember that the Chicago dog is a specific thing: A steamed, all-beef hot dog with yellow mustard, Day-Glo relish, chopped onion, tomato wedges, pickle spear, sport peppers, and celery salt on a poppy seed bun. That neon relish is made with sweet pickles and dyed a bright green (sort of like the Chicago River on St. Patrick's Day). Dunk their deep-fried pickles into sauces that reach as high as "truffle-mushroom" or as low as "bacon-bacon." Another inordinately famous and faithful hot dog and burger base is **Poochie's** in Skokie. For a more retro experience, approach the iconic **Superdawg**, with its dancing hot dogs dressed in spotted gear. This family-owned and operated drive-in will make you feel as if you've just entered the set of *American Graffiti*. With its super menu of super-dogs (made with pure beef), burgers, sandwiches, beverages, and soda fountain specialties including floating scoops of ice cream in bubbling root beer, this is as much a family tradition as it is a landmark since 1948.

True fast foodies pay homage to the golden arches at the McDonald's Museum in Des Plaines. The building is a re-creation of the original store, with massive displays of fresh potatoes being peeled and root beer drawn from a barrel by a uniformed crew of mannequins, fashioning a diorama that is as visually authentic as it is weird. It is no surprise that Chicago has its fair share of highway fast food stops. After all, the concept was virtually invented here when the Fred Harvey Company (which Hollywood immortalized in Judy Garland's *Harvey Girls* film), went from catering to railway passengers to a constant roster of motorists. It partnered to build the visually imposing series of mid-century "oases" stretching over the Illinois Tollway now catering to modern-day travelers. Speaking of travelers, those looking for a natural nibble should stop by **wilde & greene restaurant + natural market** brimming with kosher, vegan, sustainable, and gluten-free items. Also on the premises are ten different food stations offering the likes of burgers, pizza, seafood, and sushi.

Ethnic Enclaves

In such a diverse cultural urban center, it is no wonder that other ethnic enclaves are also thriving. Along Devon Avenue, you will find one of the country's larger South Asian communities. This corridor of South Asia showcases sincere and genuine restaurants (*desi* diners included),

shops, and grocery stores serving a largely Indian and Pakistani clientele. Come for terrific *tandoori* and leave with an elaborate sari! Presenting everything Japanese under one roof is **Mitsuwa Marketplace** in Arlington Heights. This enormous supermarket carries everything from top-notch beef and sashimi to Japanese groceries, baked goods, books, and cosmetics. Also housed within this marvel is their version of Restaurant Row replete with restaurants offering everything from traditional Japanese dishes to fast-food Chinese and Korean selections. Journeying from Asia to the Middle East and closer to Park Ridge, Des Plaines, and Niles, find an array of ethnic supermarkets filled with Greek and Middle Eastern specialties. The influence of a massive Mexican population is found here as well within deliciously authentic tacos, tortas, and other foods at the many taquerias dotting these sprawling suburbs. There is a new generation of casual eateries and fast-food concepts booming here— **bopNgrill** is frequented for its fantastically messy burgers and Korean fusion; **Buffalo Joe's** is *the* go-to spot for chicken wings on Clark St.; **Rollin' To Go** is a pearl among Northwestern students; and **Al's Deli** is a neighborhood fixture. With fast-food forgotten, end a day here at **Amitabul**. This fusion Korean restaurant prepares delicious and healthy items. Also on the menu are Buddhist delicacies with organic vegetables and spicy sauces for a vegan-friendly meal that, somehow, couldn't be more American. It is truly a gem that transcends all traditional tastes.

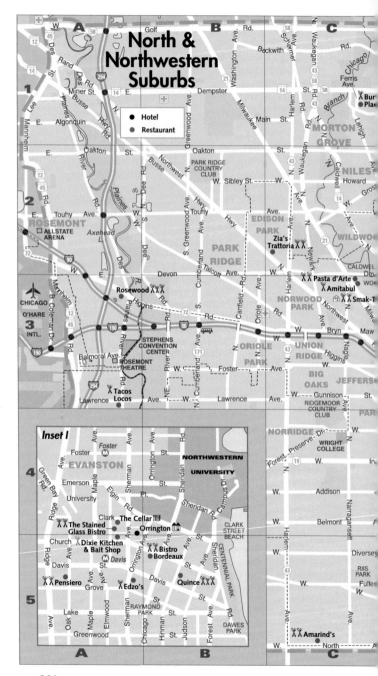

North & Northwestern Suburbs

Legend:
- ● Hotel
- ● Restaurant

MORTON GROVE
NILES
WILDWOOD
CALDWELL
ROSEMONT
ALLSTATE ARENA
EDISON PARK
PARK RIDGE
PARK RIDGE COUNTRY CLUB
Zia's Trattoria
Pasta d'Arte
Amitabul
Smak-T
Rosewood
CHICAGO O'HARE INTL.
NORWOOD PARK
STEPHENS CONVENTION CENTER
ROSEMONT THEATRE
ORIOLE PARK
UNION RIDGE
BIG OAKS
JEFFERS
Tacos Locos
RIDGEMOOR COUNTRY CLUB
NORRIDGE
WRIGHT COLLEGE
Bur Pla

Inset I

EVANSTON
NORTHWESTERN UNIVERSITY
Foster
The Stained Glass Bistro
The Cellar
Orrington
Dixie Kitchen & Bait Shop
Bistro Bordeaux
CLARK STREET BEACH
Pensiero
Edzo's
Quince
RAYMOND PARK
DAWES PARK
CENTENNIAL PARK
RIIS PARK
Amarind's

264

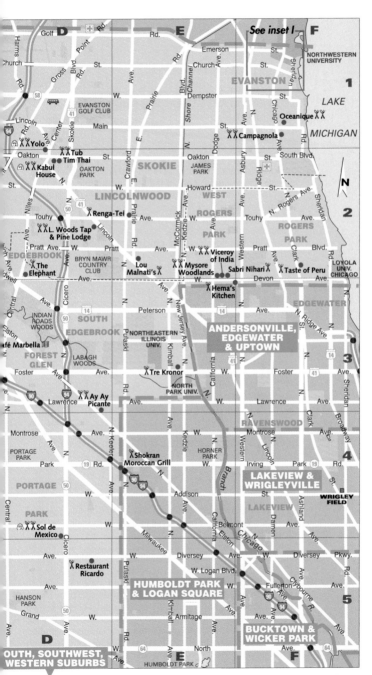

Amarind's

Thai

C5

6822 W. North Ave. (at Newcastle Ave.)

Phone: 773-889-9999
Web: www.amarinds.com
Prices:

Lunch Tue – Sat
Dinner Tue – Sun

Amarind's corner location and turret-like entrance is a favorite of Oak Parkers and others looking for affordable, solid Thai food in a family-friendly environment. Weekday specials and accommodations for kids keep tables filled day and night. A bright and pleasant décor dotted with Thai artifacts, tapestries, and artwork set the scene.

Start with deliciously filled chive dumplings served with a dipping sauce of soy, chili, and black vinegar. Follow with spicy grilled pork loin coated in a savory marinade of lemongrass, shallot, garlic, scallion, mint, lime juice, and chili paste (note that if you like things spicy, ask your server to alert the kitchen). Accompany tasty dishes like these with a cold glass of sweet and creamy Thai iced tea.

Amitabul

Korean

C3

6207 N. Milwaukee Ave. (bet. Huntington & Raven Sts.)

Phone: 773-774-0276
Web: www.amitabulvegan.com
Prices:

Lunch & dinner Tue – Sun

With its Korean-inspired menu of "Healing Buddhist Spiritual Vegan Cuisine," Amitabul strives to heal all that ails you (and even if it doesn't, the food is still really tasty here).

Get those immunities humming again with dishes like "Green and Greener Nirvana," or perhaps the ultimate panacea, "Dr. K's Cure All Noodle Soup." Munch on steamed *mandoo* vegan dumplings, with flavors that come alive in a duo of salty red-chili and sweet soy dipping sauces. Spice lovers tuck into the "Yin and Yan," coin-sized slices of chewy brown rice cakes stir-fried in a spicy red chili sauce with a host of perfectly fresh and crunchy vegetables. Libations are limited to energizing juices and cozy teas, which may not be enough to brighten the lack of ambience here.

Ay Ay Picante

D3

Peruvian ✗✗

4569 N Elston Ave. (bet. Kennicott & Kiona Aves.)

Phone: 773-427-4239

Web: www.ayaypicante.com

Prices: 💲

Lunch & dinner daily

🚇 Irving Park (Blue)

Incans, Andeans, and conquistadors have shaped Peru's cultural and culinary history, and Ay Ay Picante celebrates them all, bringing flavor to an otherwise bland neighborhood. Murals of mysterious images of the Peruvian desert decorate the dining room, and pan flute melodies trill in the background.

Leave the carb-phobic at home; Peruvian staples of corn, potatoes, and rice are all over this six-page menu so vegetarians won't go hungry. Authenticity strikes a chord in classic dishes like crispy fried empanadas stuffed with hard-boiled egg and ground beef; or *tamal Peruano*, steamed banana leaves filled with chicken, nuts, and black olives, and paired with *salsa criolla*. Their signature *aji verde* is so much in demand it's now sold by the bottle.

Bistro Bordeaux

B5

French ✗✗

618 Church St. (bet. Chicago & Orrington Aves.), Evanston

Phone: 847-424-1483

Web: www.lebistrobordeaux.com

Prices: $$

Lunch Sun

Dinner nightly

🚇 Davis

Bistro Bourdeaux hits that American ideal of the classic "French" bistro right on *le nez*. The old-world ambience is created thanks to details such as smoky mirrors, ancient pots and pans hanging on hooks, pressed-tin ceilings, and the list goes on. The service is well timed, and the prices just right for a night out.

Just as the décor meets the "Frenchified" brasserie expectations, so, too, does the food. The onion soup is classically done in an American style, with caramelized onions and a blend of rich melted cheeses. Choose from roasted skate wing, chicken liver pâté, or escargots for classic French flavor. Desserts meet expectations, too. You won't find a berry coulis bathing your *île flottante* in Lyon, but in Evanston, it's just fine.

Burt's Place

C1

8541 Ferris Ave. (bet Capulina & Lincoln Aves.), Morton Grove

Phone: 847-965-7997
Web: N/A
Prices:

Lunch Wed – Fri
Dinner Wed – Sun

If you're dedicated to deep-dish pizza, follow these three rules to guarantee a memorable meal at Burt's Place: make a reservation and place your order a few days in advance, call as soon as or just before the restaurant opens to reliably reach a staffer, and arrive on time to ensure a still-hot and bubbling pizza. Why go to all this trouble for a pizza? Quite simply, because Burt's, a neighborhood favorite that looks the part with its tchotchke-covered, wood-paneled dining room, makes great deep-dish and that's it.

With limited oven space, timing is paramount. But when a generous slice with a thick, caramelized crust, tangy tomato sauce, piles of toppings, and the perfect balance of cheese hits your table, you'll know why you made the effort.

Café Marbella

D3

5527 N. Milwaukee Ave. (bet. Bryn Mawr & Catalpa Aves.)

Phone: 773-853-0128
Web: www.cafemarbella.com
Prices: $$

Dinner Tue – Sun

The unassuming location of this tapas spot is perfect for large groups who want to pass around plates, tasting a little bit of everything. The décor is understated, with red clay tile floors, brick archways, and simple booths, all the better to allow diners to focus on the authentic food.

The restaurant's talented team of chefs have cooked in some of the city's most favored Spanish-style kitchens, and the tapas are prepared quite well here. Look for classics like gazpacho *Andaluz*, *gambas al ajillo*, and *piquillos con atún*. Tortilla *Española* is cooked as if the kitchen were in Spain, not on the northwest side; while sautéed Rioja-style chorizo lounges among large, buttery, tender white beans and sautéed strips of red pepper and onion.

Campagnola

Italian

F1

815 Chicago Ave. (at Washington St.), Evanston

Phone: 847-475-6100 Dinner Tue – Sun
Web: www.campagnolarestaurant.com
Prices: $$ Main

Who says you have to head downtown for a fabulous night out on the town? Campagnola is proof that the suburbs can sizzle. From its sultry and soft lighting to the exposed brick walls and comfortable banquette seating, this Italian jewel seems to be designed with a tête-à-tête in mind.

The subdued sophistication of the dining room is echoed in the kitchen, where the chef ensures that the best designs are indeed simple. You won't find a high-falutin carte filled with adjectives describing fancy ingredients or fussy cooking techniques. Instead, this menu is purely about simplicity where dishes like chicken *al mattone* and linguini tossed with spicy shrimp headline. From start to finish, Campagnola satisfies with every beautiful bite.

The Cellar

International

A4

820 Clark St. (bet. Benson & Sherman Aves.), Evanston

Phone: 847-425-5112 Dinner nightly
Web: www.thecellarevanston.com
Prices: 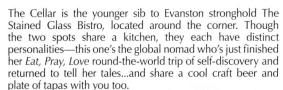 Davis

The Cellar is the younger sib to Evanston stronghold The Stained Glass Bistro, located around the corner. Though the two spots share a kitchen, they each have distinct personalities—this one's the global nomad who's just finished her *Eat, Pray, Love* round-the-world trip of self-discovery and returned to tell her tales...and share a cool craft beer and plate of tapas with you too.

What the Stained Glass does for wine drinkers, The Cellar does for beer. These far-reaching brews pair seamlessly with the small plates menu divvied into sections labeled A Hint of Europe, All-American, and Worldwide. Dive into varied bites like blue cheese beignets with roasted mushrooms and Port wine syrup; before going whole hog on the fried chicken with sweet garlic gravy.

269

Dixie Kitchen & Bait Shop

Southern

825 Church St. (bet. Benson & Sherman Aves.), Evanston

Phone: 847-733-9030   Lunch & dinner daily
Web: www.dixiekitchenchicago.com
Prices:

 Davis

Kitsch and college campus combine at this paean to Southern food. The inexpensive prices and considerable portions have made it a favorite of budget-driven students, so be prepared to wait for a table.

Meals start with a cornmeal griddle cake and progress to plates of flavorful fare like fried chicken, jerk catfish, crayfish étouffé, Dixie ribs, jambalaya, and other classics from south of the Mason-Dixon line. The catfish Po'boy is perfectly fried without a touch of oiliness, layered on a French roll with lettuce, tomato, and remoulade. The rich gumbo is deliciously swimming with shrimp, chicken, and andouille sausage.

Desserts like peach cobbler or pecan pie sweeten the deal and their breakfast makes for an over-the-top start to any day.

Edzo's

American

1571 Sherman Ave. (bet. Davis & Grove Sts.), Evanston

Phone: 847-864-3396   Lunch Tue – Sun
Web: www.edzos.com
Prices:

 Davis

Burger shop plus nearby college campus usually equals one thing, but Edzo's somehow takes the formula and gets a different answer. Yes, this close to the Northwestern University campus Edzo's attracts a lot of students and faculty. And, yes, the menu is burgers, fries, and shakes. But this isn't just a shack—there's plenty of room for dine-in eating.

And perhaps a burger is a burger is a burger. But these are some burgers. Order yours as a single, double, or triple, then pick your cheese and toppings—how about pepperjack and hot *giardiniera*? Or there's always the crowd-pleaser: the patty melt. Side your burger with some heavy-duty fries; buffalo, truffle or loaded fries top the list. A spicy Mexican chocolate milkshake rounds out the decadence.

The Elephant

Thai

D2

5348 W. Devon Ave. (bet. Central & Minnehaha Aves.)

Phone: 773-467-1168
Web: www.theelephantthai.com
Prices:

Lunch & dinner Mon – Sat

Mood-lifting hues and brightly painted pachyderms perk up the walls of this small, cheery neighborhood favorite, where fragrant classics loaded with fresh ingredients make it the go-to spot for local families dining in and taking out. Notes of lemongrass, Thai basil, galangal, and Kaffir lime leaves wafting through the air remind everyone of the deeply infused flavors that are soon to come in traditional dishes like Panang curry or basil roasted duck.

Warm the belly with a bowl of *tom kha kai*—a silky yet tangy broth of coconut milk, lime, and herbs with sliced chicken breast. Heat-seekers should tackle the spicy chicken, sautéed with bamboo shoots, bell peppers, and carrots, tossed in an intensely flavored red curry sauce with steamed jasmine rice.

Hema's Kitchen

Indian

E3

2439 W. Devon Ave. (bet. Artesian & Campbell Aves.)

Phone: 773-338-1627
Web: www.hemaskitchen.com
Prices: $$

Lunch & dinner daily

Bustling Devon Avenue is the go-to neighborhood for Indian and Pakistani vittles, music, movies, clothing, and other delights. And Hema's Kitchen is one of the stalwarts of the area, a favorite of locals (so much so, a second location opened in Lincoln Park), despite the fact that there is no shortage of restaurants from which to choose.

The menu, by Hyderabad native chef Hema Potla, includes some old favorites and twists on the classics. The chicken roll is basically an Indo-wrap, with a kebab rolled in butter-brushed *paratha*, along with verdant green chutney. Lamb *rogan josh* is a mouthwatering curry; sweet, nutty, spicy, and tart, seasoned with cardamom, cloves, and other spices. And pistachio *kulfi* is a creamy, sweet ending to a spicy meal.

Kabul House

Afghan   ✨✨

D2

4949 Oakton St. (at Niles Ave.), Skokie

Phone: 847-674-3830

Web: www.kabulhouse.com

Prices: $$

Lunch Tue – Fri

Dinner Tue – Sun

Set on a bright and airy corner in the heart of Skokie, Kabul House is now an established hit and beloved local spot. Its mix of contemporary cream-and-wood décor interspersed with Afghan art and tapestries lends a visual complement to the menu's authentically spiced dishes.

Two kinds of tender steamed dumplings–*aushak* with leeks and scallions, or *mantoo* with ground beef and onion–burst with flavor when drizzled with spicy tomato-meat sauce and minted yogurt; while each of the meats in a three-kabob combo of chicken, lamb, and beef are moist, smoky, and perfectly seasoned. Finish with a bowl of *firnee*, the traditional Afghan pudding infused with cardamom and topped with pistachios, or relax with a sweet cup of black tea with bergamot oil.

Lou Malnati's

Pizza   ✨

E2

6649 N. Lincoln Ave. (bet. Avers & Springfield Aves.), Lincolnwood

Phone: 847-673-0800

Web: www.loumalnatis.com

Prices: ⎊⎊

Lunch & dinner daily

Lou Malnati got his start in Chicago's very first deep-dish pizzeria. In 1971, he opened his own, and it's been golden ever since. With 30 locations around Chicago (the original is a bit of a time warp), Lou's remains family-owned and operated with great food and devoted service.

They have an extensive menu of pizzas, pastas, and other Italian classics. Portions are colossal: begin with stuffed spinach bread–that great Chi-style garlic, spinach, and cheese combo with tomatoes stuffed into bread–and you'll struggle to stay upright. Try the "Lou" pizza—buttery pastry-like crust crowned with spinach, mushrooms, and sliced tomatoes then doused in sauce and slathered with gooey cheese.

Bonus: you can ship Lou's anywhere in the U.S. through their website.

L. Woods Tap & Pine Lodge

American 🍴🍴

D2

7110 N. Lincoln Ave. (at Kostner Ave.), Lincolnwood

Phone: 847-677-3350
Web: www.lwoodsrestaurant.com
Prices: $$

Lunch & dinner daily

Under light-decked antlers and exposed wood beams, families crowd warmly into the leather booths at this popular Lincolnwood lodge for American comfort cuisine. Large portions mean you'll likely be taking half your meal home, so don't be afraid to ask for a doggie bag.

Try nostalgic favorites like baked meatloaf, chicken pot pie, and baby-back ribs, or lighter options like the L. Woods chopped salad, house-made veggie burger, and pesto-topped flatbreads. The messy but tasty pulled-barbecue chicken sandwich piles crunchy coleslaw and crispy fried onion straws onto a heap of tender, slow-cooked meat. A wedge of tangy, creamy Key lime pie is a bracing refresher after a bowl of outstanding turkey and vegetable chili that is hearty enough for a full meal.

Mysore Woodlands

Indian 🍴🍴

E2

2548 W. Devon Ave. (bet. Maplewood Ave. & Rockwell St.)

Phone: 773-338-8160
Web: www.mysorewoodlands.info
Prices: 💷

Lunch & dinner daily

Mysore Woodlands rises above this competitive strip of south Asian eateries thanks to its unique focus on South Indian delights, vegetarian style. It may feel like a banquet hall and the service is quick, but the flavors here are bold, intense, and uniquely delicious across the vast menu of authentic stews, curries, and specialties. It is the local favorite for *dosas* and *uthappam*, each with a variety of fillings.

Those who are unsure of what to choose have an advantage here with the tasty *thali*—a large, traditional platter of assorted metal bowls boasting their spectrum of spices and tastes. These may include *sambar* (tamarind broth with vegetables); *poriyal* (fried okra, carrot, onion, potato, and zucchini), and creamy rice pudding for dessert.

Oceanique

F1

505 Main St. (bet. Chicago & Hinman Aves.), Evanston

Phone: 847-864-3435   Dinner Mon – Sat
Web: www.oceanique.com
Prices: $$$$ Main

Chef Mark Grosz opened this romantic seafood gem in 1989, and loyal clients have been fishing for excuses to make the trip to Evanston ever since. In this soft-toned dining room with hand-painted touches and wavelike fabric billowing from the ceilings, servers treat each meal as a special occasion.

The chef's affinity for French techniques expresses itself on a constantly changing menu that may include tender quail with apricot-chanterelle stuffing; seared scallops with a lobster-soy broth; and dark chocolate cake layered with rich crème Chantilly and chestnut ice cream. If the impressively thorough wine list makes drink decisions difficult, Grosz's son, dedicated wine director Philippe Andre, is happy to guide guests through pairings and selections.

Pasta d'Arte

C3

6311 N. Milwaukee Ave. (bet. Highland & Mobile Aves.)

Phone: 773-763-1181   Lunch Tue – Fri
Web: www.pastadarte.com   Dinner nightly
Prices: $$

If there were such a contest, Pasta d'Arte could easily be a frontrunner for friendliest restaurant in Chicago. The chef-owned, family-run trattoria is a local favorite, owing in part to its staff, which combines personal warmth with professional knowledge. Guests can view the same level of skill reflected in the semi-open kitchen, as they settle into the intimate dining room or make their way to the heated courtyard patio. Hearty and traditional Italian dishes comprise the bill of fare, perhaps including tender veal saltimbocca in a silky butter-white wine sauce, or a warming bowl of vegetable-barley soup that is the perfect antidote to a blustery Chicago evening. Lunches are lighter yet still satisfy with several types of pizzas and panini.

Pensiero

1566 Oak Ave. (bet. Davis & Grove Sts.), Evanston

Phone: 847-475-7779
Web: www.pensieroitalian.com
Prices: $$$

Dinner Thu – Sat

 Davis

Located in the lower level of the Margarita European Inn, Pensiero is one of those Evanston eateries that doesn't get overrun with Northwestern students. Rather an adult crowd dines here, appreciating the upscale setting with tall windows, rosy faux-finished walls, and perceived refined service.

Pensiero isn't particularly inventive, but serves solid and flavorsome Italian fare that's generally crowd-pleasing. A mint-scented pea flan with Maryland crab salad tossing peppery arugula and carrot vinaigrette is a colorful way to begin your feast. Pastas are pretty straightforward, but meat and seafood delights like the grilled red snapper with potatoes, crispy prosciutto, and a roasted red pepper vinaigrette are memorable to say the least.

Quince

1625 Hinman Ave. (bet. Church & Davis Sts.), Evanston

Phone: 847-570-8400
Web: www.quincerestaurant.net
Prices: $$$

Dinner Tue – Sun

Quaint and charming Quince, discreetly tucked away in Evanston's The Homestead, is the perfect setting for a romantic tête-à-tête or elegant family repast. The dining room mimics the ambience of the inn which draws on Southern colonial style for its décor inspiration. Mauve and wood-paneled walls along with cream furnishings dress the intimate space embellished with a bookshelf-framed fireplace.

The polished staff brings forth a bevy of Chef Andy Motto's preparations and may unveil keen creations such as squash blossoms stuffed with ground chicken and dressed with artichoke purée and pistachio foam; or pan-seared halibut sauced with basil-shellfish emulsion and teamed with garlic-dressed romaine chiffonade, poached quail egg, and white anchovy.

Renga-Tei

Japanese

E2

3956 W. Touhy Ave. (at Prairie Rd.), Lincolnwood

Phone: 847-675-5177
Web: N/A
Prices:

Lunch Mon & Wed – Fri
Dinner Wed – Mon

 There's no glitz but plenty of piscine glory at Renga-Tei, set among a nondescript row of businesses in a Lincolnwood strip mall. The first hint that you're getting a genuine Japanese sushi experience comes from the staff's synchronized and punctual greeting announcing your arrival. Behind the counter, Chef/owner Hisao Yamada foregoes a smiling hello to remain focused on working the steel like an old pro.

A bright, clean, and minimalist décor matches the quality of food on the plate. This is not the place for gimmicky rolls smothered in sauce, but pristine fish with sublime sticky rice. Sunomono *moriwase* or *tekka* rolls with julienned cucumber are perfect palate teasers; while a single novelty roll, the Chicago Super Crazy, displays a dash of humor.

Restaurant Ricardo

Mexican

D5

4429 W. Diversey Ave. (bet. Kilbourn & Kostner Aves.)

Phone: 773-292-0400
Web: N/A
Prices:

Lunch & dinner daily

 Though it's often referred to as Taqueria Ricardo, this authentic Mexican restaurant adjoining the Latin-American market Carniceria Ricardo is so much more than a quick stop for tacos. In a small, cheerful room festooned with Mexican artwork, quick and friendly servers crisscross the tiled floor to grab plates from the mosaic-lined kitchen, where a wood fire permeates the food with smoky goodness.

Those in the know plan their shopping trips to leave time for the moist *pollo a la leña* straight from the rotisserie, grilled skirt steak with scallions and peppers, and incomparable tacos *al pastor* with roasted pork, pineapple, and fresh cilantro on white corn tortillas. Wash it all down with a glass of perfectly sweet and cinnamon-spiced *horchata*.

Rosewood

Steakhouse ✗✗✗

A3

9421 W. Higgins Rd. (at Willow Creek Dr.), Rosemont

Phone: 847-696-9494
Web: www.rosewoodrestaurant.com
Prices: $$$

Lunch Mon – Fri
Dinner nightly

The Windy City loves its steakhouses, and nowhere is it more apparent than at this independent restaurant that has been thriving for more than two decades amid the popular chains near O'Hare. Inside the serene space, coffee-colored leather chairs and wood paneling create a classic Rat Pack vibe.

Succulent USDA Prime steaks get top billing here, such as the 16 oz. Kansas City strip, cooked perfectly to order. Spend the extra dollars on a peppercorn, Cajun, blue cheese, or horseradish crust on any steak for an added indulgence. French onion soup, smoked salmon on flatbread, shrimp cocktail, mashed potatoes, and baked apples round out the menu. Fresh seafood, like the horseradish-crusted ahi tuna, is a good option for those who want something different.

Sabri Nihari

Indian ✗

E2

2502 W. Devon Ave. (bet. Campbell & Maplewood Aves.)

Phone: 773-465-3272
Web: www.sabrinihari.com
Prices:

Dinner nightly

On a stretch of Devon filled with halal meat stores, fabric shops, and Indo-Pak groceries, this long-standing gem is a feast for the senses. Wearing a slightly formal aspect, Sabri Nihari focuses on an array of gratifying Pakistani-influenced dishes. Whether eating at a place that serves only *zabiha* meat (slaughtered in strict accordance with the Islamic faith) is important or not, this well-maintained spot is well worth a visit.

The *bhindi gosht* (succulent okra cooked with beef, tomato, and garlic) offers a lovely balance of heat and tenderness; while the signature *haleem* is a lusciously rich stew of lentils and beef. The Karachi chicken rubbed with garlic, ginger, and herbs is a delightful ode to the classic South Asian flavor spectrum.

Shokran Moroccan Grill

E4

4027 W. Irving Park Rd. (bet. Keystone Ave. & Pulaski Rd.)

Phone: 773-427-9130   Dinner nightly
Web: www.shokranchicago.com
Prices: ⊜⊗   🚉 Irving Park (Blue)

Judging by the ordinary façade, commercial surroundings, and hovering highway, you may be tempted to pass right by. But, oh, the delights that would be missed! Arabic for "thank you," Shokran is a scrumptious spot for homemade Moroccan, where rich silk fabrics billow from the ceiling; framed mother-of-pearl artifacts hang on burnt sienna walls; and hookah pipes and copper chargers bedeck the room.

Brace yourself for the couscous royale—melt-in-your mouth braised lamb; juicy merguez (spicy sausage stuffed with ground lamb and beef); tender zucchini, rutabaga, carrots, and chickpeas snuggled into fluffy couscous. Satiate the sweet tooth with handmade cookies—from almond pastries to *fekkas*, each morsel is fresh and irresistible. Thank you, Shokran.

Smak-Tak 😊

C3

5961 N. Elston Ave. (bet. Markham & Peterson Aves.)

Phone: 773-763-1123   Lunch & dinner daily
Web: www.smaktak.com
Prices: ⊜⊗

Set on a desolate stretch, Smak-Tak ("taste it" in Polish) and its skilled team of old-world cooks prepare some of the city's best Polish food. With knotty pine paneling covering the walls and ceiling, wood tables, and a faux fireplace, the space resembles a cozy mountain cabin.

Tiffany-style glass lamps bestow a gentle glow on large portions of food. Patrons should plan their ordering so they can try a little of everything including a delicious pickle soup bobbing with chunks of potatoes, cucumber, and fragrant dill; or tender and plump veal meatballs tossed in a well-seasoned mushroom gravy and coupled with a side of creamy carrot and cabbage sauerkraut. Pierogis filled with cheese and potato pancakes served with applesauce are other stomach-busters.

Sol de Mexico 🏠

Mexican ✗✗

D4

3018 N. Cicero Ave. (bet. Wellington Ave. & Nelson St.)

Phone: 773-282-4119   Lunch & dinner Wed – Mon
Web: www.soldemexicochicago.com
Prices: $$

Mama Mexicana leads the *mole*-making magic here at Sol de Mexico, firing up dishes with awe-inspiring authenticity. Creative, moan-worthy, and true-blue delights weave their way across the menu: Alaskan sablefish with *hoja santa, chile güero,* and sweet plantains; or New Zealand rack of lamb in a classic Oaxacan black *mole.* Belly buzzing in anticipation? Get to it with *ayamole,* a creamy roasted pumpkin soup kissed with *guajillo* chiles; heavenly *chuleta de puerco en mole verde,* wood-grilled pork chops laid across a *mole* served with a stack of smoky tamales and crunchy chayote; and bliss out with *natillas,* a cinnamon rice pudding drizzled with mango purée.

Take the edge off with one of several tequilas from their extensive selection.

The Stained Glass Bistro

American ✗✗

A4

1735 Benson Ave. (bet. Church & Clark Sts.), Evanston

Phone: 847-864-8600   Dinner nightly
Web: www.thestainedglass.com
Prices: $$

All are welcome to worship at the altar of the wine grape here, where wines by the glass, on tap, and in flights are served nightly. Exposed ductwork and beams snaking across high ceilings lend an urban-chic feel to the romantic, pendant-lit space warmly lined with wooden wine racks.

Complementing the global drink list is soul-satisfying American bistro fare with eclectic influences, from a foie gras BLT with applewood-smoked bacon and white truffle mayonnaise, to crispy-skinned barramundi paired exquisitely with a creamy pea, artichoke, and *fromage blanc crustade.* Dessert may feature Chocolate3 or a trio of decadent treats. A true community gem, The Stained Glass Bistro offers deals to Northwestern students and faculty who may inquire.

Tacos Locos

4732 N. River Rd. (at Lawrence Ave.), Schiller Park

Phone: 847-928-2197   Lunch & dinner daily
Web: www.tacoslocosllc.com
Prices:

There are no missteps at this table-service taqueria, a happy corner in the Chicagoland suburbs. Despite the fact that it is tucked into a small strip mall in Schiller Park, Tacos Locos is a cozy, family-run spot that pairs friendly service with high quality Mexican food prepared with care at a superb value.

The solid menu is loaded with tried-and-true tacos, tortas, and other classics, but it's the little details that stand out. Cooks quickly grill each massive burrito for an extra-crispy exterior, and addictive *choriqueso* blends Chihuahua cheese with chorizo, roasted poblanos, and mushrooms for a decadent take on *queso fundido*. Locals know to stop by on weekends when tamales, menudo, and other specialties are available on a limited basis.

Taste of Peru

6545 N. Clark St. (bet. Albion & Arthur Aves.)

Phone: 773-381-4540   Lunch & dinner daily
Web: www.tasteofperu.com
Prices: $$

Don't be put off by the plain-Jane exterior. Inside, wood masks mingle with posters of Peruvian destinations atop desert-toned walls; red tapestries cover the tables; and lively (sometimes live) music reveals the passion of Cesar Izquierdo. This chatty owner has been touting his peppery cuisine in East Rogers Park since 1974.

The menu shows off a wide range of Peruvian food, from the classic *papa rellena* stuffed with tender ribeye cubes, walnuts, and raisins, to a steamed rice- tomato- and onion combo in *lomo saltado*. If the complimentary *aji verde* sauce tingles the taste buds a little too much, take a swig of cold and refreshing Inca Kola. Should you choose to BYOB, take note that Chilean *pisco* won't be welcomed—this is a Peruvian place, after all.

Tre Kronor

Scandinavian ✗

E3

3258 W. Foster Ave. (at Spaulding Ave.)

Phone: 773-267-9888
Web: www.trekronorrestaurant.com
Prices: 💰💰

Lunch daily
Dinner Mon – Sat

If you had a Swedish grandmother, this is the food she would pile in front of you for breakfast: thick waffles laden with bananas, berries, and whipped cream; light and buttery pancakes soaking up warm and tart lingonberries; or a Stockholm omelet filled with Havarti and *falukorv* sausage. Should your palate prefer savory dishes, Tre Kronor has also got you covered with a *Reubenssen* of slices of tender corned beef, oozing *Jarlsberg* cheese, and tangy sauerkraut on toasted rye bread; or Swedish meatballs with pickled cucumbers and lingonberry sauce.

After satisfying your cravings amid adorably Nordic wood furnishings and wall murals, burn a few calories by walking across the street to the Sweden Shop to outfit your home in Scandinavian imports.

Tub Tim Thai

Thai ✗✗

D2

4927 Oakton St. (bet. Niles Ave. & Skokie Blvd.), Skokie

Phone: 847-675-8424
Web: www.tubtimthai.com
Prices: 💰💰

Lunch & dinner Mon – Sat

A casual stop in suburban Skokie, this Thai find is as accommodating as they come. The setting is pleasant, with dark wood furnishings and pastel walls showcasing a revolving display of artwork typically for sale.

The affordable menu is equally accommodating and the kitchen delights with tasty recipes and quality ingredients. Diners can request the level of spice desired; but if it's not hot enough, there are pickled chilies, chili paste, and chili powder on the table. Choices run the gamut of the traditional Thai options such as shrimp dumplings; spicy basil chicken; pad Thai; and sweet coconut sticky rice with mango for dessert. Tub Tim Thai is never a splurge, but lunch is a particular bargain with an appetizer, salad, and main course for under $10.

Viceroy of India

Indian ✕✕

E2

2520 W. Devon Ave. (bet. Campbell & Maplewood Aves.)

Phone: 773-743-4100   Lunch & dinner daily
Web: www.viceroyofindia.com
Prices: ⬡⬡

A walk down Devon Avenue is like a daycation to India. Each storefront is packed with saris, Bollywood videos, snack shops, restaurants, and other retail businesses offering up a taste of home to Chicago's enormous Indian population. Streets are packed (and, as a result, parking sometimes a challenge) most nights, making for great people-watching.

Viceroy of India is a favorite among the many options on Devon both because of its small café, for sweets and take-out, and its upscale dining room, which accommodates large parties. A reasonably priced lunch buffet; a particularly good *dosa* served with coconut-based chutney; and fragrant lamb *saag* are a few of the draws. The tamarind rice, with its nuts and herbs, has a perfect sour, yet fragrant, note.

Yolo 😊

Mexican ✕✕

D1

5111 Brown St. (bet. Floral & Lincoln Aves.), Skokie

Phone: 847-674-0987   Dinner Tue – Sat
Web: www.yolomexicaneatery.com
Prices: $$

Yolo is that friendly and delightful Mexican restaurant you wish were in your neighborhood. Their hospitable service ensures a consistent crowd of Skokie residents who know a good thing when they taste it...perhaps in the dining room which is an attractive arena punctuated by Mexican art and linen-topped tables.

This destination boasts some of the best salsas and sauces in town. Fresh ingredients and bold flavors combine in dishes like *tlacoyitos Veracruz*, fava-packed corn cakes with Mexican sausage, sautéed mushrooms, and steak, topped with sour cream and cheese. *Ceviche de camaron*, citrus-marinated shrimp tossed with mango and cucumber, or *pollo Yucateco*, grilled chicken immersed in an *achiote* sauce, are staples elevated by first-rate flavors.

Zia's Trattoria

Italian XX

C2

6699 N. Northwest Hwy. (at Oliphant Ave.)

Phone: 773-775-0808
Web: www.ziachicago.com
Prices: $$

Lunch Tue – Fri
Dinner nightly

This venerable neighborhood standby welcomes a steady flow of business lunches that turns into a dinner parade of locals, all coming for the relaxed atmosphere and approachable, rustic Italian fare. Exposed brick walls and wrought-iron lantern sconces approximate the feel of an authentic trattoria, and the white linen tablecloths belie the affordably mid-priced meals.

Pastas are as rich with flavors as they are generous, and Italian classics like *vitello saltimbocca* and *pollo al limone* are offered along with more contemporary main courses like *gamberi Calabrese*, balancing fiery Calabrian peppers with cooling mint. Soups and specials change daily—try the velvety cream of potato with rich undertones of caramelized garlic when it's on the menu.

Good food without spending a fortune? Look for the Bib Gourmand 😊.

South, Southwest & Western Suburbs

South, Southwest & Western Suburbs

With perhaps a few high-profile exceptions (here's lookin' at you, President Obama's Hyde Park), the neighborhoods of the city's west and south sides and the west and south suburbs rarely make the pages of traditional visitors' guides. Instead, they're saved for those residents who work and live in these city environs.

Feeding Families

While it's certainly true that these neighborhoods may not have the museums, hotels, or 24-7 service of those more centrally located, they are a foodie's dream come true, with lesser-known groceries, tasty takeout joints, and other ethnic eateries. Back in the day, some of these neighborhoods, including Back of the Yards, once home to the famous Chicago Stockyards, changed the food industry. Today the Marquette Park neighborhood, where, in 1966, Martin Luther King, Jr. brought his civil rights marchers, may seem questionable after dark. But it is still worth a ride for no reason other than the mighty mother-in-law. No, not visiting a relative. That's the name of **Fat Johnnie's Famous Red Hots'** best dish: A tamale, a kosher hot dog, chili, and (processed) cheese poised on a bun, handed through a window. This may be a shabby and shaky trailer, but Fat Johnnie's hot dogs (a mainstay for over 30 years now) have a reputation of their own and have been luring hungry hot dog lovers from the world over. The rest of Marquette Park (near 63rd St.) features predominantly Mexican storefronts, taquerias, and other food vendors. Film buffs love the fact that Marquette Park (the 600-acre actual green space, not the neighborhood) was featured in the iconic movie *The Blues Brothers*.

Eastern European Eats

Closer to Midway International Airport, near Archer Heights, is a concentration of Eastern European shops mixed among classic Chicago-style brick bungalows. One favorite is **Bobak's Sausage Company**, with its 100-foot-long meat counter. This meat lover's paradise is a Chicago-based organization that caters mainly to food entities, grocery stores, and delis. Shopping here is entertainment in and of itself. Purchase a hot lunch to eat on the spot or buy a range of delicious sausages (Polish-style) and other deli meats to take home for the family. For a bigger and better taste of Chicago, you can also choose to buy from their bulk-pack items, retail-pack items, and imported specialties. Want to try this on your own? They also proffer a list of recipes. For a more Polish and Lithuanian take on deli dishes, try Evergreen Park's **AJ's Meats**.

Ireland in Chicagoland

Nearby Beverly is the hub of the city's Irish bar scene, something many people first discover during the raucous South Side Irish St. Patrick's Day parade. But all year long, bars serve corned beef, cabbage, and plenty of cold beers. Beverly's Pantry for instance sells cookware and teaches locals how to use it in a series of ongoing classes. Non-food attractions in Beverly include a number of Frank Lloyd Wright houses and other significant architectural monuments (not to mention a real castle). Farther north and closer to Lake Michigan, cerebral hub Hyde Park attracts Obama fans, academicians, students, and more architecture buffs. Professors and students at the University of Chicago crowd the surrounding cafés, restaurants, and bars geared towards the smarter set.

During the summer months and baseball season, don't miss the White Sox at the U.S. Cellular Field. A lick of the five-flavor ice cream cone from the **Original Rainbow Cone**, a Chicagoland staple since 1926, promises an equally thrilling experience. Housed in a pretty pink building, the original menu may also unveil a range of splits, shakes, and sundaes; as well as a decadent carte of ice cream flavors such as black walnut, New York vanilla, and bubble gum-banana.

Chicago's Beloved Bites

Those without any heart or cholesterol problems for that matter ought to try the beloved breaded steaks (with a mélange of toppings) from **Ricobene's**, which has several locations on both the south side and in the south suburbs. Ricobene's also caters to the beefy best in everyone by serving up those Chicago classic pan, deep-dish, or thin-crust pizza pies alongside other delectable offerings like mouthwatering barbecue specialties (try a full slab dinner); Italian-esque sandwiches (imagine the Sloppy Joe and Vesuvio Italian classic sandwich); Chicago-style hot dogs; and char-broiled burgers. Suburban Oak Park may be more famous for past residents like Ernest Hemingway and Frank Lloyd Wright, but nonetheless, foodies care more about vinegar-maker Jim Vitalo. His amazing, subtle herb-infused **Herbally Yours** vinegars are sold in bulk at the **Oak Park Farmer's Market** on Saturdays in the summer.

Grazing Through the Middle East

Suburban Bridgeview, home to Toyota Park, where the Chicago Fire soccer team usually plays, is one of the region's best stops for authentic and fine Middle Eastern cuisine. Throughout this area, you'll find restaurants outfitted with grills and bakeries galore. Visit a myriad of centrally located stores, and be sure to take home snacks like pita, hummus, and baba ghanoush; as well as fresh groceries for a night of magnificent Middle Eastern cooking. In closing, it would be simply blasphemous to end your meal without a taste of sweet. So after you've consumed your fill of falafel and the like, move on to sweeter respites in this Middle Eastern Corridor, namely **Elshafei Pastries** for some sticky-sweet baklava and other pistachio-pocked delights. Need more saccharine satisfaction? Linger at **Albasha Sweets** and **Nablus Sweets**. One bite of these syrupy, luscious, and creamy pastries will leave you smiling for the rest of the evening. Can there be any other way to end such fresh, fun, and divine fare?

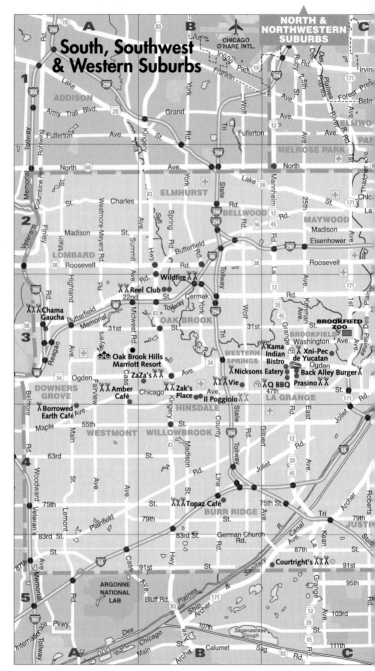

South, Southwest & Western Suburbs

CHICAGO O'HARE INTL.

ADDISON

ELMWOOD PARK

MELROSE PARK

ELMHURST

BELLWOOD

MAYWOOD

LOMBARD

Wildfire

Reel Club

Chama Gaucha

OAK BROOK

BROOKFIELD ZOO

BROOKFIELD

Oak Brook Hills
Marriott Resort

WESTERN SPRINGS

Kama Indian Bistro

Xni-Pec de Yucatan

ZaZa's

Amber Café

Zak's Place

Nicksons Eatery

Vie

Back Alley Burger

Q BBQ

Prasino

DOWNERS GROVE

Il Poggiolo

LA GRANGE

Borrowed Earth Café

HINSDALE

WESTMONT

WILLOWBROOK

Topaz Café

BURR RIDGE

JUSTI

Courtright's

ARGONNE NATIONAL LAB

Saganashkee Slough

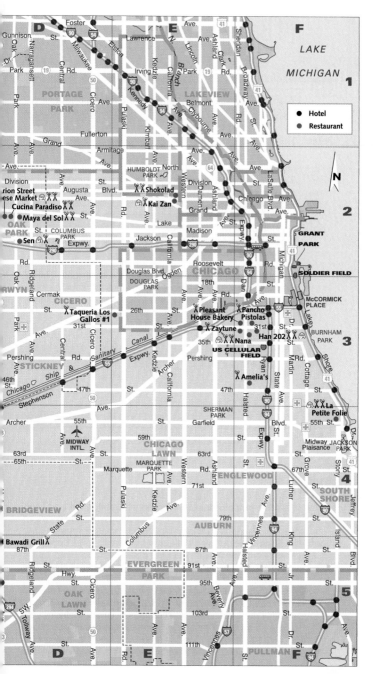

Al Bawadi Grill

D5

Middle Eastern

7216 W. 87th St. (bet. Harlem & Oketo Aves.), Bridgeview

Phone: 708-599-1999   Lunch & dinner daily
Web: www.albawadigrill.com
Prices: $$

Housed in a former fast food joint on busy 87th Street, Al Bawadi Grill doesn't exactly shout "peaceful oasis," but the owners have done a lot with what they've got. Water fountains, faux palm trees, and etched glass set the scene for the kind, hospitable service. A colorful pile of pickled vegetables as well as a smoky eggplant salad are brought to the table for diners to enjoy while they peruse the grill-centric menu.

Hummus is velvety and artfully presented, dotted with olive oil, chilies, and sumac accompanied by warm pita. The Al Bawadi mixed grill includes three kinds of kebabs–shish, *kefta*, and chicken–accompanied by grilled onion, tomato, and two styles of rice. Wash it all down with a freshly squeezed juice or smoothie.

Amber Café

A3

American ✗✗

13 N. Cass Ave. (at Burlington Ave.), Westmont

Phone: 630-515-8080   Dinner Tue – Sat
Web: www.ambercafe.net
Prices: $$

Set on the main drag of Westmont, Amber Café has been serving a touch of elegance since 2004. The dining room exudes calm with walls cloaked in seafoam green and exposed brick. Paved with rosy, polished wood floors, tall windows replete with steel-hued sheer drapes, and tables boasting white linen and fresh flowers, Amber Café is *très* romantic.

Stroll past the pebbled-glass wine cabinet to the cozy micro-tiled bar. Catch dinner here from a menu based on American ideals with Mediterranean sensibilities. Grilled octopus gets flavor and pep from charred tomatoes and pickled chilies; pan-roasted Alaskan king salmon is pristinely plated over a bed of vegetables; and a light cheesecake is balanced with a perky citrus compote spiked with ginger and kumquats.

Amelia's

Mexican ✗

F3

4559 S. Halsted St. (at 46th St.)

Phone: 773-538-8200   Lunch & dinner daily
Web: www.ameliaschicago.com
Prices: 💰💰

This neighborhood bright light offers Mexican cuisine with a creative slant. The well-maintained space is generously sized, great for families, and is attractively done—brick walls are hung with colorful paintings of mountainside scenes and baskets of flowers, tall slender windows are dressed with crinkly orange drapes, and gently swirling ceiling fans lend a chill vibe.

Lunch serves tortas, fajitas, and enchiladas, while dinner offers starters such as the *tamal nejo*, revealing a toothsome cornmeal filling topped with shredded white meat chicken and a complex and richly satisfying red *mole* made from a family recipe. Globally-flecked entrées include the likes of grilled pork tenderloin with a ginger rice cake, hominy, andouille sausage, and tomatillos.

Back Alley Burger

American ✗

C3

13 S. La Grange Rd. (bet. Burlington & Harris Aves.), La Grange

Phone: 708-482-7909   Lunch daily
Web: www.backalleyburger.com   Dinner Mon – Sat
Prices: 💰💰

Everything here–from the décor to the menu–is industrial and rugged, yet polished and enticing. A brown wooden fence divides a narrow row of booths and handful of tables from the kitchen. Place your order at the brightly polished counter, then take a number and lots of napkins.

Plump hot dogs, huge salads (like the "garbage" topped in onion rings) and more than 15 supreme variations on the humble burger top every table. Half-pound beef patties might be decked with salami, mustard, onion, and Merkts cheese on a fresh soft pretzel roll, and accompanied by a tasty mound of shoestring potato fries. Finish with a hand-dipped vanilla Oreo-cookie shake, thick with lumps of ice cream.

Apple slices are a kids' menu option, but so is chili and cheese.

Borrowed Earth Café

Vegetarian ✗

A4

970 Warren Ave. (bet. Highland Ave. & Main St.), Downers Grove

Phone: 630-795-1729   Lunch & dinner Tue – Sat
Web: www.borrowedearthcafe.com
Prices: $$

This suburban stalwart is as earnest as they come. The environmentally friendly dining room cleverly encourages diners to learn to appreciate a raw food way of life. The aesthetic is more Woodstock than Gwyneth Paltrow, but the food is good enough for any health-conscious Hollywood celeb.

Enjoy a guiltless lasagna made with thin sheets of zucchini, juicy tomatoes, grated carrots, loads of creamy pesto, and fluffy cashew "ricotta." It arrives with a side of kale-licious salad: kale, hemp seed, and cabbage tossed with the house dressing. For even more of the leafy power green, try the addictive and delicious kale chips. The out-of-this-world cheesecake is a revelation and easily surpasses run-of-the-mill dairy cheesecakes, minus the guilt.

Chama Gaucha

Steakhouse ✗✗✗

A3

3008 Finley Rd. (at Butterfield Rd.), Downers Grove

Phone: 630-324-6002   Lunch Mon – Fri
Web: www.chamagaucha.com   Dinner nightly
Prices: $$

Chama Gaucha is a sort of carnivorous carnival that will have you crying uncle after devouring pounds of delicious skewered meats grilled over the open-fire *churrascaria*. Meals begin at the bountiful salad bar, but save plenty of room for the piping hot and juice-dripping meats. Chicken, pork, sausage, bacon-wrapped filet, lamb—it's all here and ready for the taking. The wine list focuses on reds for a good reason, but go Brazilian and order a caipirinha.

The mood feels theatrical, with *passadores* or gauchos flaunting machismo in slicing spit-roasted meats from long metal skewers, Zorro-style right at the table. Just be sure to have your red and green signs at the ready, so servers know when to stop. It's glorious gluttony at its best.

Courtright's

French 𝖃𝖃𝖃

C5

8989 Archer Ave. (bet Cemetery & Willow Springs Rds.), Willow Springs

Phone: 708-839-8000
Web: www.courtrights.com
Prices: $$$

Dinner Tue – Sun

The beauty of situating a restaurant in Willow Springs is that the forest is waiting as a natural backdrop—such is the case in Courtright's genteel and hospitable dining room. Floor-to-ceiling windows showcase a woodsy panorama of the landscaped gardens abutting the Cook County Forest Preserve, echoed by floral carpeting, upholstered booths, and freshly cut flowers throughout the well-kept space.

The menu appetizingly marries classic French techniques with farm-fresh produce, though the kitchen's ambition sometimes exceeds its expertise. Simple preparations like an English pea soup with lovage and romaine get a briny kick from black olive tapenade; while generously seasoned and juicy *poussin*, or pan-roasted duck breast is admirable on its own.

Cucina Paradiso

Italian 𝖃𝖃

D2

814 North Blvd. (bet. Kenilworth & Oak Park Aves.), Oak Park

Phone: 708-848-3434
Web: www.cucinaoakpark.com
Prices: $$

Dinner nightly

 Oak Park (Green)

For nearly 20 years, Cucina Paradiso has been playing the role of the charming Italian bistro, and Oak Park regulars keep eating up its cinema-perfect style. Vintage posters of Fernet Branca and other emblematic brands adorn exposed brick walls, soft lighting flickers on shimmering mosaic columns, and the awning-covered sidewalk patio entices commuters from the nearby Metra station.

Good thing there's white butcher paper covering the linen tablecloths as locals lick their plates clean of hearty standbys like rigatoni Bolognese with sweet Italian sausage crumbles; and crisply pan-fried chicken pistachio with roasted red pepper cream sauce. Half portions of fresh pastas and smaller plates like grilled calamari Abruzzi-style sate smaller appetites.

Han 202

Chinese 🍴🍴

F3

605 W. 31st St. (bet. Lowe Ave. & Wallace St.)

Phone: 312-949-1314   Dinner Tue – Sun
Web: www.han202.com
Prices: 🥜

 ♿

Named after the Han dynasty, most are pleasantly surprised by this restaurant's sparkling clean and minimalist décor. The dining room is replete with white walls, dark wood floors, and red-stained tables. The small, tidy kitchen is partially open and offers a peek at an orderly staff churning out Chinese food incorporating a touch of fusion. But, they require you to BYOB, so don't pull up a seat at the bar.

The $25 five-course prix-fixe showcases fine product, expertly prepared and may begin with crispy fries dressed with truffle oil, followed by delicate shrimp tempura garnished with fried candied walnut halves. Meals end on a decadent note— imagine dark chocolate mousse dusted with cocoa powder and neatly plated with a fresh raspberry and blueberry.

Il Poggiolo

Italian 🍴🍴

B3

8 E. 1st St. (bet. Garfield Ave. & Washington St.), Hinsdale

Phone: 630-734-9400   Lunch Mon – Sat
Web: www.ilpoggiolohinsdale.com   Dinner nightly
Prices: $$

♿

A charming turn-of-the-century building in downtown Hinsdale gets a new lease on life with Il Poggiolo. The balcony, or *il poggiolo*, of this former silent movie theater now gives mezzanine diners a bird's eye view of the handsome bar framed in dark wood and the burgundy tufted banquettes below—as well as the massive fringed red lampshades dangling from the ceiling.

Beyond a fire engine-red meat slicer, the showcase kitchen turns out modern versions of regional Italian cuisine like melt-in-your-mouth meatballs bobbing on fresh marinara sauce in an iron skillet; or handmade ravioli filled with goat cheese, resting on a pea purée and creamy herb-speckled tomato sauce. Airy chocolate mousse surprises those who indulge with its slow-building spiciness.

Kai Zan

Japanese ✗

2557 ½ W. Chicago Ave. (at Rockwell St.)

Phone: 773-278-5776   Dinner Thu – Tue
Web: www.eatatkaizan.com
Prices: $$

How small is a restaurant with 1/2 in its address? Pretty darn petite. However, Kai Zan packs a heap of personality into its narrow footprint on far west Chicago Avenue. Shimmering surfaces like glossy white tiles, mother-of-pearl coasters, and a marble sushi counter impart a pristine feel to this buzzed-about Japanese respite.

Go with the fishy flow and sample from the menu of seared and raw contemporary sushi. Squares of escolar soaked in a soy-truffle sauce with addictive fresh pickled wasabi; salmon slices wrapped around scallops, then seared with a citrus glaze; and tidy one-bite *makimono* walk the line between overly complex and simply inspired. Though the bites are budget-friendly, the register tally can add up—good thing the place is BYOB.

Kama Indian Bistro

C3

Indian ✗

8 W. Burlington Ave. (bet. Ashland Ave & La Grange Rd.), La Grange

Phone: 708-352-3300   Lunch Sat – Sun
Web: www.kamabistro.com   Dinner Tue – Sun
Prices: $$

Across from the Metra, find this petite, inviting Indian storefront. Per Hinduism, Kama (or desire) is one of four goals in life, and as a nod to tradition, this bistro entices via aubergine walls hugging a portrait of the amorous Kamadeva (God of Love) himself. Purple is a running theme throughout the slender space; while fresh lavender roses and beaded tea candles add an elegant touch to the tables.

Jeweled throw pillows lay across banquettes and hypnotic sitar music wafts through the room. But seducing one's appetite is the chef's playful intent with unlikely ingredients like shrimp *koliwara* bathed in onion, chili, ginger; and *achari masala*, chicken massaged with an exotic blend of 18 spices. The PB & J naan leaves tiny tots with big smiles.

La Petite Folie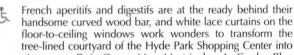

French 🍴🍴

F4

1504 E. 55th St. (at Harper Ave.)

Phone: 773-493-1394
Web: www.lapetitefolie.com
Prices: $$

Lunch Tue – Fri
Dinner Tue – Sun

French aperitifs and digestifs are at the ready behind their handsome curved wood bar, and white lace curtains on the floor-to-ceiling windows work wonders to transform the tree-lined courtyard of the Hyde Park Shopping Center into picturesque Paris. Owner Mary Mastricola, a Le Cordon Bleu and UIC alumna, has returned to her collegiate roots with this *très charmant* bistro.

Her Gallic palate shines through in elegant dishes showcasing in-season ingredients from local markets. Highlights have unveiled smoked pheasant salad punctuated by dried cherries and earthy walnuts; or hazelnut-crusted salmon atop squid ink fettuccine. The all-French wine list has enough Burgundy, Bordeaux, and Chinon to make a satiated diner burst into song with the *Marseillaise*.

Marion Street Cheese Market

American 🍴🍴

D2

100 S. Marion St. (at South Blvd.), Oak Park

Phone: 708-725-7200
Web: www.marionstreetcheesemarket.com
Prices: $$

Lunch & dinner daily

🚇 Harlem (Green)

In its mission to bring together nothing less than the best seasonal and local ingredients, this Oak Park *fromagerie* has spawned a bistro that elevates the market's purpose to new heights. Within this cozy space with tin ceilings and warm woods, find affluent droves nibbling on cheese and charcuterie plates. Others can be seen dining on more substantial fare like chorizo quiche or lamb-chestnut stew. A list of purveyors on the menu shares the kitchen's ingredient sources, from local bison to nearby hot sauce producers.

The adjoining market lets you replicate this artisan meal at home with honey, preserves and jams, wine and craft beer, local chocolates; and other specialty foods. Make sure you save your café receipt for a same-day discount in the market.

Maya del Sol

 D2

Latin American

144 S. Oak Park Ave. (bet. South Blvd. & Pleasant St.), Oak Park

Phone: 708-358-9800
Web: www.mayadelsol.com
Prices: $$

Lunch Sun
Dinner nightly
 Oak Park

Holiday lights may twinkle in the window, but this Latin jewel's inventive and tasty plates lure food lovers year-round. The divided den features an ample bar, tables, and TVs on one side; on the other, exposed brick and sunflower-stenciled lamps surround snug booths. Dusky ochre hues set a calming vibe for a family-friendly feast.

Aloof teens and jubilant toddlers share tables with adults who are here for such *delicioso* dishes as champagne gazpacho finished with *cajeta* cheese and crispy tortilla strips; *calabaza rellena* smothered in a sweet corn-butter sauce; and *crepas de cajeta*, lacy crêpes folded over caramelized goat milk syrup, pecans, and plantains.

The fiery stretch limo parked out front is a thrill, but it's truly the food that steals the show.

Nana

F3

Latin American

3267 S. Halsted St. (at 33rd St.)

Phone: 312-929-2486
Web: www.nanaorganic.com
Prices: $$

Lunch & dinner daily

Nana Solis raised her kids just up the stairs from this family-run and convivial Bridgeport favorite—thus, the authentic and evocative moniker. With a menu centered on organic ingredients from local farmers, the big "nana" of Mother Nature gets a shout-out too.

Every seat in this deceptively big space between the front coffee bar and rear open kitchen gets a workout. Devoted breakfast droves pile in (sometimes in their jammies during the regular pajama brunch) for creamy grits infused with Latin swagger via chopped poblanos; or a savory-sweet Monte Cristo with thick-sliced ham and smoked cheddar layered between brioche French toast.

Lunch and dinner options like maple-glazed chicken with *tostones* and Cara Cara orange *mojo* sate with flavor and flair.

Nicksons Eatery

C3

30 S. La Grange Rd. (bet. Calendar & Harris Aves.), La Grange

Phone: 708-354-4995   Lunch & dinner Mon – Sat
Web: www.nicksonseatery.com
Prices: $$

Make sure you're starving (and have rescheduled your appointment with the cardiologist) before heading to Nicksons Eatery, as this charming spot in downtown La Grange celebrates country American cooking. Tin ceilings, homely wood floors, and a cowhide-covered banquette lend a barn-like aura to the dining room.

The Baca family, which includes husband and wife Nick and Carson (thus the name), and brother Rick, run the show with finger-lickin' good food. Tasty Texan brisket tacos, pan-seared pork chops, pork ribs, and soft shell crab Po'boys—this is country cooking with a gourmet slant. Those crispy sweet potato fries will hook you! In the sweet vein, Key lime pie, double chocolate pecan fudge, and old-fashioned root beer floats offer a slice of Americana.

Pancho Pistolas

F3

700 W. 31st St. (at Union Ave.)

Phone: 312-225-8808   Lunch & dinner daily
Web: www.panchopistolas.com
Prices: ⅗

Since 1997, South Siders and White Sox fans have flocked to this red brick building with the pistol-packing Pancho sign for serious steak that's tender and seasoned just so. From carne asada with grilled scallions and peppers to a stuffed skirt steak burrito, the perfectly cooked medium-rare beef can be added to several dishes on the menu and is worth the upgrade.

Beyond just steak in its juicy forms, the lively spot does right by its Mexican fare, which keeps the spice levels low but still tastes great when married with margaritas from the glass-block bar. If you can handle the 17-inch-long Pancho *grande* burrito, it might be wise to arrive with an extra plate—the multi-tortilla wonder is so long, it hangs over the platter upon which it's presented.

Pleasant House Bakery

English ✗

F3

964 W. 31st St. (bet. Farrell St. & Lituanica Ave.)

Phone: 773-523-7437 Lunch & dinner Tue – Sun
Web: www.pleasanthousebakery.com
Prices: ⊗⊗

The British royal pie, a rarity in Chicago, has found a home at tiny Pleasant House Bakery—and though U.K. expats go gaga for their savory meat pies, carnivorous Midwesterners can learn to love them too. The jovial staff welcomes everyone at the walk-up counter, bringing traditional British delicacies to marble-topped tables in this wedge-shaped dining room.

A meal of a Jamaican meat, or steak and ale pie wrapped in all-butter crust with a side of shucked green peas massaged in butter and fresh mint couldn't be more proper. Until, of course, you add a plate of crispy spud chips tossed with cheese, chopped ribeye, and gravy; or *banoffee* pie and snickerdoodles for dessert.

Reservations are only accepted for Sunday high tea with sandwiches and scones.

Prasino

American ✗✗

C3

93 S. La Grange Rd. (bet. Cossitt & Harris Aves.), La Grange

Phone: 708-469-7058 Lunch & dinner daily
Web: www.eatgreenlivewell.com
Prices: $$

Prasino means "green" in Greek and this eco-friendly arena lives up to its moniker by using organic ingredients from local farmers and purveyors. Additionally, its décor features recycled or reclaimed materials where possible. This oversized space in La Grange feels easygoing and cozy with lighting salvaged from corrugated cardboard and wood tables. The same philosophy extends to its sister restaurant in Wicker Park.

Broiled shishito peppers are a game of spicy roulette: most are fairly tame, but white miso-ginger aïoli cools down any unexpectedly searing bites. Sustainably sourced black cod pan-roasted with a soy glaze is tender and brightly sauced; while at dessert, carrot cake with sugar-frosted walnuts walks the line between virtuous and indulgent.

Q BBQ

Barbecue ✗

C3

70 S. LaGrange Rd. (bet. Cossit and Harris Aves.), La Grange

Phone: 708-482-8700   Lunch & dinner daily
Web: www.Q-BBQ.com
Prices: ⊜⊜

Look for the line snaking out the door and you'll know you've found Q—even city folk walking from the Metra will spot it easily. Once inside this warmly hued lair, gander at their chalkboard listing the daily smoked meats and sides denoting regional barbecue from across the country. Also watch out for the hickory and applewood cords lining the floor.

Chopped Texas brisket is tender and lightly smoky with a well-done crust; Carolina pulled pork is tangy and moist; and Memphis chicken wings get a dry rub with brown sugar for a sweet finish. Don't forget the football-shaped hush puppies for the table, and a jar or two of smoky, spicy, and tangy mustard- or vinegar-based sauces to take home. Grab a six-pack of Minnesota-brewed Hamm's beer while you're at it.

Reel Club

Seafood ✗✗

B3

272 Oakbrook Center (off Rte. 83), Oak Brook

Phone: 630-368-9400   Lunch & dinner daily
Web: www.reel-club.com
Prices: $$

Shopping in the behemoth Oakbrook Center could work up an appetite for almost anyone. Reel Club, a Lettuce Entertain You offering tucked amidst this mega mall, gives weary shoppers and longtime locals a great alternative to the staid food court. Its foyer leads to a bar and lounge area closely chased by a dark wood-paneled dining room.

A basket of irresistible cheddar cheese popovers shows up on every table here, and the menu spotlights seafood with a highlight being the Sunday brunch seafood and salad buffet. There are other American standards like the juicy ahi tuna burger slathered with a lemon-ginger aïoli and served on toasted brioche with hand-cut fries. You may also create your own flight of four of their wines by the glass.

Sen

Japanese ✗

814 S. Oak Park Ave. (bet. Harrison & Van Buren Sts.), Oak Park

Phone: 708-848-4400   Lunch & dinner Tue – Sun
Web: www.sensushibar.com
Prices: $$ Oak Park

It may be a subunit of currency, but it is no coincidence that Sen rhymes with Zen. From river stones pressed into a concrete entryway to a serene poplar-paneled room, minimalism and natural textures form the main strain in this sushi temple. New-age spa music drifts over the warm scene outfitted with benches and stools.

Bento lunches are all the rage here, yet witness a bit of artistry in such stunning creations as crab and pineapple wontons that take the Rangoon to a new level. Inventive maki like the *goka* stuffed with hamachi, avocado, and crowned with seared *otoro*; as well as red dragon with spicy tuna, *tai*, and red *tobiko* show off the *itamae's* shining skill. Tempura-fried ice cream kissed with raspberry sauce beautifully blends bright and sweet.

Shokolad

Eastern European ✗✗

2524 W. Chicago Ave. (bet. Campbell Ave. & Rockwell St.)

Phone: 773-276-6402   Lunch Tue – Sun
Web: N/A
Prices: ⊜⊝

Ukrainian, Russian, and Eastern European dishes are comfort food to much of Chicago's population, and diners come to Humboldt Park's Shokolad to indulge their cravings in a bright, casual setting. Must-tries include the potato and cheese *varenyky*, the Ukranian answer to the Polish *pierogi*, and the *pelmeni*, tender, spiced ground pork dumplings.

Sure, cheesecake lollipops aren't authentic Eastern European treats, but these dark or white chocolate-covered cheesecake rounds are favorites of regulars. In fact, they may be responsible for introducing many people to Shokolad. Highlighting the prowess of the pastry department, there's a bakery showcase with sweets to take away.

Regulars tout the Sunday brunch, by far one of the best around.

Taqueria Los Gallos #1

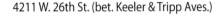

Mexican

 E3

4211 W. 26th St. (bet. Keeler & Tripp Aves.)

Phone: 773-762-7452   Lunch & dinner daily
Web: N/A
Prices: Kostner (Pink)

 It's more of a Mexican diner than a taqueria, though tacos here are an authentic highlight, simply adorned with onions and cilantro. Inside, the red and white décor combines the colors of a radish with rooster-themed accents. Servers in yellow shirts and paper hats are remarkably fast.

If you're eating in, go directly to a numbered table and take a seat. Most everyone seems to be relishing the signature dish of *carne en su jugo*, a flavorful broth teeming with beef, bacon, and beans with onions, avocado and cilantro. *Tacos de carne asada, tacos al pastor*, seafood cocktails, and ceviches are simple and traditional.

Days here can begin with *desayunos* but skip dessert and instead, visit their *panaderia* next door and take home a whole box of goodies.

Topaz Café

American 🍴🍴🍴

B4

780 Village Center Dr. (at Blue Ridge Pkwy.), Burr Ridge

Phone: 630-654-1616   Lunch Mon – Fri
Web: www.topazcafe.com   Dinner nightly
Prices: $$$

 Dining at the tony outdoor Burr Ridge Village Center might be as sexy as mall eats can get, and Topaz Café stands out as the epitome of suburban chic. At lunch, the columned space fills with power shoppers toting bags, then hits a sultry note as the lighting dims softly to amber for dinner. Get intimate with nightly specials at the bar, but be forewarned that your date might get distracted by the sporting event du jour on one of the multiple TVs.

 Steaks, seafood, pastas, and salads dominate the pleasantly contemporary American menu. Standouts include dense and hearty homemade potato gnocchi, or roasted Amish chicken set atop creamy polenta and drizzled with rich jus. Dark chocolate crêpes with Grand Marnier cream are an appropriately refined finish.

Vie

American ✗✗✗

B3

4471 Lawn Ave. (bet. Burlington Ave. & Elm St.), Western Springs

Phone: 708-246-2082   Dinner Mon – Sat
Web: www.vierestaurant.com
Prices: $$$

Vie is a showcase of contrasts: industrial elements like shiny concrete floors, brushed aluminum chairs, and menus presented on metal clipboards play off the earnestness of framed rural landscapes depicted abstractly in black-and-white photos on pale gray walls. And, as if to reiterate its sense of gravitas, find a culinary focus on seasonality and support of farmers and food artisans from the Midwest.
Bellota *lardo* from Iowa's La Quercia meats with pickled fennel and asparagus from Chef Paul Virant's garden meld with Russet potato gnocchi; and Skuna Bay salmon is silky-smoky from a quick sear on the wood grill. The glossy veneer on vanilla bean crème brûlée shatters to reveal smooth custard topped with Seville orange cream and almond streusel.

Wildfire

Steakhouse ✗✗

B3

232 Oakbrook Center (off Rte. 83), Oak Brook

Phone: 630-586-9000   Lunch & dinner daily
Web: www.wildfirerestaurant.com
Prices: $$$

This 1940's-inspired steakhouse has a cozy vibe, despite the location looking out at the mall parking lot, and the crowds who pack these tables. The music playing in the background and the low lighting contribute to the attractive ambience.
A shopping mall chain restaurant might not have been high on the "must eat" list, but like the Lettuce Entertain You folks are inclined to do, Wildfire exceeds expectations. The menu bulges with sandwiches, salads, and pizzas at lunch. At dinner, steaks and seafood platters are added. Each entrée, like the filet mignon, is cooked tender and to order. High-quality, lean meats add to the pleasurable experience. The classic steakhouse creamed spinach is heavy on the cream and seasoned with butter and nutmeg.

Xni-Pec de Yucatan

Mexican ✗

C3

3755 Grand Blvd. (at Prairie Ave.), Brookfield

Phone: 708-387-0691
Web: www.xnipec.us
Prices: **$$**

Lunch Fri – Sun
Dinner nightly

 Some city-dwellers may find it a trek, but every step is well rewarded with brilliant Mexican cuisine. Inside, red walls, Mayan posters, and a wooden menu seem simple, as if to belie the fact that their food is spectacular. This becomes clear as the supremely friendly staff presents their fresh corn tortilla chips, ideal for scooping up tart salsa or dipping into a ramekin of wicked habanero relish.

As expert servers lead you through a serious menu of Mexican specialties, consider stopping at the *pescado tikin-xic*, fish cooked in a banana leaf, doused with *guajillo-adobo* sauce. A string of adjectives from enchanting, perplexing, and lush could be used to describe the *mole rojo*, marrying ground chiles and spices. Suffice it to say this: order it.

Zak's Place

American ✗✗

B3

112 S. Washington St. (bet. 1st & 2nd Sts.), Hinsdale

Phone: 630-323-9257
Web: www.zaksplace.com
Prices: **$$**

Lunch Mon – Fri
Dinner Mon – Sat

 A modern, sophisticated tavern in the heart of Hinsdale, Zak's Place is equally suited for a family night out or romantic hideaway. The spacious room with handsome brass and dark accents ratchets up the comfort level, while wooden wine crates double up as intimate divisions. Solo diners may peruse the wine list or slurp down a bowl of fresh pasta at the front bar before heading home.

Sandwiches dominate this "place's" lunch menu, while dinner items like pork belly hash studded with buffalo sausage and potatoes; chocolate-braised short ribs; and a light, fluffy cheesecake kissed with tangy blueberry compote show versatility. However, don't bother looking around for Zak to thank him for a wonderful repast—this particular gem was named after a family pet.

Zaytune

F3

Middle Eastern ✗

3129 S. Morgan St. (at 31st Pl.)

Phone: 773-254-6300
Web: www.zaytunegrill.com
Prices:

Lunch & dinner daily

🖼 Halsted

Don't dismiss this tiny, value-oriented Middle Eastern lair as just another passable Bridgeport eatery. Zaytune, marked by a black awning and brick façade, is a well-kept place putting out seriously good eats. Owner Daniel Sarkiss is a graduate of Kendall College's culinary program; his love for and flair with fresh ingredients and bold seasonings keeps Zaytune ahead.

Order at the counter and await carefully composed classics like tabbouleh, hummus, baba ghanoush, and fava bean stew that have more than just the local vegans swooning. The grilled flatbread is something you'll want to wrap yourself in on a cold day. Golden brown falafels and chicken shawarma wraps are a sight to behold; while pistachio *kinafa* and walnut baklava are a teeny splurge.

ZaZa's

B3

Italian ✗✗

441 W. Ogden Ave. (bet. Richmond & Woodstock Aves.), Clarendon Hills

Phone: 630-920-0500
Web: www.zazasclarendonhills.com
Prices: $$

Lunch Mon – Fri
Dinner nightly

Despite its location among a bevy of car dealerships, this neighborhood favorite carves out a relaxing enclave for itself on a heavily trafficked stretch of road. A hedged patio framed by tiki torches is a pleasant summer perch, and warm mustard walls and cherry wood blinds temper the not-so-*belli* views from the dining room.

The oft-changing menu always has something to please. Carnivores may not be able to resist the one-two punch of pancetta and homemade Italian sausage in *penne Abruzzese*, while those looking for lighter flavors might veer to the plump, crab-filled gnocchi in a creamy vodka-style sauce. Pasta dishes are big enough to satisfy, but the kitchen also churns out hearty and fresh entrées like salmon *acqua pazza* or *vitello limone*.

Where to Stay

Blackstone

636 S. Michigan Ave. (at Balbo Ave.)

Phone:	312-447-0955 or 800-468-3571
Web:	www.blackstonerenaissance.com
Prices:	$$$

 Harrison

328 Rooms

4 Suites

The Blackstone Renaissance Hotel

It might be owned and managed by Marriott, but there's nothing cookie-cutter about this significant property. First, the location is noteworthy—it is the place to begin your exploration of the Magnificent Mile and the rest of the city. Walk to Grant Park, Shedd Aquarium, Soldier Field, or the Art Institute, but it's not just the "steps-away" status that gives this hotel its pedigree. Since 1910, the Blackstone has been the beloved choice of celebrities and chief executives, hosting every president since William Taft.

While it may be historical, it is certainly not creaky—this thanks to a spot-on face-lift that took the hotel into the new millennium. The Beaux-Arts exterior makes a stunning first impression, but the sizzle resides solely indoors. There is a bit of wit and whimsy in the public spaces: from gilded leather tufted couches, to the 1,400 pieces of original art, the Blackstone puts a fresh spin on classic details. Rooms and suites are truly modern and wear earthy tones; while bathrooms are boldly decked with white-and-black palettes.

Staggering views of the lake are a draw. Speaking of the outdoors, guests also enjoy recreational activities like a jogging or biking trail.

Blake

500 S. Dearborn St. (bet. Congress Pkwy. & Harrison St.)

Phone: 312-986-1234
Web: www.hotelblake.com
Prices: $$

 LaSalle

158
Rooms

4
Suites

Ralph De Caro/Panomedia Productions

Chicago ▶ Chinatown & South Loop

Spacious rooms, reasonable rates, and a top-notch restaurant prove that the Blake is indeed worth its salt. Housed within the historic Morton Building (the former home of the Morton Salt Company), this hotel effortlessly blends past and present with its modern style and amenities.

Espresso-hued wood-paneled walls with red accents set a handsome tone in the appealing lobby. The attractive minimalist décor is striking, yet the ambience has a relaxed ease; while a glass-walled business center with a separate conference room caters to your work needs.

The rich chocolate and soft beige color scheme is continued in the various guest rooms. The accommodations are large and comfortable—pull back those expansive blinds and take in the stunning view of Chicago. Other amenities like large desks with ergonomic leather chairs, have business travelers in mind, but it's not all work and no play at the Blake. Fine linens dress the beds, pleasing artwork adorns the walls, and iHome iPod docking stations replace alarm clocks. But for a further taste of luxury within your own room, order a full array of in-room spa services that may include restorative treatments and revitalizing facials...nirvana!

The Drake

140 E. Walton St. (at Michigan Ave.)

Phone: 312-787-2200 or 800-553-7253
Web: www.thedrakehotel.com
Prices: $$

 Chicago (Red)

461 Rooms

74 Suites

The Drake Hotel

It doesn't get more old-time Chicago than The Drake and this esteemed hotel retains its status as one of the finest in the city. Opened in 1920, The Drake oozes with history. The rich and royal all flocked here in its heyday and while today's guests are more likely to be here for business meetings, not state meetings, the hotel maintains its regal presence.

The grand architecture and impressive lobby are a sign of what's to come. Expect old-world elegance in the rooms and suites. Standard rooms are quite small, but all accommodations are well appointed with a traditional design (think antique furnishings, gilded mirrors, and ornate lighting fixtures).

The walls may not be able to talk in this historic nest, but the Cape Cod Room's bar can show off a bit—Joe DiMaggio and Marilyn Monroe are among the many who have carved their initials in it. Today's guests will do better to save their knives for buttering the scones at the properly elegant afternoon tea at the Palm Court. From its delicate finger sandwiches to its fine bone china, this rite of passage is a tea to make the Queen proud (in fact, Queen Elizabeth II did have tea here, along with other royals throughout the years).

Four Seasons Chicago

D4

120 E. Delaware Pl. (bet. Michigan Ave. & Rush St.)

Phone: 312-280-8800 or 800-819-5053
Web: www.fourseasons.com
Prices: $$$$

Chicago (Red)

175 Rooms

168 Suites

Four Seasons Hotel Chicago

Four Seasons knows how to pour it on. This elegant hotel has it all—white-glove service, impressive facilities, elegant accommodations, fine dining, and a prime location just blocks from Lake Michigan and within a stiletto's throw of some of the world's best shopping.

Whether you choose a lake view or city view, all guest rooms and suites are outfitted with a fresh, contemporary décor and are crammed with creature comforts including a sleek LCD flat-screen. The beds, dressed with dreamy linens and soft colors, are exceedingly inviting; and the marble bathrooms make a grand and glamorous statement. There are plenty of places to put your feet up and relax, but the window seat is arguably the best. Is there anything better than soaking up the scene in a fluffy bathrobe? From the doormen and front desk to the dining and spa staff, the service is seamless and spot on.

Coveted by affluent clusters, the Four Seasons hosts many a wedding with an on-site expert who works to ensure an unforgettable experience. Want a ballroom wedding? The bride and groom will even receive a complimentary suite with every amenity including savory delights and a changing room for use on their wedding day.

Chicago ▲ Gold Coast

Indigo

1244 N. Dearborn Pkwy. (bet. Division & Goethe Sts.)

Phone: 312-787-4980 or 800-972-2494
Web: www.hotelindigo.com
Prices: **$$**

Clark/Division

163
Rooms

2
Suites

Shanae Diewold Photography

There is nothing remotely pretentious about the Indigo. This boutique hotel, part of the InterContinental Hotels worldwide chain, is proof that budget doesn't have to be boring. Located on a quiet residential street in the Gold Coast and within minutes of Oak Street's boutique row (a revered shopping haven), the Indigo is a breath of fresh air with its summer's dream décor. It is all very beach house on the Scandinavian coast with its white-painted patio-style wood furnishings, white beadboard, gleaming blonde wood floors, and indigo blue and lime green colors.

This hotel has the cottage look down pat, and the upbeat personality extends to the guestrooms. Banish the wintry blues in these ambient and uplifting beach shack-style accommodations, where wood floors add a particularly homey aura and walls covered in floral murals bring the outside in.

The luscious colors and inviting ambience are surefire mood boosters. Niceties like Aveda bath products, flat-screen televisions, and coffee makers add a final touch. Amid all the shopping and sightseeing, take the time to unwind by ordering room service—available in the mornings. The lobby bar/restaurant features light fare throughout the day.

Park Hyatt

800 N. Michigan Ave. (at Chicago Ave.)

Phone: 312-335-1234 or 877-875-4658
Web: www.parkchicago.hyatt.com
Prices: $$$$

 Chicago (Red)

185 Rooms

13 Suites

Andy Barnes Photography

The Park Hyatt is the place to stay when you want to sneak a peek at how the other half lives. Situated catercorner to the historic Water Tower on the Magnificent Mile, this luxurious getaway occupies the first 18 floors of a sky-reaching tower, home to some of the city's most exclusive private residences.

Park Hyatt is the A student in the Hyatt hotels chain, and this particular Chicago sibling is no exception. It is understated sophistication at its best, offering luxury and comfort to its privileged guests. The contemporary-styled guestrooms don't skimp on size or style, and they offer plenty of conveniences and goodies like high thread cotton bedding, butler service, large safes big enough to hold and charge laptops, and video checkout. The sleek marble and granite bathrooms are equally spacious (oversized tubs, separate walk-in showers) and stocked with deluxe bath salts, Blaise Mautin products, and candles.

Sip in the height of style in your own room, or enjoy a thrilling array of cocktails on the outdoor terrace, replete with spectacular views. From valet parking and turndown to a weekly sommelier-guided wine and spirit tasting, courteous and efficient service is a staple.

Chicago ▶ Gold Coast

313

Public

1301 North State Pkwy. (at Goethe St.)

Phone: 312-787-3700
Web: www.publichotels.com
Prices: **$$**

 Clark/Division

250 Rooms

35 Suites

PUBLIC Chicago

Put that tired, age-old public vs. private debate to rest—at least in Chicago, where Public takes the cake. The arrival of Ian Schrager's latest hotel breathes new life into the Gold Coast landmark Ambassador Hotel and brings style to the masses.

The unassuming exterior makes way for interiors that are the very definition of sleek sophistication. White, white, and more white lend a modern touch to the otherwise stately lobby, but it's not the chic design that is most surprising... it's the price! You don't need a black card to soak up the atmosphere, where style comes at a sensible (gasp!) price. But, with such delicious dining and entertainment options—there is a screening room in the back adorned with plush loungers and intimate seats—Public feels much more like a private club than budget bore.

Don't mistake their quietly neutral palette and cantilevered furnishings of the rooms and suites for simplicity. There's substance behind this style, with Frette linens, state-of-the-art technology, and an eye-catching collection of photography and vintage postcards. Oh, and it's really all one phone call away. Press just one button for everything from a personal attendant to room service.

Chicago ▶ Gold Coast

Raffaello

E5

201 E. Delaware Pl. (at Seneca St.)

Phone: 312-943-5000 or 800-898-7198
Web: www.chicagoraffaello.com
Prices: $$$

 Chicago (Red)

97
Rooms

73
Suites

Mitchell Freeland Design

Craving champagne but on a beer (imported, of course) budget? The Raffaello might just be your biggest and best boon ever. This stylish boutique hotel gives you a swanky Gold Coast address without the pomp–and price–of its fussy competitors.

Located next door to the John Hancock Tower, Raffaello is also just steps from Water Tower Place and the shops of 900 North Michigan. So it goes without saying that this treasure has a prime location, and the hits just keep on coming at this contemporary spot. The soaring ceilings capped off with an oversized chandelier, and the sparkling marble floors of the lobby are a sure sign of good things to come. Rooms are on the smaller side, so upgrades are worth the extra bucks; but the soothing spirit will leave you smitten. Creams, beiges, and dark woods define the current look, and amenities like high-quality bath products (think Gilchrist and Soames) and high-tech extras like 32-inch flat-screen LCDs and iHome players maintain the modern theme.

Never quite made it into the cool clique? Book a nook at the hotel's outdoor oasis, Drumbar. This handsome lounge decked in wood-paneling will have you feeling like part of the "in" crowd, instantly.

Chicago ▶ Gold Coast

The Ritz-Carlton Chicago

160 E. Pearson St. (bet. Michigan Ave. & Seneca St.)

Phone: 312-266-1000 or 800-621-6906
Web: www.fourseasons.com/chicagorc
Prices: $$$$

Chicago (Red)

344 Rooms

91 Suites

John Russo

It just does not get any better than this. The Ritz-Carlton Chicago, managed by esteemed Four Seasons, has one of the city's most coveted locations. Situated at Water Tower Place, the shopping of Magnificent Mile is practically served up on a silver platter for guests of The Ritz-Carlton (and there is also direct access to the indoor shops at Water Tower Place).

Valets graciously welcome patrons and then whisk them away to the classically elegant world of the 12th floor lobby. The gentle trickle of the central fountain alludes to the serenity found here. While the lobby shows off a traditional aesthetic, the gloriously updated guest rooms and suites are decked with a definitively modern take. Thick, plush, and geometric-patterned carpets set the tone for the well-appointed (lavish furnishings, deluxe amenities) and well-planned (plentiful storage, spacious dressing areas, large desks) rooms, ideal for both business and leisure travelers.

From access to the refined Carlton Club, a spa/indoor pool/fitness facility with a seasonal sundeck, to the glass-enclosed Greenhouse with breathtaking Lake Michigan and city views, there are plenty of perks as a guest of this exclusive hotel.

Sofitel

20 E. Chestnut St. (at Wabash Ave.)

Phone: 312-324-4000 or 800-763-4835
Web: www.sofitel-chicago.com
Prices: $$$

 Chicago (Red)

382
Rooms

33
Suites

Sofitel Chicago Water Tower

Some of architecture's greatest minds built their masterpieces in Chicago, and the Sofitel continues the city's long-held tradition of innovative design. Imagined by French architect Jean-Paul Viguier, this structure is comprised of a 32-floor prism of white glass and steel. The result? A fantastic landmark in a city synonymous with stand-out buildings.

Of course, the location doesn't hurt either—this sanctum is delightfully central and just a short walk from Gold Coast shopping and the Museum of Contemporary Art. Neither does great service, nor elegant designer guest rooms with plentiful amenities and services.

The hip vibe is immediately felt upon entering the lobby, where towering ceilings and a polished décor set the stylish tone. The accommodations continue the cool theme with modern furnishings, marble bathrooms, and abounding creature comforts—maybe Frette robes, and complimentary movie channels. From corporate (staffed and self-service business centers) to personal (concierge), needs are met with grace and know-how by an intuitive staff. Grab a book from the charming library and bone up on architecture while enjoying a concoction in the hugely sought-after bar and lounge.

Chicago ▶ Gold Coast

Talbott

D4

20 E. Delaware Pl. (bet. Rush & State Sts.)

Phone: 312-944-4970 or 800-825-2688
Web: www.talbotthotel.com
Prices: $$

Chicago (Red)

120 Rooms

29 Suites

The Talbott Hotel

Want to feel like a resident of the swanky Gold Coast? Check right in to the boutique Talbott. This hotel feels like a private residence blending old-world charms with modern fixings. And, with a location just two blocks from the Magnificent Mile, you can hit the shops and still have energy to walk home.

Inside, the Talbott feels like a classic English estate; dark wood-paneled walls lined with hunting scenes and a roaring fireplace feel straight out of the princely countryside. Far from fuddy-duddy, the hotel displays its sense of humor with a lady bug-dressed cow sculpture scaling the façade. Designed by artist Brian Calvin for the 1999 Chicago Cow Parade installation, the cow adds a serious touch of whimsy to this otherwise traditional hotel.

The accommodations offer a respite from the city pace with their quiet elegance and high-quality amenities that may include Frette linens and Aveda toiletries. While it has been awarded a Green Seal certification for its eco-sensitive choices, guests' comfort is never compromised. If the hotel's 24-hour room service has you over-eating, work off those extra calories by making use of the complimentary access to nearby Equinox Fitness Center.

Waldorf Astoria

11 E. Walton St. (bet. Rush & State Sts.)

Phone: 312-646-1300 or 800-500-8511
Web: www.waldorfastoria.com
Prices: $$$$

Chicago (Red)

38
Rooms

150
Suites

Waldorf Astoria Chicago

What was once the Elysian is now the super-luxe Waldorf Astoria. Walk through the cobblestoned motor court that resembles a French château, and step into the striking lobby—you'll think you've died and gone to haute heaven at this grand dame. The seductive space is the very picture of contemporary minimalism. Its striking chandelier and gleaming marble floors are sure to make a lasting first impression.

The good looks extend to the rooms and suites, where champagne and platinum color schemes and tailored furnishings give off a current British sensibility. It is all very glamorous, and the Carrara marble bathrooms (showers come with leg rests for shaving!) are over-the-top gorgeous.

Within this palatial establishment, not only do guests resemble ladies and lords of the manor, but the uniformed staff delivers polished service. It doesn't end there. Dining is a first-rate affair; while the tucked-away Bernard's Bar with its bevy of thirst-quenching libations, has that wood-paneled elegance down pat. Even exercise is elevated to an art form at the spa and health club, where you can unwind with a homeopathic facial or succumb to a "lava shell" massage after hoofing it on the treadmill.

Chicago ▶ Gold Coast

Whitehall

 105 E. Delaware Pl. (bet. Michigan Ave. & Rush St.)

Phone: 312-944-6300 or 866-753-4081
Web: www.thewhitehallhotel.com
Prices: $$

Chicago (Red)

214 Rooms

8 Suites

Gerilyn Frey

Chicago ▶ Gold Coast

Smack dab in the middle of it all sits the Whitehall hotel. This independent boutique hotel is right in the thick of it, nestled among the shops, restaurants, theaters, and entertainment of the Magnificent Mile and the nightlife of Rush Street. Many of Chicago's major attractions (Millennium Park and Navy Pier to name a few) are also just down the road.

This elegant red brick building was once home to full-time residents who occupied apartments, but today's temporary residents are treated to a gloriously old-world, European sense of style. The lobby may as well be a love letter to the past, with sparkling chandeliers, tufted leather chairs, and polished wood paneling. If that doesn't feel nostalgic enough, many of the furnishings have been restored to their former grandeur.

The guest rooms and suites also have the feel of another era, exquisitely appointed with four-poster beds, wrought-iron headboards, leather-topped mahogany desks, and hand-painted armoires. But rest assured, as the amenities (luxurious Egyptian cotton sheets) are definitely 21st century.

Indulge in a regal repast at Fornetto Mei—bringing together the foods and flavors of Asia and Italy in an intimate dining room.

Majestic

528 W. Brompton Ave. (bet. Lake Shore Dr. & Pine Grove Ave.)

Phone: 773-404-3499 or 800-727-5108

Web: www.majestic-chicago.com

Prices: $

🚇 Addison (Red)

48 Rooms

4 Suites

The Majestic Hotel

Need to find yourself a temporary den while hitting up a Cubs game? Opt for the Majestic. This boutique haven is the closest hotel to Wrigley Field, so you can have your fill of beer and dogs and even stay for extra innings without worrying about a long trip home. Just because it's near the ball park doesn't mean this hotel doesn't know how to pour on the sophistication—as indicated by its moniker, the intimate space is reminiscent of old-world Europe.

Once ensconced inside one of their guest rooms or suites, you'd never know that you're in bustling Lakeview. Instead, it's peace and quiet in an elegant setting. From the sleek mahogany furnishings and landscape paintings that are riffs on Monet, to the gold-toned fabrics, the accommodations are clearly inspired by an English country estate. Try to upgrade to a suite since the standard rooms are on the small side.

Guests are treated to complimentary breakfasts and afternoon cookies. Don't worry about parking headaches, especially on game day, since the hotel does offer a garage. The amenities are limited, so you'll need to dine in an area restaurant and work out in a local gym. But with a price point and location this good, who cares?

Chicago ▶ Lakeview & Wrigleyville

Willows

555 W. Surf St. (bet. Broadway & Cambridge Ave.)

Phone:	773-528-8400 or 800-787-3108
Web:	www.willowshotelchicago.com
Prices:	$

 Wellington

51 Rooms

4 Suites

The Willows Hotel

Maybe it's the quaint tree-lined street in the heart of a residential neighborhood. Maybe it's the designation as a historic landmark (the building dates back to 1926). Or, maybe it's just the charming country inn ambience, but the Willows rightfully boasts a distinctive experience within the Windy City.

Just a mile from Wrigley Field and a short walk to notable Lincoln Park and lovely Lake Michigan, Willows invites guests to unwind in gracious European-style comfort. French reproduction furnishings and French-influenced wall coverings add sophistication, while honey, green, and brown color schemes lend an inviting, slightly homey, touch.

The Willows is definitely not for those high maintenance or testy travelers who seek hotels brimming with modern services. There is no business center or exercise facility (though they do provide access to a nearby gym), and a simple breakfast is served in the lobby. If you want manicures and martinis, go elsewhere. But if you are the type who wants to live like a local while stretching out in a comfortable and copious guest room, the Willows is a sure bet. Besides, who can resist a place that has an afternoon social with freshly baked cookies?

Chicago ► Lakeview & Wrigleyville

Villa D'Citta

2230 N. Halsted St. (bet. Belden & Webster Aves.)

Phone: 312-771-0696 or 800-228-6070
Web: www.villadcitta.com
Prices: $$

 Fullerton

6
Suites

Chuck Gullett

What's that? The genteel townhouse you were crossing your fingers for was willed to another family member? Forget about it. Just book a room at Villa D'Citta and you'll get the same feel, without the pesky property taxes. Originally built in 1887, this B&B was a private residence until 2009. Stately, sophisticated, and steps from Lincoln Park's main strip, Villa D'Citta is a luxurious and quiet alternative to the anonymity prevalent in larger hotels.

The residential mien and bed-and-breakfast style lures couples, discerning travelers, and adventurous types who want to really feel at home in the Windy City. And feel at home they do, where guests have the run of the place. Totter around the gourmet kitchen, grill on the outdoor deck, or hop into the Jacuzzi—it's all part of the experience. There are just a handful of rooms and suites, all decked with a modern, slightly masculine appeal. Or, empty out the piggy bank and rent the whole kit and caboodle.

Ralph Rousseau, the host, and his tiny dog Whiskey, will not only make you feel welcome the instant you walk in, but will also remind you of the pet-friendly policy. From restaurant recommendations to sightseeing, Ralph has you covered.

Chicago ▶ Lincoln Park & Old Town

Allegro

B2

171 W. Randolph St. (at Wells St.)

Phone: 312-236-0123 or 800-643-1500
Web: www.allegrochicago.com
Prices: $$

Clark/Lake

452 Rooms

31 Suites

James Spada

Not on the A list? Check in to the vibrant Allegro and you'll certainly feel like a very important person! Adorned in a slick Hollywood Regency manner, the demeanor here is relaxed, fun, and youthful. Part of the Kimpton hotel group, the Allegro has that cool boutique-esque ambience, yet it offers the top-notch amenities of a major hotel chain.

Brush up on your geometry before heading to the rooms and suites at the Allegro, since geometric patterns are everywhere. From the silver and white wallpaper to the royal blue carpets to the decorative pillows, it is pattern play throughout. The accommodations have a stylish blend of old Hollywood glamour and contemporary dazzle.

Kimpton is known for its many amenities, so expect extras like evening wine receptions, complimentary morning coffee, and no fee/no restrictions pet policies. From KimptonKids programming and in-room spa services to well-equipped fitness facilities, state-of-the-art conference and meeting rooms, and eco-friendly practices, the Allegro lives up to its promises. Relive the days of the three-martini lunch at the Encore Lunch Club + Liquid Lounge or settle in to a comfy booth for some yummy Italian food at 312 Chicago.

Burnham

1 W. Washington St. (at State St.)

Phone: 312-782-1111 or 866-690-1986
Web: www.burnhamhotel.com
Prices: $$

 Washington

103 Rooms

19 Suites

Hotel Burnham/Kimpton Hotels

Hotel Burnham has pedigree and panache. A historic landmark built in 1895 as one of the first skyscrapers, the building has been reworked, revamped, and reinvigorated with a dramatic décor. Housed in Daniel Burnham's Reliance Building, Burnham's property has a fiercely independent spirit and delivers a well-rounded, unique, and first-class experience.

From caged elevators and mosaic-tiled floors to mailbox slots on the guestroom doors (there's no delivery—they're sealed shut), traces of the building's past add a distinct charm and unique flavor. There's nothing sedate about these accommodations, where regal guestrooms pop with sensational bursts of color and patterns. It's all very fancy, with gilded furnishings and tasseled silk canopy beds, but it's good to be king. Even the closet has a few surprises with leopard- and zebra-patterned bathrobes.

The customary services and amenities (including a concierge staff) are here, but the unusual touches are most memorable (try parenting a goldfish during your stay). A complimentary wine hour in the evening is the perfect way to kickoff a night on the town. There is also 24-hour room service for those who have no desire to budge from bed.

Chicago ▶ Loop

Fairmont

200 N. Columbus Dr. (bet. Lake & Water Sts.)

Phone: 312-565-8000 or 800-526-2008
Web: www.fairmont.com/chicago
Prices: $$

State/Lake

622 Rooms

65 Suites

Fairmont Chicago

The Fairmont has always enjoyed a fantastic location convenient to Michigan Avenue and Millennium Park, but now, with its fashionable lobby decked in sleek lines, natural hues, and handsome woods, this hotel sizzles with a fresh style. Whether you're here with family or to honeymoon with your new honey, this exquisite property provides the perfect vacation refuge. The look is very mod and the lobby could double as the latest "it" spot, but there is substance behind this style with Fairmont's superior comfort and plush amenities.

The rooms and suites are a study in upscale modern design, where earth tones set a soothing slate, interesting patterns (zebra-striped carpets, bamboo leaf-inspired pillows) inject an upbeat flavor, and artist Warwick Orme's floral artwork captures the eye. Comforts abound, and the Fairmont even offers allergy friendly rooms (PURE) and a dedicated floor for corporate travelers (GOLD).

This glorious getaway may boast divine dining, but the Fairmont really has guests at "hello" with its impressive lobby capped off by an outpost of ENO, where 500 varietals of wine (60 types by the glass!), 35 different types of cheese, and artisanal chocolates await gourmands.

Hard Rock

D2

230 N. Michigan Ave. (at Water St.)

Phone: 312-345-1000 or 866-966-5166
Web: www.hardrockhotelchicago.com
Prices: **$$**

 State/Lake

370 Rooms

11 Suites

Daniel Newcomb

It is likely that you know the Hard Rock shtick. Like a laid-back Smithsonian for rock and roll memorabilia, the Hard Rock has made its name by sharing the hard-living rock star lifestyle with diners and hotel guests, but this lively Chicago sibling strays a bit from the standard and shows off some local pride. Housed within the historic Carbide & Carbon Building, the Hard Rock mixes its expected look with art deco architecture. This fun and upbeat hotel offers reasonable prices for the cool vibe and central location.

The guestrooms take the rocker lifestyle quite seriously. If the celebrity costumes displayed in the hallways doesn't clue you in, the rock star-themed artwork certainly will. Dark colors and low lighting are ideal for late night revelers, though business travelers might have trouble getting work done.

The sleek and modern lobby is home to two popular establishments—crowded Angels & Kings with a clubby vibe to match the hotel's reputation, and Chuck's Manufacturing for some cool cocktailing alongside an array of American treats. In case you don't already have one of those ubiquitous Hard Rock t-shirts, you can always pick one up in the lobby's namesake store.

Chicago ▶ Loop

Hotel 71

71 E. Wacker Dr. (at Wabash Ave.)

Phone: 312-346-7100 or 800-621-4005
Web: www.hotel71.com
Prices: $$

 State/Lake

331 Rooms

26 Suites

Hotel 71

It's not your age, the year, or even your shoe size; Hotel 71 is named for its E. Wacker Drive address. This modern jewel pivoted upon the "Magnificent Mile" enjoys a spectacular riverfront setting near the pedestrian riverwalk and directly across from Trump International Hotel & Tower. Here, less is more as far as design goes.

The sleek, modern decor is soothing and warm. Tan, brown, and golden hues run throughout, while the accommodations add plaid patterns and animal prints as interesting accents. The rooms are expansive, fitted with flat-screen televisions, desks armed with ergonomic chairs, large bathrooms with Cali Tarocco products, and complimentary in-room coffee. From mini-stereos to three telephones, electronics are plentiful. Those wishing to take in the sights should be sure to book rooms with river views.

Hoyt's on the first floor offers a spectrum of international small plates along with hearty American fare. After an exquisite revamp, Hotel 71 is now, more than ever, ready for its close-up. Its windowed top floor ballroom was a stand-in for Bruce Wayne's penthouse in *The Dark Knight*, and more recently it was used as a backdrop in *Transformers: Dark of the Moon*.

Chicago ▶ Loop

328

JW Marriott Chicago

 B4

151 W. Adams St. (bet. LaSalle & Wells Sts.)

Phone: 312-660-8200 or 888-717-8850
Web: www.jwmarriott.com
Prices: $$$

🚇 Quincy

581 Rooms

29 Suites

JW Marriott Chicago

The JW Marriott is a perfect blend of old and new. Housed in the Continental & Commercial National Bank building, which opened in 1914 and was designed by acclaimed Chicago architect David Burnham, this hotel has seriously good bones, but its interiors wow even further with a fresh, contemporary design.

The rooms and suites are handsomely furnished with a dash of art deco (Lucite light fixtures) and a sprinkle of Chinoiserie (Asian-influenced furnishings and artwork). Even the bathrooms show off a touch of glamour with granite, sparkling marble, and chocolate brown wall coverings. However, it's not just about good looks at this sumptuous hotel—JW Marriott spares no comforts, whether it's plush bedding or comfy leather desk chairs, no detail is overlooked.

With 44,000 square feet of meeting space, it's no surprise that this Loop respite is a favorite for conferences and pow-wows, but don't worry that it's all work and no play. The Lobby Lounge, complete with light bites and libations, is an ideal refuge for hotel guests as well as business groups. Spend an hour or more in VALEO Spa, Fitness, and Wellness Center, or take a dip in the pool and wash away the stresses of the day.

Chicago ▶ Loop

Monaco

225 N. Wabash Ave. (bet. Haddock & Wacker Pls.)

Phone: 312-960-8500 or 866-610-0081
Web: www.monaco-chicago.com
Prices: **$$$**

State/Lake

172
Rooms

20
Suites

David Phelps

There is not much one can say but hats off to the Monaco, housed in a former...you guessed it...hat factory near the Chicago River. While it may rest within walking distance of the Loop, Michigan Avenue, shopping, and the theaters, this hotel certainly doesn't rely on its location alone.

Everything about the property speaks to its gracious style and demeanor. The staff, from the first greeting by the doorman to the efficient and helpful front desk clerks, seems genuinely concerned with guests' comfort. The lobby is tastefully appointed with a modern romantic European style and feels elegant without being stuffy.

Stripes and diamond patterns create a pleasing contemporary aura in the guest rooms and suites, but it is truly the river and twinkling city views that stand out. Accommodations are even furnished with cushioned window nooks, known as meditation stations, for relaxing and day-dreaming with a view. Many thoughtful amenities such as in-room spa services and goldfish companions soothe the body and soul after a windy day. Adding to Monaco's appeal, the South Water Kitchen serves three meals a day, while a hosted wine hour at 5:00 P.M. allows guests to enjoy complimentary glasses.

Palmer House

17 E. Monroe St. (at State St.)

Phone: 312-726-7500 or 800-445-8667
Web: www.palmerhousehiltonhotel.com
Prices: **$$**

 Monroe

1584
Rooms

55
Suites

Palmer House Hilton

It doesn't get any more legendary than the Palmer House. This great-granddaddy of Chicago hotels was built 13 days before the great fire of 1871; it was then rebuilt and reopened in 1873 as the world's first fireproof hotel. Back when a nickel got you a vaudeville show, the lobby was a true spectacle; and despite a massive nip and tuck, it continues to soar as a serious scene.

Palmer House embraces the Old World: the ceiling, painted with Greek mythological characters, was restored by the same craftsman who worked on the Sistine Chapel. Italian marble, gilded candelabra, carpeted hallways, and grand staircases—it's like a page was ripped from the grand lobby handbook. Where else can you sleep where Mark Twain, Liberace, and Charles Dickens once laid their weary heads?

If walls could talk—this glamorous nest has seen and done it all. Electric lighting and elevator service were all pioneered here. At every turn the hotel honors its history, and yet, guests are never asked to forsake today's comforts. From spacious, attractive, and updated accommodations to fine dining at the lovely Lockwood restaurant, the Palmer House lives as comfortably within the 21st century as it did in the 19th.

Chicago ▲ Loop

The Wit

201 N. State St. (at Lake St.)

Phone: 312-467-0200 or 866-318-1514
Web: www.thewithotel.com
Prices: **$$**

 State/Lake

256 Rooms

42 Suites

theWit Hotel Chicago

There's definitely a bit of whimsy at The Wit. Just listen to the sound piped in to the hallways—usually chirping birds by day, crickets by night, and roosters in the morning. Even their wake-up calls are unusual—when was the last time you were awoken by Harry Caray?

This hotel is definitely not your grandfather's Doubletree, though it is in fact managed by the same. Instead, The Wit is ultra-modern in both design and décor. The rooms and suites pack a punch with vibrant orange chaise lounges and plentiful high-tech amenities. Widescreen TVs are loaded with movies and music channels, while suites are equipped with complete kitchens.

Boasting a lively setting, the lobby alone exudes a sophisticated energy. Additionally, dining is definitely not an afterthought at this boutique-inspired hotel: State & Lake feeds the bustling scene with its American cooking; and ROOF–the 27th floor indoor-outdoor space complete with fire pits and a sweeping view of the city–is *the* place to be. This hot spot with DJs galore draws a young, swank crowd. You may find yourself jostling for space in the elevators with these revelers ready for a big night out, but it's all part of the fun at The Wit.

Conrad

521 N. Rush St. (at Grand Ave.)

Phone: 312-645-1500 or 800-266-7237
Web: www.conradchicago.com
Prices: $$$

Grand (Red)

283 Rooms

28 Suites

Conrad Chicago

It starts with a great location. The city's business and theater districts are close by, while the parks and shores of the lake are a few minutes east, but what makes the Conrad Chicago stand out is its appeal to label lovers—the hotel is adjacent to Nordstrom and the high-end shops of The Northbridge Shopping Center.

It continues with no expense spared in-room treats. The Conrad spoils its guests with a seemingly endless stream of luxury amenities: Pratesi sheets, Acca Kappa bath products, Bose surround sound, and lavish 42-inch plasma TVs. Services are equally plentiful, and include indulgent options like bath butlers and pillow menus. If your credit card got more of a workout than your stroll down the Magnificent Mile gave you, the hotel's fitness center is available 24 hours a day.

And it doesn't end there. The hotel has three inviting and distinct venues. The Terrace Bar exudes a casual sophistication perfect for light meals or drinks (try the signature chocolate martini), while the Terrace Restaurant at Conrad steps it up with American and global cooking. Open during warmer months, The Terrace Rooftop is a sure bet for cozy outdoor enjoyment—movies are even shown on Sundays.

Chicago ▶ River North

dana hotel and spa

660 N. State St. (at Erie St.)

Phone: 312-202-6000 or 888-301-7952
Web: www.danahotelandspa.com
Prices: $$

 Grand (Red)

194 Rooms

22 Suites

Hedrich Blessing

Get to know dana. This boutique hotel certainly has its number on you, that is if you're a young, discerning traveler with a penchant for fine living and high-priced tech toys. The dana hotel perfectly complements its creative, art gallery-filled neighborhood. It captures the essence of industrial chic with stone, wood, and natural design elements. The calling card of this design philosophy–exposed ductwork and piping–is found throughout the hotel in the lobby and private accommodations.

Rich, hand-hewn Jarrah wood floors make a striking statement in the guest rooms, but it is the floor-to-ceiling windows that are the unmistakable star. Exposed concrete and unfinished support pillars show off the signature style, but oversized showers capped off with rain showerheads and pillow-topped beds ensure that you can be cool and cosseted at the same time. Hipsters will find plenty to add to their gadget wish lists after a stay here—the Zeppelin-Bowers & Wilkins sound systems sync to guests' MP3 players for a state-of-the-art sound.

From the modern, spacious spa and rooftop Vertigo Sky Lounge, to the delightfully playful menu at Argent restaurant and bar, the facilities are all top-notch.

Felix

111 W. Huron St. (bet. Clark & LaSalle Sts.)

Phone: 312-447-3440 or 877-848-4040
Web: www.hotelfelixchicago.com
Prices: $$

 Chicago (Red)

225 Rooms

Hotel Felix

Is this where Al Gore stays? He may not be camping out here, but the Felix would certainly warm his heart. This innovative boutique hotel was the first hotel in Chicago designed to meet the specifications of Silver LEED certification. From design elements (carpets are made from recycled materials; floors are cork and bamboo) to practices (paperless front desk; eco-friendly cleaning products), the Felix takes eco-conscious living very seriously.

The rooms and suites perfectly complement the hotel's relaxed modern sophistication. The soft and earthy palette, simple furnishings, and upgraded amenities like an iHome are the very definition of urban living.

Cast your worries aside—this is not a hippie commune by any stretch. It doesn't just do good, but it looks good too at this chic, contemporary hotel. Take a seat in the inviting lobby bar (with a working fireplace) and discuss carbon footprints over cocktails or dine on French favorites from the newly minted LM Bistro (which also provides room service). The Spa features a comprehensive variety of treatments, all guided by the healing properties of plant and flower extracts.

The best part? It doesn't take a lot of green to stay here.

Chicago ▶ River North

James

  F2

55 E. Ontario St. (at Rush St.)

Phone: 312-337-1000 or 877-526-3755
Web: www.jameshotels.com
Prices: $$$

 Grand (Red)

191
Rooms

106
Suites

Spa

The James Chicago

It is not surprising that the James has a loyal following with European travelers and stylish young professionals. A great location in River North coupled with a trendy atmosphere make this hotel the perfect package.

It is chic from top to bottom in that Californian/Scandinavian minimalist way. Blonde woods, simple lines, and contemporary furniture all effortlessly create the understated look. Thankfully, the staff eschews that "too cool for school" philosophy found in other hotels that resemble the James.

Standard rooms outfitted with streamlined platform beds give a taste of the scene, but the lofts, one-bedroom apartments, and penthouse, with more space and better views, are certainly worth the splurge featuring a formal living area complete with an Apple iBook-based entertainment system. The accommodations also come with plenty of goodies; bathrooms are stocked with roll-in showers and wet bars boast full-sized bottles.

The business lounge is a boon for corporate visitors (work spaces are not included in all rooms), while guests develop a soft spot for neighboring JBar and Lounge. Their tasty concoctions and intimate vibe are perfect for starting or concluding a night on the town.

Chicago ▶ River North

Palomar

505 N. State St. (at Illinois St.)

Phone: 312-755-9703 or 877-731-0505
Web: www.hotelpalomar-chicago.com
Prices: $$

🚊 Grand (Red)

238
Rooms

23
Suites

Chris Molina

Just like its guiding force, the World's Fair, the sparkling Palomar brings innovation, style, and panache to the Windy City. Situated in the heart of River North, this 17-story hotel is one of the more recent Kimpton properties to hit the scene. Enter through the pristine glass doors, glide past the elegant living room-style lobby, and let the elevators whisk you away to a cosmopolitan and contemporary world.

Bright couches, deep-colored drapes, and carpets covered in big red blossoms create a dramatic look in the rooms and suites alike. Bathrooms continue this modern-chic style with gleaming cream marble tiles, dark wood furnishings, and stainless steel fixtures. The pièce de résistance at the Palomar is its 17th floor sundeck, pool, and fitness center, where you can sunbathe, swim, or sweat with a skyscraper view.

In-room spa services, complimentary morning coffee, and an evening wine hour are among the niceties this hotel extends to its guests. Don't miss Sable Kitchen & Bar's inventive New American food and glamorous setting evocative of the sexy 1940s. All this and you can bring your biggest four-legged friend too, since the Palomar doesn't discriminate against larger pets.

Chicago ▶ River North

The Peninsula

108 E. Superior St. (bet. Michigan Ave. & Rush St.)

Phone: 312-337-2888 or 866-382-8388
Web: www.peninsula.com
Prices: **$$$$**

Chicago (Red)

257 Rooms

82 Suites

The Peninsula Chicago

From the elegant lobby to the ultra-luxe guest rooms to the top-notch spa and restaurants, The Peninsula delivers an all-around exceptional experience. No detail is overlooked at this pristine sanctum and everything looks and feels very plush—from oversized marble soaking bathtubs, to bedside electronic panels controlling everything including lighting and temperature.

The Peninsula Spa offers a temple of serenity in the heart of the Gold Coast. The pool, surrounded by glass and offering jaw-dropping views, is quite simply the best in town, while the fitness center is *the* place to sweat and be seen. The luxury quotient also extends to the hotel's many dining selections and glorious beverage offerings. The Peninsula bar is truly fantastic and exudes a dark, luxurious, and clubby ambience. Hugely raved about and regarded as one the best "scenes" in Chicago, the bar is buzzing and lively on weekends. Ritzy crowds flock here to savor some seriously divine cocktails along with a wonderful selection of light bites.

Whether sipping on afternoon tea in The Lobby, noshing on deliciously flaky croissants at Pierrot Gourmet, or hitting one of the hotel's other concepts, it's all very posh here.

Chicago ▶ River North

SAX

333 N. Dearborn St. (bet. Kinzie St. & the Chicago River)

Phone: 312-245-0333 or 877-569-3742
Web: www.hotelsaxchicago.com
Prices: $$$

 Chicago (Red)

333
Rooms

21
Suites

Thompson Hotels

Bring your lover and leave your work behind when you check into the SAX. A member of the Thompson Hotel group, this hot lair is located in Marina City, defined by its two iconic Bertrand Goldberg-designed buildings (yes, the ones known as the corn cobs). Set upon the north bank of the Chicago River, and steps away from the House of Blues, not only is it surrounded by parks, shops, and restaurants, but it also pays respect to the best of what Chicago has to offer.

The SAX has you at first glance. The lobby has a classy bordello, hip vampire look (think lots of crystal and 18th century-style red velvet upholstered chairs). The guestrooms are identical in spirit to the lobby and are decorated with the same romantic and fresh vibe, though softer colors are also used.

Many guests play hard at the SAX, where entertainment comes in many forms. There is a 10-pin bowling alley for a little retro fun and a sixth-floor lounge powered by Microsoft, but the Crimson Lounge is the jewel in the crown. It is the happening haunt where bright young things gather for VIP bottle service and DJ or live music. Don't worry if you're not a night owl, since not all of the fun happens when the sun goes down.

Chicago ▶ River North

Trump International Hotel & Tower

 401 N. Wabash Ave. (bet. Hubbard St. & the Chicago River)

Phone: 312-588-8000 or 877-458-7867
Web: www.trumpchicagohotel.com
Prices: $$$$

🚇 Grand (Red)

229 Rooms
110 Suites

William Huber

Go big or go home seems to be Donald Trump's mantra, and the Trump International Hotel & Tower shows off these principles in all of its glorious, shimmering style. The hotel, part of a 92-story mixed use tower, stands out among the Loop's skyline for its curvaceous, elegant design of sleek stainless steel and tinted glass. It grabs your attention, but there's nothing flashy about the well-heeled sophistication peddled here.

Bright with large windows, the Italian limestone-clad lobby has a surprisingly intimate character. The highly professional staff handles everything in a seamless manner. Trump Attachés or personal concierges offer the highest level of personalized attention.

The Donald's own gold-loving style is never evident; the guestrooms and suites are the very definition of cool and contemporary with grey, black, and soft brown color schemes. Whether it is Bose clock stereos and iPod chargers on the bedside tables or Miele cooktops and Bernardaud china in the kitchenettes, the accommodations showcase the world's leading brands.

From the glorious guest rooms and health club, to the exquisite, buzzing scene in Terrace at Trump, the real VIP here is the show-stopping view.

Chicago ▶ River North

Westin River North

320 N. Dearborn St. (bet. Kinzie St. & the Chicago River)

Phone: 312-744-1900 or 877-866-9216
Web: www.westinchicago.com
Prices: $$$

 Chicago (Red)

407
Rooms

17
Suites

The Westin Chicago River North

It may be located across from the legendary House of Blues, but all visitors at the Westin aren't singing the blues. Instead, they're whistling a happy tune, thanks to a good night's sleep in one of the many rooms and suites. This modern respite enjoys a great location. Sitting at the edge of the river, the hotel is a convenient base and is a business traveler's favored perch—they flock here as much for the conferences held in the more than 28,000-square-feet of meeting space as they do for the food scene and accommodations.

The guest rooms and suites are appointed with a subtle style. Clean, simple furnishings crafted from polished woods and soft, muted colors are used to create a soothing and relieving atmosphere. Westin's signature beds will make you want to jump right in after a busy night on the town; while the bath, replete with therapeutic spa showers, is ideal for helping you wake you up or wind down.

Some of the better trappings of the Westin are its three distinctive entertainment venues. Ember Grille sates all carnivores with fire-roasted entrées and prime steak; Kamehachi Sushi Bar serves basic Japanese; and Hana Lounge is just right for catching up over cocktails.

Chicago ▶ River North

Allerton

A1

701 N. Michigan Ave. (at Huron St.)

Phone: 312-440-1500 or 877-701-8111
Web: www.theallertonhotel.com
Prices: $$

 Chicago (Red)

359 Rooms

84 Suites

Nathan Kirkman Photography

Relive a part of the Windy City's history while staying at the Allerton. This Streeterville landmark was built in 1924 and was one of the first high-rises on North Michigan Avenue. With its beautiful Italian Renaissance design, intricately carved stone details, decorative brickwork, and iconic neon signs, this vestige is an architect and history buff's dream come true.

Regarded as a gorgeous getaway, The Allerton represents a welcome departure from the modern towers that line the Magnificent Mile. But there's nothing formal or antique here: checkerboard terrazzo flooring sets a stylish tone in the lobby, though it is in the rooms and suites where the design really gleams. From the plush white tufted leather headboard to the Lucite cube bedside lamps, it is art deco all the way.

Each evening, this inviting home-away-from-home hosts a complimentary wine hour for guests to mingle and munch. Other trappings may include a 24-hour health club and the sleek M Avenue Restaurant and Lounge with its upscale dining and comfortably chic setting. The lobby-located flightboard displaying airport departure times and accompanying printer kiosk is certainly one of the most convenient gestures.

Chicago ▶ Streeterville

342

Inn of Chicago

A2

162 E. Ohio St. (at St. Clair St.)

Phone: 312-787-3100 or 866-858-4430
Web: www.innofchicago.com
Prices: $$

Grand (Red)

339 Rooms

20 Suites

Scott Thompson

If you have caviar taste but a burger budget, the Inn of Chicago is just the place for you. It may be a half-block away from the Magnificent Mile, but you don't need a lot of moolah to stay at this value-oriented hotel that offers the same coveted neighborhood without the sticker shock.

The Inn of Chicago has enjoyed a long history–first opening in 1928 as the Hotel St. Clair–but this space is rooted firmly in the present with its modern design and high-tech amenities. It may not be pricey, but this hotel does not skimp on the extras either—large screen plasma televisions, dazzling views, and massive walk-in showers are among the standard offerings. All guests are welcomed with open arms, but business travelers are especially well cared for here, with conference rooms, a business facility, and a fitness center.

Though the hotel does not have its own restaurant, the Lavazza Café hits the spot with its spectrum of tasty pastries and sandwiches; while the InnBar is the in-place for a post-work or post- sightseeing signature cocktail. Of course, the hotel's real pièce de résistance is the 22nd floor Skyline Terrace, which opens during warmer months and showcases stunning city views.

Chicago ▶ Streeterville

InterContinental

505 N. Michigan Ave. (bet. Grand Ave. & Illinois St.)

Phone: 312-944-4100 or 800-628-2112
Web: www.icchicagohotel.com
Prices: $$

Grand (Red)

717
Rooms

75
Suites

InterContinental Chicago

Like an aging starlet with a story to tell, the historic InterContinental has lived many lives. Like old photographs or letters, there are several signs of the hotel's former incarnations—there is even a blue Majolica-tiled pool complete with terra-cotta fountain of Neptune that was the training site of Olympic athlete Johnny Weissmuller.

Don't be put off—just because it revels in its history doesn't mean it ignores modern needs. The 24-hour room service is timely, but if you need to stretch your legs, their dining choices are enjoyable. The exquisite lobby is the showpiece of the InterContinental. They just don't make grand entrances like this anymore and this magnificent four-floor rotunda with handcrafted mosaic tiles of onyx and marble is worthy of attention. Though not as grand, the accommodations are decorated in the same old-world vein.

InterContinental spices up the old with the new at its dining establishments. ENO is a unique concept managed by the master sommelier and offers flights of wine, chocolate, and cheese from around the world. Their take-home gifts make wonderful souvenirs. The hotel's main restaurant, The Continental, has a modern American flavor and feel.

Orrington

1710 Orrington Ave. (bet. Church & Clark Sts.), Evanston

Phone: 847-866-8700 or 888-677-4648
Web: www.hotelorrington.com
Prices: $$

257 Rooms

12 Suites

Hilton Orrington/Evanston

The Orrington now is proof positive that everything old can be new (and renewed) again. This hotel first opened its doors in 1925 and has achieved landmark status, but a multi-million dollar renovation brought this elegant attraction seriously up to snuff. The location, not far from downtown Evanston's shopping, dining, and entertainment scene, is ideal for those journeying on business, pleasure, or visiting nearby Northwestern University. The convenience factor is par none.

Striking black wood furnishings set against dramatic red and yellow walls, striped fabrics, and clean lines set a modern tone in the diverse range of rooms and suites. The accommodations are well-suited for corporate travelers with ample work spaces and comfortable chairs, as well as for families with pets in tow—look out for the bowls of biscuits and water at the entrance. Whether you need to check in to the office, or check out after a weary day of sightseeing, the Orrington has your every need covered.

Famished after all the fun? Two dining options include the Globe Café & Bar for all-day dining with a focus on lighter fare (salads, sandwiches, et al), and Indigo Lounge for martinis and mixed drinks.

North & Northwestern Suburbs

Oak Brook Hills Marriott Resort

3500 Midwest Rd. (at 35th St.), Oak Brook

Phone: 630-850-5555 or 800-228-9290
Web: www.oakbrookhillsmarriottresort.com
Prices: $$

347
Rooms

39
Suites

Marriott International

The Oak Brook Hills Marriott Resort is a business traveler's dream. Visit this suburban Chicago resort with the confidence that you won't feel "stuck" at a conference or the like. It's not just about the event and meeting space, though there certainly is a lot of it. This Marriott branch entices guests with an 18-hole golf course, indoor and outdoor pools, fitness center, tennis courts, and easy access to area shopping.

All the rooms and suites are sunny, spacious, and extremely comfortable. From plush duvet covers to ergonomically designed desk chairs, the accommodations treat guests to a wonderful plethora of amenities.

Of course, all of the action takes place outside the rooms. The Audubon certified Willow Crest Golf Course is a definite morale booster. Lessons, equipment rentals, and putting green are all part of this first class facility. Need to calm your colleagues? Take them to one of three area spas or hit up the Oak Brook Center or Yorktown Mall. Brought the whole family along for the company conference? Take them to nearby Brookfield Zoo. Back at the Marriott, there are four restaurants all showcasing American cuisine, and many of them boast scenic views of the golf course.

● Where to **Eat**

Where to **Stay**

Indexes

Alphabetical List of Restaurants

Restaurants by Cuisine

Vegetarian

Vietnamese

Cuisines by Neighborhood

CHICAGO

ANDERSONVILLE, EDGEWATER & UPTOWN

SOUTH, SOUTHWEST & WESTERN SUBURBS

Indexes ▶ Cuisines by Neighborhood

Starred Restaurants

*W*ithin the selection we offer you, some restaurants deserve to be highlighted for their particularly good cuisine. When giving one, two, or three Michelin stars, there are a number of elements that we consider including the quality of the ingredients, the technical skill and flair that goes into their preparation, the blend and clarity of flavours, and the balance of the menu. Just as important is the ability to produce excellent cooking time and again. We make as many visits as we need, so that our readers may be assured of quality and consistency.

A two or three-star restaurant has to offer something very special in its cuisine; a real element of creativity, originality, or "personality" that sets it apart from the rest. Three stars – our highest award – are given to the choicest restaurants, where the whole dining experience is superb.

Cuisine in any style, modern or traditional, may be eligible for a star. Due to the fact we apply the same independent standards everywhere, the awards have become benchmarks of reliability and excellence in over 20 countries in Europe and Asia, particularly in France, where we have awarded stars for 100 years, and where the phrase "Now that's real three-star quality!" has entered into the language.

The awarding of a star is based solely on the quality of the cuisine.

Bib Gourmand

This symbol indicates our inspectors' favorites for good value. For $40 or less, you can enjoy two courses and a glass of wine or a dessert (not including tax or gratuity).

377

Brunch

Late Dining

Alphabetical List of Hotels

Notes

Notes

Notes

The Michelin Adventure

It all started with rubber balls! This was the product made by a small company based in Clermont-Ferrand that André and Edouard Michelin inherited, back in 1880. The brothers quickly saw the potential for a new means of transport and their first success was the invention of detachable pneumatic tires for bicycles. However, the automobile was to provide the greatest scope for their creative talents. Throughout the 20th century, Michelin never ceased developing and creating ever more reliable and high-performance tires, not only for vehicles ranging from trucks to F1 but also for underground transit systems and airplanes.

From early on, Michelin provided its customers with tools and services to facilitate mobility and make travelling a more pleasurable and more frequent experience. As early as 1900, the Michelin Guide supplied motorists with a host of useful information related to vehicle maintenance, accommodation and restaurants, and was to become a benchmark for good food. At the same time, the Travel Information Bureau offered travellers personalised tips and itineraries.

The publication of the first collection of roadmaps, in 1910, was an instant hit! In 1926, the first regional guide to France was published, devoted to the principal sites of Brittany, and before long each region of France had its own Green Guide. The collection was later extended to more far-flung destinations, including New York in 1968 and Taiwan in 2011.

In the 21st century, with the growth of digital technology, the challenge for Michelin maps and guides is to continue to develop alongside the company's tire activities. Now, as before, Michelin is committed to improving the mobility of travellers.

MICHELIN TODAY

WORLD NUMBER ONE TIRE MANUFACTURER
- 69 production sites in 18 countries
- 115,000 employees from all cultures and on every continent
- 6,000 people employed in research and development

Moving
for a world

Moving forward means developing tires with better road grip and shorter braking distances, whatever the state of the road.

CORRECT TIRE PRESSURE

RIGHT PRESSURE

- Safety
- Longevity
- Optimum fuel consumption

-0,5 bar

- Durability reduced by 20% (- 8,000 km)

-1 bar

- Risk of blowouts
- Increased fuel consumption
- Longer braking distances on wet surfaces

forward together
where mobility is safer

It also involves helping motorists take care of their safety and their tires. To do so, Michelin organises "Fill Up With Air" campaigns all over the world to remind us that correct tire pressure is vital.

WEAR

DETECTING TIRE WEAR

MICHELIN tires are equipped with tread wear indicators, which are small blocks of rubber molded into the base of the main grooves at a height of 1.6 mm. When tread depth is the same level as indicators, the tires are worn and need replacing.

Tires are the only point of contact between vehicle and the road, a worn tire can be dangerous on wet surfaces.

NEW TIRE

WORN TIRE
(1,6 mm tread)

The photo shows the actual contact zone on wet surfaces.

Moving forward
means sustainable mobility

INNOVATION AND THE ENVIRONMENT

By 2050, Michelin aims to cut the quantity of raw materials used in its tire manufacturing process by half and to have developed renewable energy in its facilities. The design of MICHELIN tires has already saved billions of liters of fuel and, by extension, billions of tons of CO2.

Similarly, Michelin prints its maps and guides on paper produced from sustainably managed forests and is diversifying its publishing media by offering digital solutions to make travelling easier, more fuel efficient and more enjoyable!

The group's whole-hearted commitment to eco-design on a daily basis is demonstrated by ISO 14001 certification.

Like you, Michelin is committed to preserving our planet.

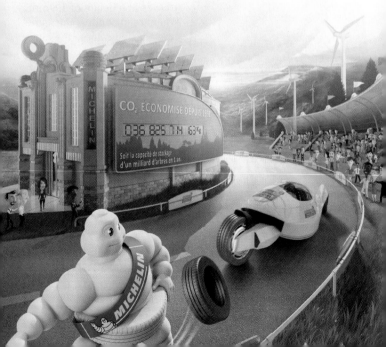

Chat with Bibendum

Go to
www.michelin.com/corporate/fr
Find out more about Michelin's
history and the latest news.

QUIZ

Michelin develops tires for all types of vehicles. See if you can match the right tire with the right vehicle...

Solution : A-6 / B-4 / C-2 / D-1 / E-3 / F-7 / G-5

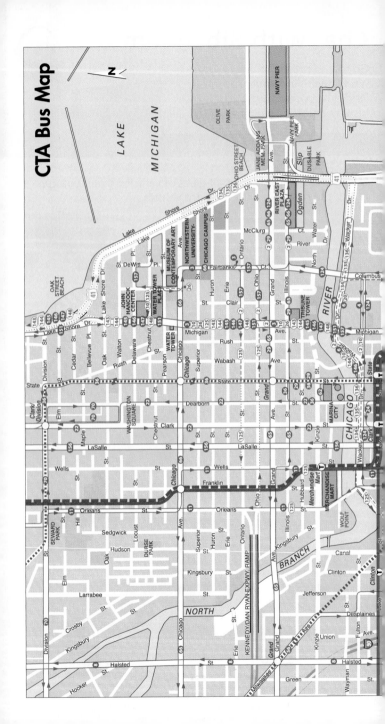

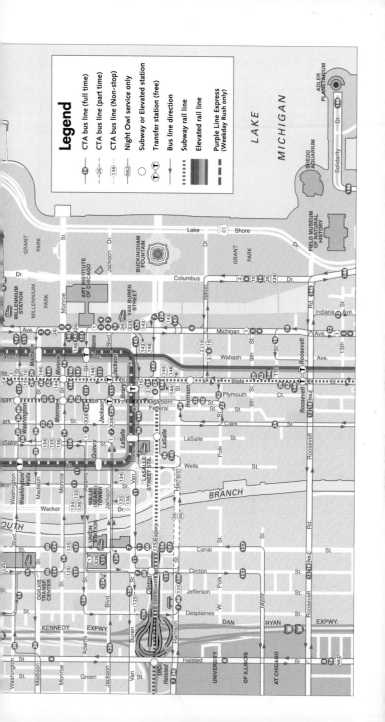